Great
STRUGGLE

Great STRUGGLE

Bishop's Story

DINESH K. AGARWAL

PARTRIDGE

To order additional copies of this book, contact
Partridge India
000 800 10062 62
orders.india@partridgepublishing.com

www.partridgepublishing.com/india

CONTENTS

TO
THOSE WHO SHAPED MY LIFE

PREFACE

I was faithful in my episcopal ministry and satisfied in life, and then unforeseen turn of events thrust me in gloom and despondency, as intolerance to my different voice begot negative energy, and conspiracy drove me into wilderness. In my loneliness, the thought of writing my experiences in the church struck me. The task of writing more or less forty years of my story (1972–2012) was challenging, much like the forty years of the Israelites' journey in the great wilderness. Hopefully, I wrote a fair and transparent account as far as I could remember, and I am glad I did it with comfort and without seared conscience.

I penned my story in the setting of John Wesley's 'holiness of life', which he also said is 'social holiness' that was missing in the church, which seems to lack the spiritual urge to practice and teach 'holiness of life', and the force of power and temporal ambition of the church leaders shifts the paradigm of life.

As for the book, who knows if it is a great story of my struggle for truth and justice? Regardless, it should inspire all, to free every human being from man-inflicted sufferings, equip each one with the truth, and to raise voice against injustice of hierarchical superiority or any other form of oppression.

I am grateful to my well-wishers and family members for their encouragement and support throughout the writing of this book.

October 19, 2014
Dinesh K . Agarwal

ALDERSGATE TO INDIA

Church is the holy institution, started and spread after the day of Pentecost. The visible church is the outward expression of the inward faith in Christ. When Jesus walked along with his disciples on the way to Caesarea Philippi, the city close to one of the sources of Jordon, built by Philip the Tetrarch, the prefect site, away from the partisan Herod's influence[1], he asked the apostles what people say about him. Their understanding of him was no way nearer to his actual identity; some thought he was John the Baptist, raised from the dead, others Elijah, the prophet, and still others thought of him as Jeremiah, the prophet. There was no single opinion about him, and the actual discovery of him was still hazy, for they were holding him in the perspective of Israel's history and not transcending him over it. Not satisfied with the answers, he then asked his apostles as what they say he was. St. Peter, one of the apostles, answered him, 'You are the Messiah, the son of the Living God.' He said, the flesh and blood did not reveal to you, but my father in heaven; on this faith [as rock], I will build my church.'[2]

The church is not merely a religious institution, there is something more to it; it is the body of Jesus Christ, or the fellowship of the redeemed people of God. After the resurrection of Christ, the Holy Spirit came upon the early church on the day of Pentecost – fifty days; the church was born, grew, and spread, beginning from Jerusalem to Samaria and all parts of the world.

Until schism, the church was undivided. In 1050, for the first time, the church split into Western and Eastern churches. Then there was a great schism in the Western church; the Roman Catholic Church emerged as the dominant church and it remained unchallenged until the days of the Protestant Reformation, spearheaded by Martin Luther, a German Roman Catholic priest. His parents were a small peasant and mineworker in Saxony, they desired their son to pursue a career in law, but because of his deep religious leaning, in 1505, he entered the monastery of Augustinian at Erfurt. In 1512, he earned Doctorate in Theology from the University of Erfurt. He became the director of studies and district vicar. He believed, salvation is a new relation to God, based not on any work of merit, but it was the gift of God's grace and absolute faith in Christ[3]. He spoke against the crying abuse of indulgences and said that they were not supported by the Holy Bible, and thus not essential for salvation. He was convinced, the scriptures or history did not support the supremacy of the Roman Catholic Church.

The church prohibited him to enter the electoral Saxony. On October 31, 1517, he pasted the famous Ninety-five Articles of Faith on the door of the Castle church at Wittenberg. Martin Luther found sympathy among humanistic intellectuals and theologians. The Roman Catholic Church insisted he must recant his articles of faith, but he refused, unless the Holy Scriptures refuted it. On April 18, 1521, Luther appeared before the assembly of nobles, at Diet of Worms, presided by Emperor Reichstag to defend himself. In his defence, he delivered one of world's greatest speeches, 'I cannot do otherwise. Here I stand. God help me, Amen[4]. He was to be seized, punished, and his books were to be burnt. Luther lived in hiding for a long time. By the conviction of his faith and the courage of his pen, the twin forces kept him focused and energized to spearhead the Reformation movement. The people who joined the protest against the beliefs and practices, not supported by the scriptures, were nicknamed Protestants and the movement became known as Protestant church. The Bible was translated into German and other languages for people to read. However, some think it is the matter of great debate whether he was the restorer of true Christianity or the destroyer of Christian unity.

The Protestant movement began to spread in Germany, France, and England. Luther's writings were received in England; however, it did not find much favour. In England, the relation between the papacy and the king Henry VIII (1509–1547) began to turn sour. He racked up the nationalistic feelings and the need to do away foreign rule. The king was a remarkable intellectual man and he had ability to mobilize and execute plans. King Henry passed the act in parliament forbidding payments to Rome. He recognized Thomas Wolsey as cardinal who was appointed by Pope Leo X. He gave him authority as papal legate before the body of clergy. The king controlled the episcopal appointment and held authority to form ecclesiastical laws. He became single and supreme lord of the Church of England (Anglican Church), as long as law of Christ allows him. He appointed Thomas Granmer as Archbishop of Canterbury. The separation from the Roman Catholic Church was not on basis of theological or scriptural differences, but on nationalistic feelings, foreign control, and ecclesiastical politics. After the death of the king, the English church was split into three groups, the Church of England, and smaller groups of Roman Catholics and Protestants, and in subsequent development, demarcation or the domain of the church and state was clearly visible.

John Wesley was an Anglican clergyman, born on June 17, 1703, in the rectory at Epworth; he was the second son of Susana and Samuel Wesley, a scholarly clergyman of the Anglican Church. He was barely three years, when fire broke in the rectory at Epworth but he was rescued miraculously. I visited the rectory in the second week of January 2001, which was turned into a museum under the auspices of the World Methodist Council. Susana Wesley was a woman of a great zeal, devotion, and strength of character who was perhaps the greatest single human influence in John Wesley's life. He was educated at Oxford.

He participated in Oxford religious study group organized by his brother Charles Wesley. The group was dubbed as 'Methodists' for their emphasis on methodical study of the Bible and devotion[5]. In 1737, they undertook social and charitable activities. After mostly an unsuccessful mission to the North American colony of Georgia, they returned to London. A year after, on their return, John Wesley was influenced by Martin Luther's theology that salvation was possible through faith alone. On May 14, 1738, a great turning point came in his life when he attended the Moravian prayer meeting under auspices of the Church of England at Aldersgate Street; he felt that his heart strangely warmed[6]. He was convinced that salvation is by faith alone. He began to preach these newfound spiritual riches to masses, calling them to holiness of life, the hallmark of Methodism, which he said, was social holiness. He then perhaps never knew it would become the commonwealth of millions around the world. In the beginning, he did not think to organize his followers into a separate church; he intended them to remain as the part of Anglican Church, and so he formed societies for spiritual care and nurture. Long after, he began to ordain ministers himself when the Bishop of London refused to do so. He travelled from place to place to preach the gospel, which gave rise to itinerant ministry, which he epitomized, in his famous and inspiring words, 'The world is my parish.' The Methodism is not the direct outcome of Reformation, but it has its origin within the Church of England and spread from England to Ireland, and then to the North America where it adapted to the American way of life.

First Methodist Church built at Nainital,
Kumaon hills, 1858

In 1856, William Butler, an American Methodist
episcopal missionary arrived on the eve of Victorian
India. After initial disappointments, he rented a house
in Bareilly. On May 31, 1857, Joel T. Janvier, William
Butler's Indian aide, preached first sermon to the
first congregation in Bareilly, 'Fear not, little, flock,
for it is your father's good pleasure to give you the
kingdom,' based on the Gospel according to St. Luke.
He inspired them with hope and promise, and within
ten minutes of the close of the sermon, the first war
of independence broke. The little flock was scattered
like autumn leaves and many of them were killed;
however, soon it began to grow and spread out from
the seed of the blood of martyrs all over India, and
even beyond India's geographical borders[7]. In 1858,
the first Methodist Episcopal Church was built at

Nainital, Kumaon hills – it was sheer co-incidence, in the same year the East India Company handed over the reign of India to Queen Victoria. In 1848, Karl Marx and Frederich Engels published the revolutionary *Communist Manifesto* that recognized class conflict between the bourgeoisie and the proletariat. In 1859, Charles Darwin, in his work, *On the Origin of Species*, postulated the theory of evolution, which was winning followers, and in 1862, Abraham Lincoln proclaimed the preliminary emancipation of slaves, leading to the end of civil war. In the mid-19th century in Europe and America, the waves of revolution and evolution shaped people's thinking; Marxism and Darwinism showed religious beliefs silly. On the social front in India, the caste system meticulously practiced purity and pollution taboos and split the vertical Varna into horizontal hierarchical sub-castes. In such milieu, the church started its work and the social holiness began to spread.

By 1871, the church was known as the Methodist Church in Southern Asia, afterward the church's jurisdiction reduced to India's geographical boundaries. In 1939, the churches with Wesleyan heritage united in North America; the united church became known as the United Methodist Church[8]. In 1953, not long after Indian independence, the church appointed the commission on the plan for the union of churches of North India and Pakistan. In 1968, the United Methodist Church passed the enabling act, empowering the church to consummate into the union of churches of North India. On November 29, 1970, the Church of North India was inaugurated in Nagpur. The Methodist Church missed the date and it could not join the union since there were still unsettled issues viz. women's work, ministries, properties, institutions endowments, Trust formation, and perhaps oblique interest of episcopal support. However, the thought of joining union of churches was not abandoned; the church was open to negotiate the unsettled issues, but the Church of North India felt it was not necessary to do so, prior to joining the union, as the church would be treated in par with other churches that have already joined the union[9]. It was an embarrassing situation for the church from the both sides – the United Methodist Church and the Church of North India. To settle the lingering issue, in 1976, the church opted to become an affiliated autonomous church to the United Methodist Church after almost two decades of unsuccessful union negotiation[10]. In 1980, the United Methodist Church authorized the Methodist Church in Southern Asia to become the Methodist Church in India. On January 7, 1981, the Methodist Church in India was inaugurated in Madras with a great excitement and aspirations. It was a defining moment; the changeover from the Methodist Church in Southern Asia, under United Methodist Church to an affiliated autonomous church with a new nametag was smooth and painless. The transfer of funds, of course not all permanent endowment funds and immovable property assets whose title deeds are sometimes not traceable and in some cases not even found or may have been stored in heavy iron safes whose number combination locks are frustrating to open, gave some cheers – until then the church was partially monitored and mentored by the American church. The church desired to continue the legacy of illustrious services to the Indian nation through its schools, colleges, hospitals, technical institutions, hostels, and orphanages spread in most part of the country, perhaps gave the sense of fulfilment and invoked responsibility. I recognized, out of historical compulsion, the church rushed into affiliated autonomy, giving birth to new positions, increased episcopal offices, and constituted the Council of Bishops, the General Conference, and Judicial Council like apex court. I remember, some senior leaders even justified and advocated affiliate autonomy under the guise of the speculation of ordaining gay ministers and such other practices that the United Methodist Church may so decide, under its cultural influence and openness. They contended that they would be free from the constitutional bindings and obligations, but could not imagine that they will be perpetually engrossed in the power struggle. The church was joyous but far too little imaginative that in the years ahead, it might face with the challenge of the holiness of life and the inferior church governance in the midst of pre-eminence of its own constitutional obligations and preoccupation, trying to meet ends, as inherited meager financial resources were insufficient to its galloping needs. As I reflect on it, I feel, affiliated autonomy did not meet its envisaged expectations; perhaps, then it was imagined.

Turning to the present scenario, the church is not facing any serious theological controversy or conflict of interpretations of the biblical texts, as in the days of Reformation, or there is no tussle between state and church and its domain of specialized power structure within generalized power structure clearly settled and recognized. I recognized, there was the rise of a different phenomenon in the church, the church hierarchy was barely living with the paradigm of holiness of life and temporal ambition conditioned it. They claimed to tend the ecclesiastical laws but gone by different rules either to gain or survive in power. The paradigm shift hugely affected the flow of truth, justice, and equity essential to the life and ministry of the church. Everything was changing; the focus of religious leaders was not in consonance with their calling. They stirred horde to break and bend rules, restricted civil liberty, devoured the church Judiciary, abused authority, and indulged in unbelievable deeds and means, contrary to the faith and practice of the church. Such political life style shifting the paradigm of holiness of life and the leaven of spiritual pathos or spiritual emptiness spreading like contagious disease, I could barely imagine it.

There were some who valued the rich spiritual heritage of the church and desired to protect it, but they faced stiff resistance from those who were at the pinnacle of the church hierarchy. They were acting in disgrace by hardening heart and becoming intolerant to the freedom of expression and suppressing the voice of their conscience. Thus, it was agonizing to practice the holiness of life in the presence of strong ambition for power and position than steel. The power ambition created tragic and chaotic situation and dissipate energies, tarnishing the image of the church and sacrificing its interests. The prophetic voice was missing; however, I played a small role[11]. Then I could not imagine that it would turn out to be the great struggle, in which one could lose friends, or friends could turn foes. However, I recognized that listening to the voice of conscience was vital, even if it meant displeasing my brother bishops. Some chose the company of lovers of power and position; others sat on a fence, waited and watched for auspicious political occasion, to be on the winning side. It seemed that such political opportunism gave rise to an anomic condition and tended to discredit bishopric. The bishops were unrestrained to take revenge and to achieve self-satisfying political ambition in their majestic religious robes. They preached the gospel of hatred and the message of love and forgiveness did not find favour. In utter insensitiveness, they felt elated in defying norms and holiness of life. Never, they wearied to influence or oppress clergy and laity by their position and inappropriate means, which did not edify their sacred calling, either to tame or to ruin church leaders who did not tread their path.

The bishops, the men of God, shackled the voice of conscience, gave distorted pictures of things to achieve self-serving ends, concealed the truth, posed as defenders of the church and in self-worth thundered, 'I am the church!' It seemed that in arrogance of power, some church leaders personified the church as themselves. Poor penitent souls in pews barely knew the great spiritual dilemma and iniquitous episodes at the religious hierarchy, and those who did know, indifference left it to the divine justice. It seemed such political behaviour of religious leaders was becoming the way of life, which was not facilitating to practicing Christian principles and the holiness of life. In the presence of defying forces, it was frustrating to deal with stubborn self-propelling tendencies; the road to overcome was long and stiff, and a great deal of sacrifice was needed to reach the end of the road. I strived to overcome, least I was thrust into the culture of silence.

Since the church is the body of Jesus Christ, followers are expected to lead a holy life, adhere to Christian teachings, and respect the voice of conscience; however, such desire was dispirited. I felt, in perpetuity of the political ambition of the church leaders, brotherly relations defined and the church's interests seized. Their enlarged self, jealousy, revenge, greed, and emotions of hatred and fear generated negative energy in the presence of spiritual emptiness. I recognized, under its influence, the men of God acted craftily and hatched conspiracy and profaned the church's spirituality. The voice of conscience tormented those who tarnished the illustrious records of the life and ministry of the church. It was a melancholic situation; bishops walked out of the holiness of life, used Machiavellian tactics to continue in bishopric, and tended to be lords and law to themselves.

From Aldersgate to India, the men of God, inflamed by the strangely warm heart, brought the treasurer of holiness of life or Scriptural holiness; it took roots in the Indian Methodism and made benevolent impact on India. However, as time passed by, it was all history. Now people were craving for power and position; it was like an epidemic that defies Christian calling and every rule of reason; consciously brutal means were used to ascend or hold on to covetous positions of power like ancient conquerors, while the holiness of life was laid dormant in the back yard of the church. I recognize that when the Christian principles and values are reduced to mere ceremonial rhetoric that led to shift from spirituality to power, stereotype religious life style and unscriptural conduct germinated negative energy, engulfing all the good the church cherished. I perceived there was virtual struggle between those who were longing to experience the Aldersgate effect and those who were high on temporal ambition. The endeavours of faithful ones to practice the holiness of life, preserve and perpetuate it were thwarted by the then-religious ruling class of the church for the sake of ascending or remaining in power. In vain, I thought my struggle for truth, justice, and equity would bear fruits, and truth would be hailed like Galileo's discovery and joy would be shared like the woman who found her lost coin. I was dismayed to experience survival in such a poor spiritual condition, and conflicting vision was a painful struggle; when it came to living by the holiness of life, assimilating it was easier. The spirituality in church did not get its due attention, and the inflamed negative energy was spreading spiritual pathos. In situations such as this, the holiness of life or scriptural holiness did not rise above its symbolism, expecting it to excel was an awesome challenge, and the struggle for the newness of life was like a caterpillar's agony.

I recognize in God's eternal purpose, power and spirituality are compatible; however, the tendency among the church leaders was anything but power obsession. For the sake of ascending to power and staying at the helm of the church's affairs, they did not hesitate to use deviant means; spirituality became a peripheral concern, as the holiness of life was not their guiding star. I found, those who desired to practice the holiness of life were marginalized, oppressed, and victimized by the power-loving leaders when they sensed the peril to their survival in chair, the church's Constitution selectively recognized or trampled at their pleasure to stick to power. In such a situation, I realized, it was a challenge to be like a prophet and yet I made feeble efforts to do right things and make things right and struggle for truth and justice – an indispensable expression of the true piety or the holiness of life. It was torturous to stick to Christian ideals or walk the way of holiness of life, and yet to survive in the self-propelling tendency in the church hierarchy was truly challenging; conforming to vicious political ways and means was a hearty welcome act. It seemed, when the faithful flock of Christ refuse to degenerate or do not cease to raise their prophetic voice against political inappropriateness in the church, they are faced with wrath; negative energy tends to thrush them into the Babylonian captivity of the 21st century[12].

EARLY YEARS

I remember, the early years of my ministry were uncertain; however, they were simulative and challenging – they enriched my spirituality, thinking, and commitment to Christian values. The years were full of challenges, risks, and possibilities; it was like sailing into deep sea waters with hope to discover under currents. I then never could imagine I would have to grapple with several problems. I seriously introspected on God's purpose for my sufferings as I recognized, he has a purpose for all of us; for some, it may be big, and for others, it may be small, and although it may look insignificant in the beginning, it takes years to show up in someone's life, while in others, it soon germinates. Some struggle for a while, others too much and too long. Of course, the early years have their own difficulties like teething problems, except for some with high connection who have smooth sailing. I understand the beginning of a career could be painful; however, it helps move forward towards a definite goal and determination to achieve something benevolent in life. The charismatic leaders in religion, business, politics, and other areas of life are the powerful example of its irrefutable reality.

In Search of Gospel Ministry

After my theology from Union Biblical Seminary, Yavatmal, Maharashtra, I was in search of some kind of gospel ministry. There were some offers on hand; however, I liked the one from Lydia Sward, a Swedish missionary of Hindustani Covenant Church. She had a PhD and was a dedicated and a lovable person and lived in Bombay. I met her at Henry Martyn Institute of Islamic Studies, Hyderabad. The institute was fully committed to Islamic studies and the Methodist Church supported it. Sam V. Bhajjan, an esteemed Islamic scholar and a Methodist, was heading the institute. I accepted her offer to work on probation.

October 20, 1972, is an important day that we remember every year as a special day of thanksgiving. It has a special significance, as on that day, I came to Bombay for the gospel work. Prior to this, I visited the city several times, but this time, I was never to leave the city. I remember, once I was in the city in the late '60s, I was introduced to an Indian Navy officer, a North Indian and a devote Christian. He was concerned about me and keen to see that I get into the Indian Navy. One day, he took me to the Indian

Navy recruitment office. As I followed him, I was a bit nervous, many questions cropped up in my mind about fitness of my height, weight, eyesight, and legs' length and posture. I wondered whether I was making a rational decision, and at times, I imagined myself wearing a Navy uniform; I liked it. I did not know then what I was doing, I was simply following him. By the time we reached the Navy Recruitment Office near Metro Cinema, Dhobi Talao, south Bombay, all my hopes and despairs vanished. On that day, the office was closed! Afterwards, I never again thought of joining the Indian Navy. Then, I did not know God had better plans to use me in some other way. I feel it happens in most of our lives: we wish something; however, we never get there, not knowing that losing opportunities do not necessarily mean the end of our future, but I think it does mean that something better and bigger is waiting for us.

From Hyderabad, I reached Bombay by train at Victoria Terminus, as it was called. I remember, it was a Friday afternoon, the sky was clear and bright, and the weather was sultry. It was the fringe of the monsoon season and occasional showers added to perspiration. October days are sultry, but there is no way; people bear it. However, I was fine with the sea climate and hectic life style of the city, some never get used to it; asthmatic attacks discomfort them and the fast-moving city life disheartens them. I started to work with the Hindustani Covenant Church and lived in Dongaji Lodge on Souter Street. The church had a special ministry among Muslims and did marvellously well. It was a challenging ministry; however, I realized I was not the right kind of person for the ministry, so I decided to quit, just after three and a half months. I did not know where I would go and what would happen to me in days to come. I did not know people, except a few ones who were very kind to me. It was providential; I moved to live with Maud Stewart on the 2nd Cross L. J. Road, Mahim, Bombay. She was a retired medical doctor and a government pensioner, advanced in age and living by herself; her brother who retired from military lived with her. He had an accident; he fell from the loft in the house and, not long after, died. She was longing to have someone who could stay with her. Maud Stewart worked for some time with Katherine Collison, a Briton and a missionary, and my spiritual mentor before government service. Her heart was full of compassion and dedicated fully to God's service; she retired and lived in her hometown Sussex, England; her death was a big loss for me. My affinity with her bound me to Maud Steward; she opened her house for me and began to treat me as one of her family members. She was a very lovable and kind person. I continued to live in the city to seek possibilities for the gospel ministry. I was a fresh seminary graduate and inexperienced, having lofty ideas of becoming big and famous like most seminary graduates do have, though I did not know how things would turn out. I felt, God was leading me wonderfully to be useful to him in some humble way and I did not feel threatened nor had any phobia of an unknown future all those years. I was simply amazed, the way God was leading me.

Methodist Connection

I remember, John Wesley's life and work attracted me from my seminary days. I was seeking some connectional relation with the Methodist Church. I started to go to Bowen Memorial Methodist Church, near the Gate Way of India – the monument which was erected on the occasion of the landing of their imperial majesties, George V and Queen Mary on December 2, 1911. The church is named after Gorge Bowen in recognition of his splendid contribution to the church growth. He was an American missionary who lived as the apostles did[1]. The pastor of the church, Manoranjan Luke, an ordained minister (pastor or priest), became friendly. He was a good pastor with evangelical conviction. I recall the Bowen church was bubbling with activities; the congregation was lively, it attracted foreigners on Sunday worship services; sermons were catchy, forceful, and evangelical in its content, and the church choir was enchanting. I became acquainted to K. K. Mukerji, a faithful church member and a cheerful giver. He was a retired undersecretary from the government of India. He had a charming personality and an impressive mannerism. He became my prayer partner and supporter. I do cherish my early memories and the support I received from so many individuals. I used to go to the Bowen Church by a B.E.S.T. city bus; a quarter of a rupee was fare and traveling by a double decker was exciting and joyous. The originating point of the bus was Mahim bus station, next to Mahim Church, famous for novena and the last stop was behind Taj Hotel, a stone's-throw-away distance from the church. There was no traffic or many traffic signals, and in early 1964, the tram services stopped. As days passed by, I came to know some of my seminary friends who had a strong evangelical leaning and who were working in different churches. We used to assemble for prayers and to explore possibilities as to what could be done for evangelistic work in the city. I was immensely influenced by evangelists like Billy Graham, preachers from Ambassador for Christ, and Theodore William, a professor in the South India Biblical Seminary, Bangarapet, Karnataka. In the summer of 1965, I attended Vacation Bible School at the seminary where I committed myself to full-time gospel ministry. Theodore William, was a speaker. I had a strong desire from the very beginning to become a revival preacher and not to work in any denominational church; it remained my unfulfilled dream. I understand; it happens in the lives of many people around the world, we do not get what we expect God to do for us; as man proposes, God disposes. In that, too, there is always a divine purpose, which we come to know sometime in life. My dream did not come true; however, I gave evangelical and revival messages within institutional setting. I was always encouraged by the feedback I received from my audience who prompted me to pen down my messages in a book; however, then I could not do it.

We decided to start an organization called the United Evangelistic Association. When Monoranjan Luke came to know about it, he criticized and tagged it as a moneymaking business. I do not particularly remember why he was so resentful. I felt, perhaps because of some freelance evangelists who smirched an independent evangelistic ministry, especially not being accountable to anyone, for their work and money. I recognize it could not be true with every independent evangelist or an organization; there were people who did awesome work, passionately led people to Christ more than any institutionalized church, which was lost mostly in who's who, the ministry to the world neglected. I believed, there was urgency and obligation on the part of the church to become leaders for evangelism, for first could not be least.

The pastor of the Bowen Church encouraged me to join the ministry of the Methodist Church and took me to Justine Harris, the then district superintendent of South Bombay District. He was an evangelical and respected church leader who did pioneering pastoral work among Tamil people in the city and started several Tamil-speaking congregations. I remember, when I first met him, he looked at me like an old-fashioned school teacher; however, as he held in respect Manoranjan Luke, assured him that he would take me to R. D. Joshi, the then bishop of Bombay Episcopal Area. Justin Harris was kind and helpful. He spoke to the bishop who then authorized him to appoint me as a local preacher on recommendation of the Bowen Church. By then, Manoranjan Luke left Bombay Conference to join Hyderabad Conference. He was not happy there and came back to join again Bombay Conference, but the situation did not favour him. Eventually, he left to the Unites States, and after some years, he died of heart attack. I recognize, although good opportunities seldom bounce back, I understand a man's life is often shaped more by losing opportunities and declining offers. Anyway, I was careful, so that I do not simply become a victim of opportunism at the cost of principles and values that I cherish.

I realized that things were political in the church, for so many church leaders tried few positions and the deserving were left out, and the undeserving held important portfolios who took policy decisions, gave direction, and led the church the way they liked. I found, a right person often got no right job, though it was so adored. I remember the church leaders took most decisions under the influence of either their family or friends or fortune and the steps taken by them did not necessarily reflect a serious God-given purpose. It often resulted in a melancholic situation, the work of the church did not move forward; however, people with vested interests reaped rich harvest.

On February 3, 1975, Justin Harris, as the district superintendent, gave me an appointment letter; I still have it. The church recognized me as one of their workers, and after initial unsuccessful attempts to send me to work in Chinchwad-Pipari, Pune; I was asked to work in Andheri (west), Bombay. I was amazed to read the letter, I was asked to work without financial support. I never heard of such kind of appointment, which did not care for one's needs, for a worker deserves wages. Regardless, not knowing how I would meet my basic needs, yet I was not shaken by it, I accepted the appointment by faith and trusted God, who provided my needs. I recognize money is important and an inevitable means to meet our ends; however, I felt there were many things in life which could not be weighed by money – serving God, of course, not. I believed I was in a divine plan to work in the church, and it was for the church to take care of my basic needs, as God takes care of the needs of his people through human beings. After accepting the appointment by faith, I was never in want, and amazingly, God provided my needs.

Inauguration of Methodist English Service, Easter 1975. (L-R) Rev. Justin N. Harris, Ms. Barbara Chase, GBGM Secretary for Southern Asia, Rev. Prasadrao Manne (Sharon's brother) & I

On March 30, 1975, Easter, the English worship service was inaugurated at Social Service & Prayer Centre on the fourth floor of the Mangal Kunj building, Borivali (west) with the support of Justin Harris, his church member Sunder Yesuvadian, and others. The area of work shifted to Borivali, as there was no permanent place in Andheri and the worship service, which was started at YMCA eventually, was disallowed. On September 7, 1975, Sunday, the congregation was organized into Quarterly Conference – a connectional unit of the church with its rights and responsibilities, and I became the founding pastor. R. D. Joshi, the then bishop of Bombay Episcopal Area received worshippers into Methodist membership, and Justin Harris organized the Quarterly Conference. At the welcome function, the congregation honoured the bishop with flower garlands, but the bishop, in his response, said he expected the congregation to give him a currency garland, so that he could donate it to Home Mission – it is unique to Methodists. Funds for Home Mission were raised by making a certain financial apportionment to local churches and institutions in a conference to subside or give full pastoral support or salary to those pastors whose local churches were unable to raise the pastoral support. I recognized, the bishop had good intension, but he did not realize that the work of the congregation just began without any financial support from the Bombay Conference and the congregation had its priority to look after their pastor. However, I was perplexed at the Bishop's response; he was a learned man and had a doctorate in religion and psychology from Boston University. I could perceive maturity and wisdom on his face; however, I was dismayed at his unreasonable expectation. It seemed he was concerned about raising funds for Home Mission, but not actually familiar with a pioneering work; expecting the nascent congregation to give a currency garland was like asking an infant to be an adult; it's thought troubled me for a long time. However, the congregation grew, I was ordained as deacon on December 16, 1975, and on November 7, 1976, I was ordained as elder and became a full member of the Bombay Conference, it was an important milestone.

First Row (L-R) Rev. Justin N. Harris, UMC Bishop
Malek B. Strokes, Bishop R. D. Joshi & others & I
am standing in the back row, extreme right

My priority was not to raise pastoral support;
spiritual care and nurture and the church programmes
were my utmost concerns. My first salary or pastoral
support was ₹ 150/–. I never complained about our
financial woes, I remember, when my elder daughter
Rayhal was 1 and a half years old, she suffered from
diarrhoea. We wanted to give her coffee, we had no
money on us, we collected some old newspapers and
sold them for a quarter of a rupee to buy coffee; sweet
little Rayhal could not figure out our impecunious
condition. Money never came on our way to serve
the church. I remember, one of my church members
originally belonged to 'Society of Friends' – a Protestant
sect that emerged in England in the seventeenth
century, and rejected Anglicanism and other Protestant
churches; they are known as Quakers who emphasized
inward apprehension of God. He said to me, 'Holy
Spirit does not need money.' He was right to that extent,

but the work of God does! There were others too, in the church who had similar attitude towards the church's mission to the world, while the rest understood the need and cheerfully supported the newly started church. Financial support is essential for the work of the church; however, I believed, ministering the church, money was no condition, for I moved forward in faith, God provided my needs.

Preaching from the pulpit of Methodist
English Church, Borivali, 1976

Justin Harris often spoke with concern and was mindful of my financial needs. He recognized it unlike R. D. Joshi and initially raised money for my ministry through the Youth Fellowship of his congregation. I had great regards for him, but some people tried to sour our relations. One of my church members, who was from his own language stock, commented, 'He was a pious pastor, but partial District Superintendent.' Agreed, although the layman was on the bitter side, but there was an element of truth in it, as he was like a parochial linguaphile; nevertheless, I did not appreciate his insensitive comment. I recognized assigning Sunday worship timings to four congregations for morning and in the same place of worship was complex and not keeping timings barely with any time gap between services and scrambling in the narrow passage on the top level of the residential building led to murmuring and bitterness and stole spiritual solace. In big cities, there were similar stories. Ideally, in one place of worship, one or two language congregations could happily worship. The church could not find money to build churches in suburbs, inasmuch as the cost of land and construction or built-up area was exorbitant, and imagining church building for each language congregation seemed wishful thinking. Anyway, assigning timings to different congregations was to be done with care and concern. After the incident, he began to distance himself from me, and some people with ulterior motives actuated it. I realized it was important for a leader to remember, some people always try to spoil relations. However, despite care, our relations soured, it could not be normal; penetrating prejudice prevailed. I heard, he was resentful and unhappy with me, so much so, he could not digest the thought of my coming up in the church leadership. I tried to clear his misunderstanding and be good to him; however, I was unsuccessful. I had an irreparable loss of a good friend in him. Often, I faced such situations in the church, and the more I tried to make up, it was as hard as catching a flying feather.

Congregation & I, February 1976

The congregation consisted of members who were migrants from different parts of the country and from other than the Methodist Church; some of them were conservative, kept their membership with their mother churches, while others easily integrated. Anyway, it was a fine blend of multiregional cultures, hailed from different linguistic groups, but English was the language of worship and communication. It was an opportunity to work with such heterogeneous group; however, our faith in Christ bound us together. Most of them fairly adjusted with the Methodist tradition, and some struggled to reconcile with the Methodist order of worship and episcopal administrative system. It was easy to hold them together as far as programmes were concerned; however, at times, it was tough when it came to the order of worship and church governance,

I experienced silent protest due to lack of conforming tendency. My commitment to the church administrative system was grossly misconstrued, as if I was dictating, unlike other pastors who were nonconformist. I felt it was essential for pastors to integrate with Methodism, so to help lay members who came from non-Methodist church traditions. I conceived, it was one of the major problems in big cities. A number of pastors who came from non-Methodist church traditions tended to be nonconformists, as far as the Wesleyan tradition was concerned. When I was on the Board of Leonard Theological College of the church, Jabalpur, I suggested to start the department of Wesleyan studies to help Methodist students and to conduct seminars in various conferences to create Wesleyan awareness. I was sad, nothing of the kind happened. During the tercentenary celebration, I noticed that there were more Methodists than I had known who had very little or no idea of Methodism, its founder John Wesley, and Wesleyan spirituality. John Wesley and his brother Charles Wesley were responsible for the rise and spread of Methodism, and yet most Methodists in India were strangers to their spiritual mentors.

In mega cities and industrial towns, there were some community churches which did not insist on membership affiliation, for their purpose was limited to provide an opportunity to worship and Christian fellowship. Christians living in cities faced hard times to travel to churches in downtown on all Sundays and on other occasions, as most of them lived far off, in uptown. They inclined to attend a church which was closer to their residence, even if it may not be their own denominational church or it could even be a community church, as traveling was strenuous and time consuming. Despite this, most of them tried to attend their denominational churches at least on holy communion Sundays and on festivals. It helped them maintain denominational ties in some way. I observed that irregular participation and fewer interactions with members of their denomination church eventually weaken the ties. The pastors of their denominational churches strenuously tried to keep their flock together; however, still they could not effectively tie the loose ends, and mere distance and time taken to travel dampened their enthusiasm. It seemed that the choice to attend other than one's denominational church or a community church was more by proximity and complexity of urban living than doctrinal beliefs or inner cravings.

Academic Pursuit

I was faithful in my pastoral ministry; whatever work I took in my hand, I put my mind and soul into it and did it with my utmost sincerity and with the best of my ability. I wanted to study further although there were no definite plans; however, as time passed by, I was clear about it. My bishop gave me permission to pursue graduate and doctoral studies at the University of Bombay.

We were still living with Maud Stewart, but we realized it was time to move out of the private house to a church house, as she was preparing to move to an old-age home, some of her distant relatives were working on it. We were happy about it, as it was good for her to move to a safe and secure place so that she could be looked after in her old age. Our work in the church could have necessitated us to move even out of the city, and it could have been very difficult for her to move with us, although we were willing to look after her.

There was latent resistance to allot the church's house on 21, YMCA Road, Bombay Central. Anyway, despite political pressures, I was successful in securing a residence by convincing S. K. Parmar, the then bishop of the Bombay Episcopal Area. He held a PhD from Iliff School of Theology, Denver, and was a professor in the Leonard Theological College, Jabalpur, in the field of the New Testament. On November 10, 1979, we eventually crossed all hurdles and shifted to women's hostel building on 21, YMCA Road. The house was in bad condition. My congregation did not have money on them to fix it, so we just managed, and long after, we could paint it. When I started to work on my PhD in Bombay University, he was still the area bishop. I felt, it was hard to read his mind, for he was a bit secretive and in idiosyncrasy shook his legs. He asked me to take charge of the Bowen Church at the Gateway of India. I convinced him, it would be difficult for me to serve the church along with my study. Not long after, he asked me to live in Igatpuri, a place 140 km away from Bombay. I learnt, once upon a time, there was a flourishing English congregation, the town had a railway colony, railway officials and others attended the church services during the British era. Both church and parsonage were in very bad stage; moreover, it was impractical to commute frequently from there to the university; mere distance could have wasted time, dampen my spirit, and worn me out, leave alone inefficient and the lack of transportation. I convinced the bishop and stayed back and continued in the same congregation.

It was testing time in terms of financial support for the study and the church ministry; however, certainly not mutually exclusive. I could manage on those counts, as I was well acquainted with the church members. In the early years of my study, I secured the Crusade's Scholarship of the United Methodist Church and long after the university awarded me research fellowship. I spent nearly seven years on the university's Kalina campus, right from my graduate study, not knowing, what I would do after my PhD, and I learnt and unlearnt many lessons during those years. It was privilege to do my doctoral work under Dhirendra Narain, the professor of sociology and a student of G. S. Ghurye – a sociologist of an international repute. He was known for his scholarship, intellectual disposition, and hard work. He had an impressive personality, penetrating look, and intellectual sharpness. I recall, while going through my thesis, he said, 'You may write everything and say nothing.' His words stayed with me since then and influenced my thinking and skill. Not long after my thesis was finalized and was under typing, he said that he would bring a book for me to read from his personal library; I do not remember the title. I was a bit disturbed in my mind; surprisingly the book did not come. In his long tenure at the university, I was one of those few students until then, awarded PhD under his guidance. I had great time in the University; I read Karl Marx, Max Weber, Emile Durkheim, Robert K. Merton, Peter L. Berger, Eric Fromm, and the work of several celebrated authors and heard eminent scholars in seminars. Marxist intellectuals were more active than capitalist thinkers; regardless, I was concerned about startling disparity between rich and poor. I became a life member of the Indian Sociological Society, got interested in academic pursuit and desired to do postdoctoral work. In the year 1984, I applied for the prestigious postdoctoral Andrew Mellon fellowship of the University of Pittsburgh, which was contested by prospective scholars from world over, with three strong recommendation letters from my professors. My research proposal of the role of religious leaders in economic development evaluated and approved by the university academic selection committee, but not offered the postdoctoral fellowship, there was stiff competition from European students. I was melancholic and abandoned the thought of applying for the following year.

Then, the Indian Council of Scientific Research, an undertaking of the government of India in New Delhi, offered me work. We declined the offer, as it would mean leaving the church's ministry, for our first priority was the church's ministry and all other opportunities had to be compatible to it.

Assaulted

I was aware, some leaders in the conference were unhappy with me for some curious political reasons. It seemed, they considered me an obstacle, as I used to raise inconvenient questions on sale and developments of church properties. One N. Kanakaraj, a lay member of the church, claimed he was an industrialist and had good rapport with some office bearers of the conference for some curious reason. He was elected as financial agent (treasurer) of the Financial Board of the Bombay Annual Conference, a registered trust of the church. On July 21, 1985, Sunday, I was returning from the church worship service. As I was walking on the footbridge of Bombay Central railway station, an unknown man, the assaulter, all of a sudden bounced on me, slapped me, pulled my spectacles, scuttled and before I could identify him, vanished in crowd. I was led to suspect his possible hand in it, as he was not comfortable with my voice against his handling of responsibility. We were set to celebrate the second birthday of Virtu, my younger daughter, the incident stole our joy; we were startled and the tiny tot stared at lighted colourful birthday candles, unaware of our sorrow, and had she known, she could have shared it. I remember, not long before the incident, when I was upset and refused meal, she stretched her little hand with morsels to feed me, and I liked it. Prior to the incident, we observed that some people suspiciously moved in a car on 21, YMCA Road, as if they were doing recce; then we could not imagine we had to go through such traumas in our life.

My colleague pastors protested the insane act; however, Eric Mitchell, the then bishop of Bombay Episcopal Area, a good man and a great storyteller, did not rise to the occasion as I expected. N. Kanakaraj was good in making friends and influencing church leaders. He posed himself as a capitalist and generous man and announced donation to various causes of the church, which I remember he seldom gave. Following the incidence, I met Stanley Downes, who was the then general secretary of the church. He was a good preacher; however, he was obsessed with his Anglo-Indian roots and flexible to the rules of the church than his inner cravings. I casually shared with him the incident, instead of condemning it, he said, 'Let us not blow the balloon too much.' N. Kanakaraj's working suggested lack of transparent handling of the church property matters and money; audit report showed that he did not account for all money, the church filed recovery suit, but barely pressed it. He also entered into the secret property deal with a property developer for the Bishop's House, Bombay. He called himself a member of the World Methodist Council and took handsome advance. The property developer filed the legal suit in the Bombay High Court, claiming the possession of the property; however, it was dismissed. I was amazed that instead of opposing, some leaders seemed to have secretly supported, and Taranath Sagar, then his pastor, was soft on him.

R. D. Joshi encouraged the greater involvement of laity in the church. In the early era of Methodism, there was protest in the church over nonrepresentation of laity in the Methodist conferences. In 1828, those who protested, separated from the main church and called themselves the Methodist Protestant Church[2]. In following years, the church joined union of churches, and the row over nonrepresentation of laity was settled by allowing lay representation. It was a good move, for there are committed and competent laypersons in the church who should be encouraged to engage in the ministry of the church. However, I found such committed laypersons kept themselves away from the church politics and election; mostly, the laypersons of a doubtful integrity took active part in the church politics and administration and frustrated the efforts of laypersons of integrity to take leadership roles. I found, some laypersons were venal, easily accessible to the church leaders to achieve their vested interests or to settle their score with their brother bishops. They acted as lobbyists, spread fictions than facts, and mobilized public opinion. The church did little or nothing to dissuade such acts and to lead the church in the right direction, deliver justice, and preach the message of love. The church government often became susceptible to latent function that reduced its effectiveness.

After the incident, I was cautious to go out or return late in the evening after my pastoral visitation; however, God gave me courage to overcome anxiety. A pastor who acted like a social activist suggested me to wear cross like a knife. I did not do it; instead, I carried a small loose pack of chilli powder in my pocket to be used like capsicum spray, to defend myself; however, there arose no such occasion to use it. I was alert and careful, prayed to God for his protection and guidance.

Push and Pull

Not long after, in November 1984, I earned my PhD in sociology from the University of Bombay. I thought, I could make a small contribution to the life and ministry of the church; however, I realized, in the church, one could either get an appointment for some covetous post that would enable him to do creative work or contest an election for some leadership position. An appointment to the post to do creative work was rare. I was in ambivalence, as I disliked contesting election; however, there was no way by which I could use my learning. I was bubbling to use my talents and experience for the service of the church; sadly, some leaders in the church were envious of my academic achievement and leadership potential; they viewed me like a political foe. In the situation, I had no other choice than to get into an election fray if I was to contribute my mite to the life and ministry of church.

It was a defining moment; I could no longer resist contesting election. Given the election culture, I was aware, I would make some church leaders either friends or foes and ugly literature machine would slash mud on me and my opponents would politically try to marginalize me. It appeared that the church leaders were immune to it, but I was not; sometimes, it got uglier than secular politics. The ideal situation did not exist, latent political inappropriateness flourished in the lack of genuine spiritual awakening. I entered into it to face it, for the sake of doing useful work. Until 1983, I was apolitical; I started to contest elections from 1984. Every time I contested an election, I was elected with ease and often in first ballot with the highest votes[3]. There were some among my colleague pastors and laypersons who opposed me; however, they could not hold me back, as by then, I gained credibility and influence in the conference. I had strong followings in the conference who expected me to take up their problems before committees and the conference. They did not approve the way some leaders irresponsibly handled serious matters; neither could they support nor speak against them, for the perils of coercion. I took up their concerns and helped pastors in their difficulties in various committees and boards. They found in me an anchor, I won their hearts as well votes, without asking them to vote for me, most of them voted for me almost for a decade until I was elected as a bishop. The threat of transfer or assignment, the correct word to use, renders most pastors as a silent spectator; it is not the exaggeration of the political milieu, it actually existed; it could be because of lack of openness to constructive criticism. Even though the right to expression was prudently exercised to edify the church, It was severely threatened or throttled; however, good leaders took cue from it. I found that church leaders at times were anything but intolerant; they turned joy into despair and failed to allow the free flow of edifying expressions.

In 1984, for the first time, I attended the General Conference of the church. I heard a lot about it that it was a highest administrative and Legislative body of the church. It was composed of ministerial and lay delegates from all Regional Conferences and ex-officio members, and active bishops presided over it by rotation[4]. I spent time to learn its working and diligently studied the rules and procedures given in the *Book of Discipline – the Constitution and Byelaws of the Church*, generally called the Discipline; sometimes Bluebook for its cover page has always been blue. I remember my colleague pastor gifted me *Roberts Rules of Orders*, which he got from the USA. I studied it. I deliberated in the General Conference held in Jabalpur, it was my maiden deliberation that put me on the committee framing, 'An Affirmation of Social Principles', I contributed my best. After the conference, I was pleasantly surprised to receive a letter from L.

R. Lance, the then bishop of Delhi Episcopal Area, congratulating me for my participation. The bishop had a good personality, he was nearing retirement; he was tall and medium built, nearly bald, and had medium dark complexion. He had a deep voice and impressive mannerism; he spoke fluent English and Hindustani – a mix up of Hindi and Urdu language. People loved and respected him. In the letter, he wrote, 'Several people were favourably impressed, the way in which you participated in the Conference.' He wished me well in my life.

Most delegates were good to me; however, some of my colleague pastors from Bombay Conference played politics. I remember the pastor who worked with social organization in Bombay, initiated by R. D. Joshi played ruse with me. He had no much formal education; however, he was amazing in the homiletic of politics and I could never match him. He came running to me while I was standing on the volleyball ground at the Leonard Theological College Campus during the General Conference Session. He said that I was nominated for the post of executive secretary of the Council of Social Concerns. Not long after, I learnt they dropped my name from the nomination list, as by then they realized that I could not be taken lightly. I felt ridiculed, until then barely interested in elections though the election politics was contagious. I could not insulate or remain unaffected by the political waves. Being human, I reacted to the politics of nomination, I entered the election fray; I felt I should have waited for a ripe time. Anyway, I lost the election to Victor Raja by a narrow margin, giving a tough fight. I was not unhappy, but I was inspired to stand for election in the future and was elected as a member of the council like a consolation prize and also to the Council of Education and Christian Nurture that brought me close to Mehar Singh, the then executive secretary of the council. Election per se was not bad; however, it led to evils; people became bias, and unfair means influenced voters and treated competitors like enemies. I realized there was no way by which the process of election could be eliminated in democracy.

In early 1987, Regional Executive Board elected me as executive secretary, which fell vacant by turn of events. Elliot D. Clive was the then bishop of the Bombay Episcopal Area. The bishop's right-hand person prompted me to contest the election, although I was reluctant, but they prevailed. The opponent candidate against me was a politically strong and influential pastor, he enjoyed support; number was in his favour, as many of the board members were his relatives. We had friendly relations; I helped him to do Bachelor of Law from Ruparel Law College, an affiliated college to the University of Bombay. I knew S. Radhakrishnan, a professor in the college who eventually became a judge of the Bombay High Court. I requested him to assist; on my request, he was glad to do so. It was a very tough election, I was elected by one vote; by chance, V. P. Gaikwad, a lay member of the board, changed his position and he voted in my favour, and I won the election. He became my close friend and we were guests in his house in Pune for a few days. He was fabulous. Interestingly, he used to argue that the onus of proof lies on an accused; contrary to accepted norm, I used to laugh over it. Anyway, my relationship with the politically influential pastor strained, resulted in bitterness, for he assumed himself as an indispensable leader of the Bombay Conference, none could dare to oppose him.

It was challenging work; the bishop thought, I would oblige him to do all things and support his even improper decisions, which I did not. I remember, once I did not sign provident papers of an influential retired pastor, not because we had any bad blood between us, it was simply the matter of rules and equity. He was in occupation of the church residence even after his superannuation. They coerced me to sign his papers without complying with the rules, whereas there was another retired pastor who met all requirements, whose papers were withheld without any valid reason. Not long after, I had to sign the papers of the influential pastor when given an indemnity bound, but the other pastor still struggled to get his provident fund released simply because he had some political differences with the conference stalwarts who mattered. After much persuasion, he received his retirement benefits. In his last days, he was a widower and lonely. He had no money on him; his son snatched away money and deserted him. Not long after, it was heart-breaking to know; he was hit by a speeding train and died. The bishop and his men were disappointed; they found me like a hot potato. I, too, was not at ease; I was melancholic to see, the way in which church leaders politically handled sensitive issues, defiled rules and had scant respect for natural justice. I felt suffocated to work in such a vicious environment. I was in a dilemma whether to fall in line or to look for an alternative – I preferred the latter over the former.

The bishop did not appreciate my concerns, even to the extent that he dissuaded pastors to meet or vote for me. He wanted to get rid of me by sending me out of the conference to teach in Leonard Theological College. I, too, thought, it was a good idea if I could get an opportunity; however, it did not work out. The political culture in the church puzzled me, I could not understand the way the church leadership behaved and did things. I was disappointed in the way some were unfairly treated; the church leaders did not act in conformity with the rules and principles they adored. The situation in the church was no different from anywhere else; it was even not edifying the church. I knew that intrinsic human behavioural patterns are the same or similar everywhere: worldliness overshadowing spirituality throughout the church history. I was inexperienced, never indulged in diplomacy or deceptive politics; however, I eagerly sought the appreciable presence of the holiness of life among the church leaders. It was perhaps my unrealistic expectation, not out of holier-than-thou-art attitude. My desire to follow the rule of law strained my relations with those in authority; some thought I was self-centred and maverick. The church leaders were easy-going and without hesitation defied rules, if it came on their way to self-fulfilment and personal preferences; however, some bishops lived by Christian values and rules. It seemed that there was an absence of ideal spiritual leaders in the church, but by no means, it dwarfed the Christian faith. I believed, if practiced, it would facilitate tolerance and understanding, for there is a relation between faith and practice. I read that Max Weber, a celebrated German sociologist, found elective affinity between certain types of beliefs and economic practices among the Calvinist sect of Protestants, in his celebrated study, *Protestant Ethics and the Spirit of Capitalism*[5]. I was striving to live by my faith like others, overcome negative energy, and hold on to truth, justice, and equity. My earnest endeavours were awfully misunderstood, and they thought I was captive to myself; maybe I was, however, never short on the church's interests – it was my first love. I was committed to the church's values and supported pastors who did not get justice, though I had to displease bishops and other church leaders. Nevertheless, I was conscious of my limitation; however, my desire to help those in need never eluded. I was not wary of right things, and in doing so, I never could think I would have to face ordeals.

Looking for Change

I was the founding pastor of the congregation for sixteen years from the time I started the church. I was keen to have change in my pastoral assignment. I requested every bishop who came to Bombay Episcopal Area; none was keen to help me. I learnt some political heavy weight pastors were opposing me; they felt that if another English congregation was assigned to me, it would mean elevating me to a better position. I did not look from their political perspective, I was not interested in the church politics, nor did I know game-changing political dynamics. I was simply a faithful worker of the church, desiring to support the right and just cause to edify the church; however, they deprived me of every available opportunity in the conference and I abandoned the thought of requesting for change in my assignment. In my despondency, I began to think of working in a church-related organization elsewhere while keeping my conference's membership intact, so to use my learning in a better and bigger way for the church at large.

It so happened, one of my seminary friends asked me to apply to the Daystar University, Nairobi. The university was looking for a research professor who could be on the team to build a Christian university in Africa. I applied for it, and Elliot D. Clive, the then bishop of the Bombay Episcopal Area, was glad to write a recommendation. After several months of correspondence and compliance of requirements, on August 3, 1988, I received a letter of appointment; three months' time was given to join. I was to raise my support with their help. By faith in God, I accepted the appointment and began to prepare to leave for Nairobi. I resigned from the post of executive secretary of the conference and sold household goods.

I was amazed to receive a telephone call from James C. Lal, the then general secretary of the church, asking me for telephone numbers of the university; for he said he was going to Nairobi. Curiously after that the university never responded and I do not know if Elliot D. Clive withdrew his recommendation as well. It seemed he smashed our hope; perhaps it was treachery, born out of jealousy. We were torn and in tears over the loss of our hope and money. It took quite some time to recover from the unexpected shock. I was not sceptic of my fellow church workers. I believed they were as good as their word, not knowing some took pleasure and pride in harming others. We were sad, helpless, and not knowing what would be our future. It deeply wounded our heart and made negative imprints on our mind, only miracle could erase it. I was appalled and thought how come the church leaders be so and would it not affect the life and ministry of the church? It was absolutely beyond my comprehension, how some people tarnish the ideal image of the church. I consoled myself; I felt I should not expect higher things from the men who were living in a lower spiritual realm, not struggling to surface over flesh and blood. I had many such experiences; later in life we realized people meant bad, God meant good. We were melancholic, broken in spirit, drained out physically; however, the words of an unknown Christian soldier in the Daystar's appointment letter gave us courage to face the future with hope and boldness:

'I asked God for strength that I might achieve

I was made weak that I might humbly obey.

I asked God for health that I might do great things,

I was given infirmity that I might do better things.

I asked God for power that I might have the praise of men,

I was given weakness that I might enjoy all things.

I got nothing that I asked for. . .

However, everything I had hoped for. . .

> Almost despite myself, my unspoken
> prayers were answered,
> I am among all men most richly blessed.'

In the moment of our sadness, we did not know God's plan for us. We were bitter in the way some church leaders treated us, became obstacles, a little, we realized then that God had a better plan, plans for our welfare, which he would fulfil in his own time. Henceforth, our life was to take a different turn, the way God planned, I never could have imagined it.

Serving the Poor
and Needy

By the providence of grace, the mantle to serve the poor and needy fell on me. It was the church's holistic response to the poor and needy in Indian society. At my personal level, I always cared for the poor and needy ones. I could help them in some small ways, within my means, and then the church gave the opportunity to help them in bigger ways. Some of my colleagues felt that I was a self-serving person, living for my own existence in my own world, barely did they recognize that it was not so. I truly felt for the poor and needy; however, those who experienced me knew that I, too, had kinder and compassionate instincts like those who are unable to bear the poverty and misery of people. Bombay City had striking contrasts in living conditions. At times, it was heart breaking to see uncared rag clad people on the side walks, curiously searching for food in thrown away stuff to satisfy their hunger unlike affluent who ran in modern sporty outfits on beaches and in jogging tracks to burn excess calories, patiently waiting to be equal with them, but only in dust. Obliviously, hunger is a global problem, it cannot be easily eradicated; however, the thought of doing something in my own small little circle for poor and needy ones in some measure never left me. On the matter of truth and justice, I was always ready to help those who suffered. I confess I am not a social activist, but out of concern, not politics, I stood by those who suffered oppression and injustice. Then, a God-given opportunity came to serve depressed and dejected ones, in the Indian society through the Council of Relief and Rehabilitation (CORAR).

Struggle to Begin Work

I heard, people say, there is an appointment in disappointment. This was true in our case as well; we were dejected, as we could not go to the Daystar University. From May 29 to June 1, 1989, Bombay Regional Conference's session was held at Union Biblical Seminary, Pune. Again, I was elected as a ministerial delegate to the General Conference's third session. There were forces as usual working against me in the conference; during the conference session, whenever I came face to face with Elliot D. Clive, the then presiding bishop, he gave an artificial smile. I could perceive his immense dislike for me; he was dissuading ministerial members from electing me as delegate, for he desired to continue in the Bombay Episcopal Area for a second term; perhaps he felt that I would come on his way. Although faced by stiff opposition from those who did not like me, I was elected without much hassle, as I had sufficient and necessary number of ministerial voting members on my side. From October 24 to 31, 1989, the Third Regular Sessions of the General Conference was held in Jabalpur; it adjourned, as it could not complete its business. Then from May 22 to 29, 1990, the Adjourned Session was held at Tambaram, Chennai; again the business could not be completed. So again, from September 16 to 23, 1990, a special session of the Third Regular Session of the General Conference was called in Bangalore. I did not plan to contest any election in the conference. Samuel R. Thomas, a cautious critique and a debate lover, was the then executive secretary of the CORAR. He was leading the episcopal election and eventually he was elected as a bishop, his post fell vacant. It was interesting; he supported me for the post of executive secretary of the CORAR. In the beginning, I was reluctant to contesting the election for the post, as it involved the handling of huge relief funds. After much thinking and persuasion from James Nathan, the then an ordained minister of Lucknow Regional Conference, one of my good friends and episcopal aspirant, I decided to enter into the election fray. A. P. Salve, my colleague pastor from Bombay Conference and other aspirants were well stocked and positioned to contest the election. On hearing me contest the election, A. P. Salve sprang up with vigour although he was in a bed with a minor illness. I took it as a challenge and canvassed tirelessly; several people positively responded and on September 23, 1990, I was elected as executive secretary of the CORAR.

The council was loaded with heavy weight politicians of the church. Karriappa Samuel, the then bishop of Bangalore Area, was assigned the chairmanship of the CORAR; a resolute and hardworking person, he earned PhD in philosophy from Rani Durgawati University Jabalpur, taught religion and philosophy in the Leonard Theological College, and counted himself among the intellectual class. Hard nut politicians: Nirmal David, James Nathan, G. M. Lal and S. Charles, John Hanchinmani, central treasurer – in short, treasurer, and others were on the council. It was not easy to work with the team, for one would never know in which way things would swing.

In the beginning, Stanley Downes seemed well disposed towards me, the then bishop of Bombay Episcopal Area, but not long after, he became unreasonable. He insisted on me for some curious reason to vacate the house, which I occupied since 1979. I was reluctant to rent a house; so without wasting time, he took up the matter before the Regional Executive Board. He was anxious to approve the resolution, making me vacate the residence; however, the board was not with him on his move. On his unimagined defeat, he was resentful; he raised his eyebrows and voice and made poignant gestures. I watched him with awe and felt as if he was waiting for some turn to revenge his defeat. However, I continued to live in the same house. There was yet another row over the allotment of office for the CORAR in the Methodist Centre, Bombay. The centre was built by the initiative of American missionaries; it was dedicated on May 29, 1971, by four active bishops of the preceding era; just after six months failing to join the union of churches of North India. The building was of its own kind in those days, centrally air-conditioned and envious to other church denominations. Perhaps, it was envisaged as a symbol of superiority of episcopal administration and the nourishing of body, mind, and soul, however as the years passed by, it seemed the body was nourished, souls starved, and the mind devoted to vicious political activities, and it became like a political ghetto. Who controlled it mattered and became synonymous to power. Stanley Downes, the then chairman of the centre, pressurized members of the Methodist Centre Committee, not to allot an office space. After much struggle, I succeeded in getting an office cabin, which was heart breaking for the bishop. I asked him to assign my membership to the local church where I served as founding pastor, he declined; I was perplexed at his unyielding and wondered if he was reacting to my not supporting him in his episcopal election. He had to make herculean efforts to be elected as bishop; the Adjourned Session was called and he was elected as bishop in 1985, at seventy eight ballots, the highest number of ballots ever cast until then. There was a pastor who assumed himself as an indispensable leader of the Bombay Conference, who seemed to have filled his ear against me, as he was envious of me; out of jealousy and grudges, he said that I did not vote for him; however, he concealed the fact that he, too, was an ardent supporter of the candidate I supported. The bishop indulged in trivial politics and tended to infringe the democratic right to choose and vote, which is essential in democracy. Sadly, he did not realize, by opposing me, he was becoming an obstacle to the ministry to the poor and needy. I could not imagine that the bishop was nurturing grudges and failed to appreciate others' preferences. I felt sad; the work of the church suffered and divided people on the issues, which were nonissues.

The CORAR run the projects and programmes funded by the United Methodist Church Committee on Relief (UMCOR). It was a commendable endeavour; many deserving people received help. It worked in the area of water development, Economic self-reliance programmes, hunger, primary health, relief and rehabilitation in general, and the rehabilitation of Tibetan refugees[1]. A number of people were helped in inside and outside the church through these projects and programmes. The UMCOR raised funds in the Unites States; 'One Great Hour of Sharing' was a great occasion to do so, negligible donation was raised within the church. I believed I must be a responsible steward when dispensing the fund. The treasurer held the funds and my duty was to ensure that money was spent on projects and programmes to help the suffering and needy people. In the beginning, it was well; however, gradually, projects and programmes' voting pattern became disappointing.

Projects and Programmes

The projects and programmes were to help the poor and needy throughout the country, irrespective of caste, creed, and religion. The aim was to address basic human needs. Thousands of people around the country were supported in the time of crises and disasters. I realized that the CORAR could have been more effective if it was an agency, having its own qualified and trained field workers and staff in the area of relief and rehabilitation like the Church's Auxiliary for Social Action (CASA) or World Vision or similar social agencies. I felt it was a major setback, as the CORAR wholly relied on local church leaders for emergency response. It was good to take local help; however, doing the work with trained field workers and project personnel could have been altogether a different story; it could have enriched its working and continuity. I felt 1981 was the good time to do so, when the UMCOR handed over its work to the CORAR. From a panel of names of experienced persons in the field of social work or relief and rehabilitation, the council members could have selected. I, too, had no specialized training; however, as a social scientist, I could understand the dynamics of rural and urban social system and development. I easily formulated and evaluated project proposals. I felt if had I some training or exposure in the area of relief and rehabilitation, my efficiency could have further excelled. However, it was by no means any obstacle to rendering faithful and honest service to the poor and needy. I had some challenging and exciting experiences, besides routine work; I cherish its memory.

On October 20, 1991, a massive earthquake shook Uttarkashi town, Uttarakhand State, the epicentre was Manheri, twenty kilometers away from the town; 9,000 feet above the sea level, and tremors were felt in radius of 400 kilometers. The urgent relief response was required. At once, I got into action and contacted Samuel R. Thomas, the then Bishop of Bareilly Episcopal Area introduced me to some local leaders who assisted me. I then contacted Tara Chand, a Methodist ordained minister from Pauri Garhwal, and Prem Lal Shah, a layman from Dehradun. We decided to assemble in Dehradun to prepare relief action plans. By the time I reached the place, these leaders were already waiting for me. After we had a preliminary discussion and planning, I along with Tara Chand proceeded to Uttarkashi. I found him a very cooperative and humble man, ready to do anything for the relief work without any hesitation. He was acquainted with the geography of the area, but for me, it was altogether a new experience. As we travelled, we came across roadblocks at several places, restaurants not seen for miles, and it was cold and windy; however, we reached Bhatwadi village, thirty kilometers away from Uttarkashi. By the time we reached, it was dark. Some relief agencies were already camped. They arranged some food for us and we managed to sleep in one of their tents; the night was very cold and windy and adjoining Gangotri River made it even colder. I had no sufficient warm clothing. I was shivering throughout the night; I curled, turned, and wriggled in my sleeping bag, trying to conquer the cold.

The next day, we inspected the area and held discussions with people who were already doing the relief work, ascertained from them emergency needs. We met some affected people from nearby villages; we could not interact with people in the villages on the higher mountainous area, as it was time consuming. Several villages were affected, houses collapsed, and dead bodies were buried under debris; approach roads and bridges were damaged. In the first half of the day, we assessed the situation, and in the afternoon, we started to return to Dehradun. It was exciting to look at beautiful and charming mountains, mostly consisting of rocks such as metamorphic, sand, and clay; they were covered with majestic cedar and pine trees and their height was high, as if touching the blue sky and declaring the glory of God and assuring everyone that God was still in the control of the precarious situation. There was no pollution, air was pure, and the river water was very clean. I could see fish, but impossible to count them. I observed people were simple, hardworking, and anxious about their life and safety, but stricken with grief and worried about sporadic aftershocks, even more. I wished I could have spent a few days more; however, the situation necessitated us to return to do something for the people in need. As we travelled back, we were faced with heavy traffic, roadblocks at several places, and the scare of fresh tremors. We travelled through risky mountain roads, pitch dark and cold night, and early in the morning we reached Dehradun. We were tired and hungry; God protected us from dacoits, wild animals, and accidents.

Having put together the pieces of the earthquake picture, we decided to arrange 500 thick plastic tarpaulins, as we found that some relief agencies had given cotton tarpaulins, which would not withstand rain and snow. A relief team was organized, consisting of teachers from Messmore Inter College, a Methodist college in Pauri Garhwal. The team reached the place along with the relief materials. I, too, reached there. On the first day, we distributed the relief material to those who were easily accessible. I returned to Bombay, the team stayed back to complete the relief work on the following days, as the houses were far off on mountains, thinly scattered, and it was difficult to reach them on the same day with the relief materials.

On our way back, we passed through the construction site of Tehri damn. We met Sunder Lal Bahuguna, a prominent leader of *Chipko* movement, committed to save the ecology. He was on protest against the construction of the damn. His supporters and admirers surrounded him. A medium-sized man with a long beard, he looked like a hermit; however, he was committed to green revolution like Vinoba Bhave. He was passionate about it; he spoke with conviction to preserve the ecology of the area. We could see massive work in progress that affected several villages and covered a very large area of land with huge heaps of soil, stone, and sand. The issue remained alive for many years. I hope there is greater awareness on the serious issue of climate change to protect our beautiful blue planet. We wished we could spend more time with him; however, it was time to move, as we had to travel through unknown and risky roads, in the middle of the night; however, we knew God was with us. I remember we reached Dehradun after midnight.

There was also relief request from the people of Pauri Garhwal; the earthquake damaged their houses. A local committee was formed, a list of affected families was prepared, and relief money was sent to D. B. Singh, a deaconess of the Moradabad Regional Conference and the manager of the Methodist Hostel. I reached on the eve of the relief distribution to Pauri Garhwal along with Paul Saraswat, an ordained minister of

Moradabad Regional Conference, energetic, active, and had years of experience in the CORAR work. The affected people assembled at the mission compound and as per the list, the relief was distributed and those who received the relief money signed on receipts. In the evening, I started to return to Kotdwar. No sooner did our car covered some distance than we saw a horde running behind us and others chased us in a jeep. They stopped our car and expressed their grievances in the manner in which names were included in the list, leaving out some affected ones. I assured them we would look into their need, but they were tough and insisted for the relief to be given to them right away though I assured they would be given relief – not long after, we sent them relief. After great perseverance, we could convince them and continued our journey. We reached Kotdwar town at midnight, eating places were closed; however, providentially, there was a dimly lit small teashop; we sipped hot tea with toasts, it was our late-night full course dinner, and we had the dingy inn to sleep in; it was all that was stored for the night. At dawn, I travelled to Delhi via Moradabad.

The next thing was to build houses to rehabilitate the earthquake-affected families. It was critical to decide about the type and size of houses, for they were to be earthquake resistant, suitable for local weather, and compatible to their culture and life style. I had several consultations with experts in the field on what type of houses were to be built. Finally, the design was chosen and the construction work was given to a contractor from Dehradun with approved cost, design, and material. Prem Lal Shah, a Methodist leader, helped the committee; thirty six houses were planned to be built on about 9,000 feet above sea level. I visited the sites again when the construction work was in progress. Thereafter, I could not go, as there was change in the leadership.

In Panahpur village – it means a place of refuse; we decided to take up rural development project. The village was located near Shahjahanpur town in Uttar Pradesh; it was primarily an agricultural community and its population was largely Methodist Christians; some claimed their ancestors migrated from Rajasthan. I learnt the church's missionaries helped very poor Christian families to settle in the village; interestingly, they continued to show the symptoms of excessive dependence. The road to the village was in a broken condition, with potholes at several places; it was more torturing to travel by a motorcar than to walk down to the village. The village school was still running in the partially ruined building, but the church and parsonage were in a stable condition; however, they needed major repairs.

Most houses in the village were of mud walls, without any drainage system, clean drinking water facilities, and primary health care facility and for any major illness, people had to go to either Shahjahanpur or Bareilly. Those who did not work on agriculture went towns to earn their livelihood; some worked in Nave Technical Institute of the Church in Shahjahanpur. Most village children studied either in the Methodist schools at Govindganj or the Nave Technical Institute at Lodipur in Shahjahanpur and lived in the Bidwell or Nave Institute hostels.

It was our desire to develop the village with local participation. A series of meetings were held with people of the village, several suggestions poured in, and sometimes, it was not easy to accommodate everyone's idea. However, it was decided to start primary health facilities, provide hand water pumps, and repair parsonage building to store grains during harvest, and restore school and repair church buildings so that they could be used for various activities. The repair work was undertaken, the extension to the parsonage carried out for the storage of grains. The church members from Bareilly and Shahjahanpur visited and interacted with them. However, as the time passed by, I was disheartened, the village people reduced their active participation; several activities started with a great enthusiasm could not be sustained, and gradually, the initial euphoria dwindled. Then I realized we were heading towards a clumsy failure, as no rural development programme could be successful without local participation. There was yet another major setback; field worker did not live in the village to interact with the people, which was the key to effective implementation of the programme. He seldom tarried in the village, lacked initiatives, commitment, and vision, and showed negligible interest. We could do some work; making the village a model for rural development remained our distant dream.

The UMCOR was committed to rehabilitating Tibetan refugees. In 1950, the Communist China occupied Tibet, and in 1959, under the leadership of their spiritual and temporal leader the Fourteenth Dalai Lama, Tibetans escaped the Chinese invasion of Tibet and established the Tibetan government in exile at Dharmsala. During one of my visits to Tibetan camps, they presented me the book *My Land and My people, Memoirs of the Dalai Lama*. I read it; there is a vivid account of the Tibetan escape, suffering, and struggles[2]. The struggle for free Tibet is on-going with faded hope by each passing day. It seems they have the critical choice, between free Tibet and autonomy. Of course, I perceive, the future will tell what they ultimately will get, one of those two or none of those.

Tibetan refugees made their home in India and settled in Himalayan ranges from Himachal to Arunachal. Perhaps Buddhism, geographic proximity and political interests led to affinities between Tibetans and Indians. During my visit to several Tibetan camps, I found them hardworking and hospitable. They run schools and monasteries and did welfare work for their community. One of their main occupations was carpet weaving; people earned their livelihood, although meager. There were many needs, but housing people in decent shelters was their greatest concern. We were committed to help the housing project at Manali camp in Himachal Pradesh as it was stalled for want of fund. Weather conditions are harsh in the area: heavy rainfall, cold winter, and snowfall. The designated UMCOR housing fund diligently spent on rehabilitating them and they also received funds from other international donor agencies.

I could visit Arunachal Pradesh, a restricted area even for Indians. I had to obtain a permit to visit the state. On landing at the Bagdogra Airport in Darjeeling district of West Bengal, Tibetan social welfare officials met me at the airport. They were courteous, cheerful, excited and greeted me in their tradition. From there, we travelled by a car to Arunachal Pradesh; all along the way, the scenery was splendid, lofty mountains and tall bamboo clusters looked gorgeous. As we got near to our destination, we escaped a major accident, the car's front left wheel skidded on the muddy road, facing a steep mountain cliff, and it was dark and raining. My heart throbbed, I thought I was going to God; however, we escaped the tragedy. They lodged me in a military guesthouse; officers were cordial and cooperative. Tibetan schools impressed me; housing and social welfare activities did fairly well. A visit to Gangtok, Sikkim, was mesmerizing, a beautiful place surrounded by enticing snow-capped mountain peaks. The sight of Kangchenjunga, 28,170 feet highest Himalayan peak in India and third highest on the earth was tranquil and transcending. A visit to Dharamsala in Himachal Pradesh settlement was interesting and educating; it is the seat of the Tibetan government headquarters in exile. I could not meet Dalai Lama, as he was on tour at that time. As said, Tibetans settled there; the second generation of Tibetans consider themselves Indians and not inclined to return to their homeland; however, they never forgot where they came from. There is a very famous church in Mcleodganj, very close to Dharamsala. People spoke high about the church bell; it was of a very big size; its sound was vibrating and far-reaching, and its resounding was enchanting.

I found elderly Tibetans had a very strong desire to go back to their own homeland and were dreaming of a free Tibet. Their enthusiasm to preserve their tradition and culture never vanished; religious ritual and functions amply demonstrated their zeal. As said, the idea of freeing Tibet from the powerful China is an on-going struggle: it will much depend on their ability to survive, sustain, and mobilize international community. The Indian government has been supportive to the Tibetans. However, its position on Tibet seems clear: Tibet is considered an autonomous region of China. India is emerging as a fastest developing nation after China and the global political scenario is changing. What will be the destiny of Tibet? Only the future will tell.

As fallout of the riot, following the Babri Mazjid demolition on December 6, 1992, many poor families in Bombay suffered and died, their houses destroyed and burnt in towns and cities. The CORAR built forty five houses for the riot-affected people in Tulsiwadi, Tardeo, south Bombay; Stanley Downes handed over the houses to them at the function organized on the occasion.

A number of the poor and needy people in different parts of the country supported. I had an opportunity to know the church work around the country. At times, it was heart breaking to see the fading glory of the work, which once flourished but now in a lamentable state or had closed down. Evangelistic endeavours received scanty attention, many church circuits were closed and buildings built by American missionaries were poorly maintained because of lack of calling and paucity of funds. Educational and medical institutions fared poorly, except a few ones. I could meet a number of the church leaders, came to know different regional cultures and political dynamics, and above all, I had privilege to preach and interact with ordinary people.

Conflict of Interest

The funds were strictly for the poor and needy; however, sometimes, the council approved some projects which did not meet the criteria. As the time passed by, my disapproval of nepotism became the cause of contempt. S. Charles, a political heavy weight in the church, was eager to corner me on some issues. I remember, he wrote a letter to me, alleging me that I gave Nelson's eye to other projects and did more for my pet projects. I once spotted him in front of the general secretary's office of the church during the recess of the council meeting held in the Methodist Centre, Bombay, moved restlessly with intention to bully me. It was a Herculean task to keep the council members satisfied and at the same time safeguard the interest of the poor and the relief and rehabilitation funds. The treasurer seemed concerned, inasmuch as compromising and politically cautious to express his views.

In September 1993, the General Board of Global Ministries (GBGM) invited me for an itineration in United Methodist Churches in the Unites States to present the CORAR work done in India with the aim to raise funds for on-going projects. Karriappa Samuel, too, was anxious to come; however, he was not invited. On September 12, 1993, Sunday afternoon, I landed at JFK and went straight to Alma Mathews House on 275, west, 11th St., New York. I frequently visited 475, Riverside Drive, the GBGM office where the UMCOR office was located. In my free time, I toured the city by subway on my own; it was like travelling by a local train in Bombay. I could visit the World Trade Centre, UNO Headquarters, and the Statue of Liberty on Ellis Island, the view from the crown of the statue was awesome. I moved from New York to Pennsylvania, Michigan, Tennessee, and south Virginia. I lived in people's houses; they were kind, generous, and caring, and having a lunch in the revolving restaurant at Renaissance Centre at Detroit was fabulous. In the Unites States, I spent a month. I found that Methodists were strongly committed to the work of the UMCOR. I travelled to many states and presented the work of the CORAR both in urban and in rural churches. I interacted with women's group, aged 60 or older, Sunday school, breakfast meetings and students, and preached in Sunday worships. It was a great opportunity to speak for the poor and needy and the ministry of the CORAR; sometimes, they asked me to speak on the Indian social system, religion, and political developments.

I had amazing exposure to American culture. I did not get any culture shock, as the love of Christ was the bonding force. In my spare time, I visited university campuses like Colombia, New York, Pittsburgh, and Michigan State University. Large and beautiful campuses and academic environment enticed me. I tried to meet some celebrated sociologists. On my way back to India, I was a special invite to the GBGM Annual Board meeting at Hilton hotel, New Jersey. It gave me a fair understanding of its working.

I could make the difference, Methodists in the United States walked second mile to help me, whereas Karriappa Samuel and his men were politically stirred, waiting to bounce on me without any valid reason or allegation and at his call. He called a special council meeting in Hyderabad to intimidate me by the vote of 'no confidence'. I successfully overcame his wrath, at least for the time being and never had I realized its apocalyptic potential. The council had no legal jurisdiction and right to indulgence in such political misadventure. I perceived it was mere pressure tactics to bend me to think alike. It was sad that leaders with vested interest, uncaring for the interest of the church, exerted such political pressures on sincere church workers. I was sad to find that those who stood to protect the interests of the church barely received support from an intelligentsia in the church. It was interesting, Karriappa Samuel used to say, 'Understanding is a shortest distance between two'; however, the distance between him and me never reduced, we differed on our priorities and perception of the church.

Some members of the council insisted that I should leave the work of distribution of relief money in their hand. It was a good proposal, practiced for some time, but when affected people began to express their dissatisfaction on it, I decided to supervise the distribution of the relief money. They persuaded me to keep myself out of it; however, I felt it was unwise to yield to such pressures. Displeased by my stand, they pursued the politics of hatred.

There was request from Cyril Charles, the son of S. Charles and the chairperson's son-in-law, for the grant of computers for his commercial computer institute in Hyderabad. There was lack of clarity in his project proposals as to how he was to help the poor and needy, but members were managed to approve his projects, I gave my vote of dissent. When the time came to release money, I could not sign the pay order, as he could not show how he would help the poor and needy. In the meantime, people whose projects were disapproved began to raise the allegation of partiality, and it was a talk of the church. I was tagged as Karriappa Samuel's man; I was good to him, but not sold to him and certainly not comfortable with his political working.

One fine morning, I was surprised to see Cyril Charles in the CORAR's office. He was throwing his weight around, pressurizing me to release the fund at once, as if I was his subordinate. I was unmoved in my position in the best interest of the church. I again asked him to clarify the way in which he would help the poor and needy. He did not do his homework, I could not release funds, and it led to further misunderstanding and ignited anger. I knew it would harm me, yet I chose to be a good steward of the project funds.

The last CORAR meeting of the quadrennium was held in Bombay, the council members were craving to have briefcases to carry home files and papers. I was against it; the treasurer, too, cautioned, but by political softness. Karriappa Samuel was in favour of giving briefcases. He even said to me, 'We should have good briefcases.' I said, 'I got one, I do not need another.' When the resolution of giving briefcases was adopted, I was duty bound to sign the pay order, for in democracy majority prevails although it may be on wrong side. No sooner was the pay order signed than James Nathan and others run to collect money from the treasurer, purchased and distributed briefcases among themselves. I felt, it was insensitive on the part of the church leaders, who often tended to become short-sighted, lacked an eagle's view, and indulged in conspicuous consumption at the cost of the poor and needy. Then I never imagined the briefcase scandal would haunt me some day in the future.

As said before, from May 22 to 29, 1990, the General Conference's session was held at Tambarm, Madras. Some politically motivated delegates wanted to change the area assignment of all bishops and chanted the slogan, 'Missionary, not stationary'. In the conference, Stanley Downes was assigned to Bombay Episcopal Area and Elliot D. Clive was assigned to Lucknow Episcopal Area without mandatory consultation. In the protest, he wrote a resignation letter, which they accepted in great haste, as if it was pre-planned. It seemed that the conspiracy was planned against him, in which Stanley Downs was one of the main players. Marvin Clive, the younger son of Elliot D. Clive, and Stanley Downes, the then chairman of Methodist Home, were at loggerhead with each other. Marvin Clive believed firmly that the Council of Bishops unfairly treated his father; it turned into volcanic uproar. Karriappa Samuel replaced Stanley Downes as chairman of Methodist Home to stop aggravating the conflict. Not long after, Marvin Clive resigned from the manager's post. John Hanchinmani was anxiously coveting the post of manager of the Methodist Home for his wife. I was amazed the approval of Cyril Charles' projects did not really concern him, but pleasing Karriappa Samuel was. He was running hither and thither to get the letter of appointment for his wife. No sooner was the letter typed in the CORAR office than he rushed to Karriappa Samuel to make him sign it, who was sitting in the smaller hall, a cabin away from the CORAR office. Then, he masterfully created for himself, the post of administrator for the Home;

the hostess and the administrator, a husband-wife duo became extremely possessive of the Home. I felt it was an unhealthy development, for in days to come; the Home would become the breeding ground of the church politics. I watched helplessly like others and felt he was thrusting his tentacles everywhere. I could only have a glance through the political window of his craze for power and position; he had barely any inclination to share work with competent persons in the church.

I understand, human beings have acquisitive urge to conquer and possess all things; it is the way, life goes on everywhere in one way or another, people tend to accumulate material things; however, I could not imagine that it would so severely infect the church. I read an amazing story of men's adventures in Leo Huberman's *'The Wealth of the Nations'*, his lucid description and the plausible reasoning for the rise of capitalism unlike of Karl Marx[3]. What is mine is mine and what is yours is also mine mindset led to unlimited greed for wealth, power, and position, often by exploitation and alienation. I felt pity, those who claimed to live for God, did the same thing in the name of God, not influenced by holiness of life, but ruled by ambition and craze for power and position that made difference to all good, the church cherished. They cared little or nothing about others, did the things, which helped them become a great and mighty in the church. It appeared, the Biblical path of becoming greatest of all, by becoming servant of all, was barely magnetic.

Sarla Lal, the GBGM's secretary for Southern Asia was visiting Bangalore to meet deaconesses; Karriappa Samuel objected her visit, as she was visiting his episcopal jurisdiction bypassing him, which created unpleasant situation. I felt it was unfair and a breach of protocol, not taking the bishop into confidence. She was also monitoring the voting pattern of CORAR's projects. There was a concern over the approval of Cyril Charles' projects and considered as an act of nepotism. There was an audit query on Cyril Charles' projects, without any prejudice I clarified it. However, Kariappa Samuel construed as if I was tarnishing his image. He kept it in his mind; he never forgot and waited for an opportune time to take revenge. The GBGM audit showed that the gain in exchange was not credited to the CORAR's fund; it became the contentious issue. The GBGM was of the firm opinion that the gain in exchange must be used exclusively for projects funding, not to appropriate towards the CORAR's administrative budget.

In April 1994, the Council of Bishops suspended Karriappa Samuel on the charges of illegal use of institutional funds, nepotism, and maladministration[4]. However, barely it suggested that the action taken against him was out of exclusive commitment to administrative or financial integrity. He challenged his suspension in the court of law, but could not succeed and then did not press it further. He grieved over the action against him and blamed S. K. Parmar, Elia M. Peters, Stanley Downes, and other bishops.

The irresponsible way of approving projects and appropriating the gain in exchange for administrative purposes led to trust deficit and lack of understanding, stringent scrutiny of project proposals, for future funding to the CORAR came into force. I recognized the loss of credibility and inaction on the part of the church leaders to modify the CORAR's structure and working deprived the poor and needy. As said, I wished the CORAR could have been a separate agency with selected or appointed members, committed and experienced in social service. The UMCOR was still open for project wise funding, provided each well-written project was submitted for their scrutiny and consideration; never it was done and no funds were received. If the church politics did not prevail over the priorities for the poor and needy, many could have been helped. The conflict of interest discredited the church and deprived the poor and needy. The ministry to them was not effectively continued because of lack of vision on the part of the church leaders, who were expected to take hard and wise decisions; occasionally and half-heartedly, the funding issue was raised before the GBGM officials or in dialogue meetings. No serious efforts made to restore the credibility of the Council of Relief and Rehabilitation; its structure exists, however, it lays dormant.

VISION CAME TRUE

On September 23, 1990, afternoon, the General Conference elected me to the office of the Executive Secretary of the Council of Relief and Rehabilitation. In the evening, I met some of my supporters who were sitting on the steps of the adjoining lawn of the Lincoln Hall of Baldwin Boys' school, Bangalore, the venue of the conference. I joined them; they looked relaxed and happy, as the conference crawled to close. We talked about the conference and the church's ministry and earnestly prayed before we departed. While praying, I felt I was in an episcopal gown; bishopric is the highest spiritual and temporal office in the church. I never imagined about it or had any idea, even in the remote corner of my conscious mind, I did not share it with anyone in the church, but whenever I remembered it, I was amazed.

It was not the first time; I had reminiscence of previous experiences as well. I remember, when I was preparing for seminary in the summer of 1968, it so happened that I spent a night in Mahila Sadan, the guesthouse of All Saints Cathedral, Nagpur. Pushpa Munnalal was in-charge of the guesthouse; she was kind to arrange a room for me. I knew her through my spiritual mentor. I fell asleep, while worrying about my future on the bed covered with a white mosquito net, and past midnight, I woke up and it seemed I had a vision; it was an incredible dazzling sight, angels descended around my bed, dressed in sparkling white robes. They said nothing; I was silent, amazed, and praised God. Angels are real and mentioned in the Bible 289 times. They warn of danger, disclose God's plan, and come to us as an unseen force to help. It was a wonderful life experience, which strengthened and encouraged me to move into the unknown future with hope and faith. I had no doubt; God would always be with me, even though I would face the saddest moments in my life.

In 1993, I dreamt I was walking on a beach, the waves were clear. I saw some people searching for something in the sea sand, covered with water. I, too, searched and none of them but I found two rings with a crown on it, lying on brown clean sand. I picked them up and then I did not understand its meaning; however, not long after, I did.

In the Biblical times, God spoke to his chosen people through dreams and visions to warn, to exhort, or to reveal future events or happenings. God is at work around the world throughout the human history, people have been experiencing it, in one way or another. I heard speakers in leadership seminars I attended, often spoke of having a vision and achieving a vision, they encouraged to write a mission statement which was to be specific and brief that would remind us its purpose, motivate us to achieve, and help us to overcome mountain-sized obstacles. It is not so with divine visions and dreams in which God reveals himself and his purpose, thereby men are inflamed with passion to fulfilling God-given purpose.

Aspiring for Episcopacy

On June 11, 1991, Mehar Singh, the then bishop of Hyderabad Episcopal Area suffered heart attack and died while he was on his way, travelling by train to Jabalpur. He was a wonderful man, soft spoken and kind, and had excellent academic record. I had privilege to be on his council as a member when he was the executive secretary of the Council of Education and Christian Nurture. We liked each other. Due to his sudden death, one post of bishop fell vacant; to fill it up, from September 11 to 15, 1991, the Special Session of the General Conference was held in the YMCA Tourist Hostel, New Delhi. James Nathan, the then executive secretary of Evangelism and Mission, and Nirmal David, the then pastor of Centenary Methodist Church, 24, Lodi Road, New Delhi, were my good friends. They were contesting the episcopal election. I remember, as we were strolling on the sidewalk of the Jai Singh Road, they asked me to contest the election. I said, 'This hour is for you, one of you must win the election. God willing, I will run next time.' B. James, the then executive secretary for Stewardship and Local Support was elected as bishop[1]. James Nathan and Nirmal David were disappointed with the election result; however, they were resolute to run next time for the episcopal office.

The thought of episcopal election hovered in my mind, although there was no definite direction or decision. While I moved all over the church, people began to consider me for Episcopacy. I realized then, there was the perception, whosoever occupied all India office was a candidate for bishopric. There were good reasons to think so; however, some prominent pastors, too, contested episcopal election, but they lacked wider exposure to the life and ministry of the church and personal interactions with the people throughout the church unlike those who held all India post. I felt then that they stood a better chance.

In democratic process, election is an important means, though it does not necessarily guarantee deserving candidates to Episcopacy. There are pit falls in the church democracy with no quick-fix solutions. One could at least hope to see that right candidates were elected to occupy the highest office of the church, it is critical to life, and witness of the church; however, episcopal vacancies were filled in a great hurry, electing wisely was not priority. It was argued, the cost of conducting the General Conference Session to elect a bishop was high with rising inflation; however, I felt it was better to pay now than pay later, bigger cost of unwise decisions, resulting into spiritual and temporal casualty. I observed, actually the church, was not serious in electing the right kind of episcopal leaders and men of God who were willing to set apart themselves to the highest office of the church with undivided loyalty to serve Christ and his church.

There was lack of spiritual sensitivity in electing episcopal leaders; it seemed those who aspired for Episcopacy, most of them lacked commitment to lead the church, manage conflicts and complexities of the church government, overcome temptation of forming political cliques, and avoid using the brutal weapon of majoritarianism. It seemed the episcopal leaders also lacked tolerance to freedom of expression, truth, justice, and equity for the sake of achieving their narrow political ambition and did not care to introspect to know if they were living by the spiritual standard as given in the Bible[2]. I felt the spiritual criterion which was vital, democratic process, often failed to take into consideration; perpetuating the episcopal forms of church government without spiritual substance was like trying to drive a motorcar without gasoline. Although Episcopacy has its roots in the Bible, it seemed to be reduced to more or less a ceremonial or constitutional necessity.

It was pathetic, most candidates aspired for Episcopacy for the glamour of power of bishopric, not for their calling; they had unquenched zeal to reap the rich harvest of the episcopal office. I remember there was a pastor in Bareilly who often said he was of bishop's soil! It was perhaps the reflection of his enlarged self and the honour of Episcopacy. There could have been a great difference in the church had delegates voted after considering the aspirants' 'calling' and spiritual standing[3]. Generally, people respected bishops out of tradition and reverence, unmindful of their spiritual standing or being above reproach. I felt sad sometimes, people looked down on bishops in contempt posthumously, as people felt pain and agony of their incongruous deeds. I was amazed, some church leaders pulled down dedication plaques of their predecessors in rage and rivalry, while others silently watched, as if they approved it. No one expressed remorse or stopped such disgraceful acts, while some bishops were crazy to fix as many dedications, rededications, and memorial plaque, they could, as if they were trying to attain immortality by performing self-glorifying rituals. They never imagined, in future, it will be broken and lie buried in the heap of rubbles. It was deplorable; some bishops even were obstacles to the free flow of God's grace and forgiveness. I wondered about the Bible's words – such ones deserve a millstone on their neck, and to be thrown into a deep sea has at all awakened their spiritual sensitivity.

I was yet to decide for Episcopacy, the push and pull of the election enticing me to get into the episcopal race. Some even often tried to get their work done by prompting me for Episcopacy. I was still thinking if I could use my research skill for the growth of the church; however, I could not see any bright future for it. Then I shared my desire for bishopric with Sharon, my spouse. I reminded her of the vision I had after my last election in Bangalore. She calmly said she would pray, 'If God wants, you would be a bishop.' It fired my imagination and energized my being, I surrendered to God and began to pray and plan.

Canvassing For Election

I decided to go through the fire of democratic process by contesting election of bishop. About thirty-six ministerial members with right to vote always rallied behind me, while there were others who lobbied against me. I always won every election I contested in Bombay Regional Conference, starting from 1984 until the last election, as a ministerial delegate to the General Conference held in Lonavala from March 10 to 13, 1994. Unbelievably, I was elected again, in the first ballot and by highest votes[4]. I was now sure to run for Episcopacy. The election campaign began with prayer and renewed dedication. On March 29, 1994, my supporters, mostly pastor colleagues who lived in Bombay, joyfully assembled in the Bowen Memorial Church. I was amazed; the church played an important role in my life and ministry without my conscious working on it. They fervently prayed for my episcopal election, laid their hands on me, and pledged their support. It was a vibrating experience, every fiber of my being was touched that vouched God's help, as I entered the election fray and their benevolent gestures humbled me. Not long after, I attended some of the then eleven Regional Conferences when the election of delegates to the General Conference was held to meet and congratulated elected delegates. Besides, I met individually most of them, both in the north and the south. I looked to God for success, began to ask their vote and support; thenceforth, I never looked back or got discouraged.

During my election tours, local supporters accompanied me; sometimes I alone met delegates in their homes to avoid getting into local politics. I did not enter any electoral pact with any other episcopal candidates. I saw Sampath Kumar and Nimrod Christian moved together to muster support. I felt, the election alliances could harm than help me, especially if the election pact is made with the candidates of doubtful integrity. I believed in an omnipotent God; no one would stop me if I was in his plan.

Sometimes, I met episcopal candidates who were canvassing in the same town or city I was. Once, I shared a room with one of them. A seasoned lay delegate from that place who was delegate to several General Conference Sessions sarcastically commented, how come two tigers could live in the same room, for there were some episcopal candidates who were intolerant, indulged in backbiting and political bitterness, not edifying the church. I was steadfast in my self-imposed principles, my goal was clear. I was firm, not to indulge in malevolent election campaign or fall into temptation of saying ill of other episcopal candidates. I decided only to talk about myself. I also did not encourage my supporters to get into mud-slashing politics, for it is not the Christian way of life. I felt I was nobody to judge my competing episcopal candidates; delegates were the best judges. I was appalled to see dirty literature littering during the episcopal election; it was filthier than one could imagine; it was the latent side of episcopal election; political carnival did not edify the church. Even during my episcopal ministry, I received hate mail and indecent literature accusing me for decisions that displeased a political few and spreading false stories; such ugly politics came to stay in the church. Sometimes, I laughed it out, other times

I was pained. It seemed, people have gone astray from the disciplined election campaigning, undermining the church's adored spirituality. After all, the church was electing a spiritual and temporal leader, not a rival political ideological leader. No serious efforts made to make delegates understand that they were entrusted with the sacred responsibility of electing a spiritual and temporal leader of the church. Anyway, there were no quick fix remedial answers to the ills of episcopal election; however, it was vital to adhere to adored election norms during canvassing.

The role of money was growing, some delegates spent a large sum to be elected, and so they strived to exploit episcopal candidates. I felt they acted like extortionists, demanded big bucks from episcopal candidates, and in anxiety to win election, some episcopal candidates gladly yielded to their greed. I was melancholic to learn that in lure of gathering plenty of votes, some episcopal candidates became prey to such tactics, doled out big sum and counted on avarice delegates who were anything but venal. The tendency grew; it is now an accepted fact that Mammon dictates election and ascension to power, shifting holiness of life. 'The *lifafa* (Envelop) Committee' was appointed to inquire into the election graft at the seat of General Conference Session in the process of episcopal ballots; however, it was not pursued to its logical end. There was lack of willing-will on the part of bishops to weed out graft and election malpractices; it seemed it was merely the political drama[5]! The church had a well-written rule, but was invoked only with political motive. I learnt, some episcopal candidates who contested the election several times spent a large sum and some of them even liquidated their immovable assets, others chose to fund their election by inappropriate means and the rest contested with utmost integrity. I recognized that in the years to come, the tendency to give gratification in election would grow steadily in the absence of holiness of life.

The church leaders spoke against the evil of graft in the episcopal election but lacked courage to deal with it. They were silent spectators to the practice, seemingly conceding the reality and there is no way unless bold and swift steps are taken to overcome it. Once, I had an interesting experience, while I was meeting delegates, one of the ministerial delegates came running to me, he caught my hand and started to itch my palm, he uttered not even a word. It seemed he was signalling that I should grease his palms, if at all, I desired his vote. It was a novel means of extortion; I did not reciprocate to his symbolism. I felt sad; some episcopal candidates, too, lured delegates, entered into all kinds of deals by make-believe covenants; if elected, they would opt for the episcopal assignment in their area and lavish on them key posts or bestow some favour; such delinquent political behaviour of some episcopal candidates tarnish the bishopric. Some episcopal candidates even lured delegates with cash, air tickets, and hotel accommodation to keep them in their safe custody and out of the reach of rival episcopal candidates.

The church leaders and officers were the election game changers; they supported the episcopal candidates of their own kind, in anxiety to make a majority in the Council of Bishops and to cleanse the prophetic voice or to keep lid on the worms of their murky deeds. They pampered delegates with handsome incentive in the form of travel claim or incidental expenses. The spiritual criterion is often smeared by political considerations. Often, episcopal candidates with spiritual leaning could not compete and win the election race. There was lack of concern over the falling standard of the Episcopacy and those who were serious about it; their voice was lost in the hustle bustle of the election politics. The tussle for who's who in the church hierarchy was becoming never-ending politics. The precious time and money of the church were spent on discussing property and finance matters, no serious thinking done to uplift spirituality, evangelism, and mission of the church for which the church exists; such tendencies shifted the holiness of life and undermined the witness of the church[6].

I observed bishops' election for years and recognized that it was crucial to cling to the ideal Biblical image of the bishop than liberally view the bishop as an organizational boss. In election off time, all were of one voice that spirituality, calling, and character of candidates were touchstone, but election interests and political compromises dwarfed them. I expected at least the bishops to conquer their political passion and remain neutral. On contrary, they acted like political manoeuvres when their beloved candidates were trailing, and while presiding, they either gave a long break to change delegates' mood and perception or allowed discussion on nonessential issues to kill time and give breathing time to their loved candidates to set-right their election strategy. It seemed the fierce competition to hold episcopal office and the inferior ministerial formation of episcopal leaders tended to extinguish the flame of holiness of life. I felt suffocated in the absence of good feelings for deserving episcopal candidates; political bickering, mud slashing, and character assassination dissuaded the spiritually minded aspirants. When General Conference's session came nearing adjournment and the election of favourite episcopal candidates could not take place and no tricks worked then prayers were offered and fiery sermons were given to facilitate election; it was merely political gimmick; prayers and sermons were used like Moses staff to perform episcopal election miracles. There was lack of earnest desire to seek God's will in electing episcopal leaders. A great haste was made to fulfilling constitutional requirement, the core spiritual criteria of calling to Episcopacy was compromised in the infinite episcopal constitutional continuum. Social factors such as language or region, people's group, and blood ties influenced the voting pattern. I am apprehensive, if the church will ever be able to elect a bishop in the spiritual atmosphere like that of the New Testament times; if it does, it would be a life-changing experience!

Every time episcopal election was held, the role of money was becoming bigger and greater, leading to as good as buying bishopric and it seemed, the church was unconcerned about the diminishing empirical value of Episcopacy. In such murkier situation, I thought perhaps there was a need to draw wisdom from other Methodist Churches and other denominational churches around the world, the way in which they elected their spiritual leaders. Actually, a mere eligibility criterion for election was not good enough, but exemplary ministerial life was. It was disappointing, candidates with inferior spiritual profile were preferred than those with spiritual standing. I remember there was one episcopal candidate who signed the deal with the municipality to give a portion of graveyard land for road widening at some consideration. He claimed the compensation, but never deposited the money in the church treasury. After years, when the municipality started to widen the road, the local congregation protested, but the municipality claimed that the deal was signed, sealed, and compensation was paid. The church filed the legal suit to stop the municipality from acquiring the land. Some conference leaders opposed his episcopal candidature and others felt it was wise to pack him out of the conference by electing him to bishopric. Another episcopal candidate was alleged to have cut teakwood trees of the church. He never denied it; however, he took shelter under the law of limitation, he was let go free though the rule was not applicable in his case[7]. When he was running the episcopal race, the memory of the teakwood episode was still alive; some raised their voices by saying, 'Teak wood trees were growing'; however, some episcopal leaders ignored the voices and rallied behind him. The list in the secret scroll did not stop there; it was longer than one could think. It did not surprise me, the bishops elected from such stock were acquainted with the means to dishonest gain, and without any hesitation repeated their past performance and escaped unhurt; it was truly disappointing, the church was indifferent to it.

It became apparent after 1981, the year when the church became affiliated autonomous, that episcopal elections were getting increasingly uglier, and as the years passed by, it became contagious, and episcopal elections were vulnerable to graft, became competitive, and spirited. Generally, more than one General Conference Session was needed to elect bishops; as years passed by, the cost of holding the General Conference Session augmented. I observed evangelism and spirituality did not receive prime attention as much as materialistic and secularist engagements, so some were rethinking to seek solace by returning to the original church like those who still adore British colonial rulers.

I did not take count of my voters by taking the cue from King David's experience, a Hebrew king who did a mistake by taking the census of his troops. I believed, God was able to multiply my votes, and so I never engaged in the arithmetic exercise. I remember one of the episcopal candidates was playing election tricks, manipulating other candidates to get more votes. He disguised, clinched give-and-take deal with three episcopal candidates severally and by concealing the secret electoral pact from each other. He assured to give them five votes each of his supporters in exchange of five votes of their supporters. He got five votes from each of them, but never asked his supporters to vote for them. He was merely playing psychological trick for good showing up that he was a leading candidate, and such inflated numbers often misled voters; however, it seldom led to election victory. I was amazed, when I did not take the count of my voters, I was gaining votes, for winning the episcopal election was not my only goal, using acceptable means was equally important.

Ordeal

On May 21, 1994, I reached the YMCA Tourist Hostel, New Delhi, the venue of the General Conference. The days were very warm; most of the delegates arrived and settled in their assigned rooms. It was a high political scenario; it happened before also, but this time it made much difference to me, as for the first time I was contesting the episcopal election, the highest office of the church. Vasant Raiborde, J. C. Fredrick, A. Sabarenjithan, and George Samuel untiredly canvassed for me. They were fully committed and several prominent delegates and leaders from all conferences supported me.

When I reached the registration counter, I sensed some uneasy political atmosphere. I fetched the conference's file and papers. I saw that some envelops were kept one side of the registration counter. I picked up one, and out of curiosity, I opened it. I was shocked to find the leaflets containing the concocted allegations of the misuse of the CORAR funds by me; it was alleged that I used them to induce voters. I did not know how to counter it. I was melancholic, however, calm and composed. It seemed that my political rivals were involved in it and no one other than the council members had the minutes of the project's approval. I was shattered and grieved to read about the scandal of giving briefcases to the council members from the CORAR funds although I was innocent. It was the shoddy politics to cut my votes and to defeat me in the election, for some leaders were worried at the prospect of my election and others were jealous and the rest intended to enhance the election prospect of their episcopal candidates. I observed, the church election politics was getting fierce and indecent over the years. I told my supporters about the mischief of my rivals and they swiftly swung into action to explaining to the delegates the truth and politics behind it.

I was overconfident like other candidates and thought that I would be elected in first ballot; however, my expectation shattered, I trailed behind due to malicious propaganda[8]. Anyway, I did not lose heart and hope, but in renewed determination, I met delegates and shook every hand I could find. A few of my supporters, out of anxiety, had gone astray, tried to influence some delegates with a little amount of money. No sooner did they indulge than I came to know about it, I was greatly disturbed, I strongly expressed my disapproval, and they abandoned the unrighteous path. As said, I strongly believed means is as important as goal. I was aware, some bishops and the church's officers opposed me and long before secretly schemed to bar me from contesting the election; however, when the result of the first episcopal ballot was out, the man who held the purse came running to me, congratulated me for my maiden showing up. I felt, he was not honest, diffused ill feeling to spoil my election chance; others rescued me from dirty politics, encouraged, and prayed for me.

I did not pull votes, as I expected for several days. Then, my supporters asked me to make a statement during the conference's session to nullify the bashing of the malicious propaganda against me by my political archenemies. I was not sure whether the presiding bishop would allow me to do so. However, I was keen to make the record straight by raising the issue through the matter of privilege when the turn of an impartial bishop would come to preside over the session. On May 26, 1994, after tea session, Samson Solomon, the then bishop of Lucknow Episcopal Area, was to preside. He was kind to me and wished well for my election. I took his prior consent during the tea break. Then, I raised, the matter of privilege, the presiding bishop recognized me. I clarified the allegation of misuse of the CORAR funds, I said it was absolutely false and frivolous; the aim was to defame and defeat me. I watched S. K. Parmar who was sitting behind the presiding bishop desperately trying to ask him to stop me speaking. I was amazed, he even asked a ministerial delegate from Punjab not to vote for me without realizing that the delegate was closer to me than to him. I had no problem with him and I did not quite understand the reason for his contemplated indulgences. Long after I learnt, he considered me as Karriappa Samuel's man, they were archrivals and that I did not recognize him to his expectation. These were his own narrow imagination; it seemed he did not recognize the importance of individual differences and preferences, moreover, my personality did not propel me to act, as per his wish; it was incompatible to my intrinsic nature. He and other bishops were supporting their favourite candidate who was tagged as *Sarkari Ghoda* (government horse) and catchwords like 'now or never' in support of their candidate were echoing ears. I was amazed, no sooner did I clarify the malicious allegations than my election results hugely improved; at times, I pulled highest votes and became one of the leading episcopal candidates[9].

Those who opposed me could become momentary obstacles; however, they could never defeat or override the divine purpose for my life.

My supporters who came as visitors helped me; one of them was Alfred Chouhan, an ordained minister of the Bombay Conference, and his brother who lived in Vadodara, Gujarat, was also a visitor. When one of the episcopal candidates saw them canvassing for me, he could not bear, although he knew they were his supporters as well. I was appalled; he forced them to leave the conference's venue through one of his ardent supporters. I felt sorry for Alfred and his brother Gilbert; they had to leave the place for the sake of good relations. It was not a setback for me and I wondered, how come some episcopal candidates could not conduct themselves like called ones, 'who care' attitude was the election reality; anyhow, the episcopal election race was to be won.

I had some amazing experiences. I learnt some delegates from the south did not vote for me because I wore short sleeve shirts. On hearing it, I had hearty a laugh; however, my supporters were serious, they did everything they could do and persuaded me to wear long sleeve shirts, as they did not like to take any chance of losing even a single vote, even for a silly reason. The weather was very warm and sweaty, long sleeve shirts were not weather friendly. I was exhausted and dehydrated due to the hectic canvassing during the balloting process. I dissuaded them; I felt, it was no reason why they should not vote for me, if they thought I was the right candidate. I doubted their genuineness, I advised my supporters to take it easy. Nevertheless, I became inquisitive about their fascination for long sleeve shirts, so I inquired about it, there were cultural, climatic, and class explanations; no exclusive reasoning seemed satisfactory. I was surprised about the way people thought and looked at me, expecting me to do things as they did.

The General Conference Session, New Delhi, could not elect any bishop. I was one of the leading candidates. The conference adjourned to meet in Bangalore in the month of November of the same year. I was happy for having deep insights into the dynamics of episcopal election and opportunity to make my record straight. Once again, I clarified the briefcases' scandal through letters and personal meetings, especially to those who were winnable delegates.

The positive ending and my leading edge in the episcopal election shook my political adversaries. Taranath Sagar and Namdeo Karkare, blossom friends, seemed sad, for they conscientiously opposed me for my different voice; however without any tangible success. They spied on our movements to spoil my election and my supporters kept a close watch on their political misadventures. Then, I did not think of them as potent political force, which could change the delegates' mood and election trend; even then, we did not take lightly. I heard Taranath Sagar's initial political success credited largely to Namdeo Karkare. Eventually, they estranged, although not for good, and turned bitter against each other, perhaps because of Namdeo Karkare conducting inquiry of the Haldwani property scam in which Taranath

Sagar was found implicated; it could be one of the reasons.

George Samuel walked me during the conference's recess to meet his acquaintance, an elderly man who lived near to the conference venue. He was interesting and talkative, the weather was bit cold, I sneezed, not once, but twice, and he spontaneously said, 'You will win; you have sneezed twice in quick succession.' I was amazed at his sense of omen. Regardless, I did well in the election, though Kariappa Samuel held back votes of the delegates under his influence from voting for me, as he was still relishing bitterness against me. I needed some more votes to reach the magic figure necessary for the election. Some of my supporters were in touch with him. They convinced him to leave behind the past and move forward for a better future. After much persuasion, he reconciled, though for a while and released votes in my favour.

Sharon, Rayhal, and Virtu neither canvassed nor accompanied me in my election tours, nor they were present during the election, for they believed in the sovereign will of God and in my humble competence; however, they devoted themselves to prayers for me to be elected if it was God's will. Sadly, one of the mischievous and influential women from Bombay accused the poor soul that Sharon came to Bangalore with a box full of money to buy votes. She intended to harm and defame us out of intense hatred and jealousy for my voice against exploitation and injustice; Sharon came to Bangalore only after I was declared elected as bishop.

Crossing the Finish Line

As the conference session was crawling to close, the election scenario dramatically changed; Sampath Kumar, Nimrod Christian, and I emerged leading candidates. The rest of the candidates who contested the episcopal election, some of them just wanted to come into a political lime light and others aimed at other positions, as their ultimate goal was not winning the episcopal election. Then they began to withdraw one by one, paving the way to have elections, two-thirds of the delegates present and voting were required for election. On the night of November 29, 1994, Tuesday, the election picture was clear in our favour and in the morning session, in one ballot Sampath Kumar, Nimrod Christian, and I were declared elected as bishops[10].

Bishop Elect: (L-R) Sampath Kumar, Nimrod
Christian & I, November 1994

It was my first and last time to contest an episcopal election. I did not contest the election several times like most episcopal candidates; it was start to finish, at one go; I never again had to contest an election. Some of my friends among episcopal candidates were envious and spewed bitterness, as they could not win election before I was elected. They thought they were older than I was, so they expected me to give up in their favour; however, the delegates did not think likewise. I was no way responsible for their election defeat and nurturing bitterness against me was insensible, for the General Conference preferred me to them. My entire election journey was shorter as compared to others, I started it in 1984 and finished in 1994; I took just ten years to reach bishopric; at 49, I became bishop. In the prevailing changing church politics, my election journey was shorter though not smooth; it was tough with many roadblocks. I was amazed though I had no family roots in the church, yet I could reach to the highest office of the church only by the divine providence, as democracy in the church seemed shattering like reeds in wind by the force of power ambition, social rigidity, and prejudice. Politically stronghold groups and blood ties had strong tendency to concentrate power among their self and block nascent aspirant like me into the arena of the church hierarchy. Some of those who were at the helm of power politics were active and vigorous to stop deserving persons coming to power in the church who were not from their stock, and the rest watched with helplessness and silence what was going on in the church, and others were kept in the dark. The people at grassroots seldom knew what happened at the bishops' levels or in the church hierarchy. It was hard to know, as if the church democracy was like despotic, even *Indian Witness*, an official newspaper of the church, was not free to express views on the issues that affected the life and ministry of the church; it was censored and controlled.

Consecration Ceremony, November 1994: UMC Bishop J. Llyod Knox, MCI Bishops & I am standing below and behind me are Sharon and Rev. A Sabarenjithan

I observed some tried to win episcopal election without caring for Christian values and principles, and the power of language or regional feelings and social affinities, though critical, did not escape the sovereign will of God. I recognized God allows men to exercise their free will, but eventually, the divine will prevail over human desires.

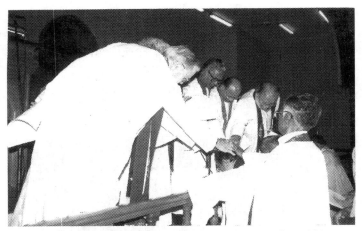

Laying of hands at the Consecration, November 1994

On November 30, 1994, Wednesday, on the same day of election, the consecration service was held in the evening in Richmond Town Methodist Church in Bangalore. Sampath Kumar, Nimrod Christian, and I were consecrated as bishops of the church. Sharon and some of my relatives were present. In solace of God's presence, I laid my hands on the Bible and the Discipline. I renewed my vows to preach and practice the Word of God, preserve and perpetuate the rule of law of the church in the presence of the large gathering. What an irony! Stanley Downes held the Discipline in his hands while I knelt at the altar and in solemn vows, placed my hands on it, though I knew, the bishop seldom cared for it.

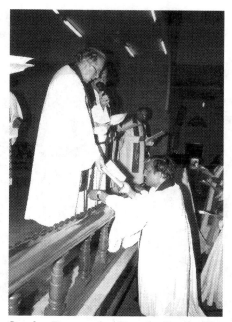

Bishop Stanley Downes holding the Book of Discipline
while lay My hands on it, November 1994

It was a happy moment in my life, as hereafter our life would change, facing the challenges and responsibilities of the episcopal ministry. Then I never knew that trying to adhere to Christian values, principles and the Discipline, my prophetic voice would turn out to be tragic for me. The church politics was embroiling, as bishops obeyed their political vibrating instincts more than the voice of their great calling.

I was amazed the vision came true; I was elected in the Lincoln hall and on the lawn adjoining the hall, four years ago, where I felt I was in an episcopal gown. It was a great experience to stand there again and thanked God, for he reveals his purpose to his chosen ones. Such things did happen in the Biblical times and they do happen even today, for God is at work in our times too, leading people to fulfil his purpose, quite often, we do not realize, but resist.

Delegates and MCI members extending greetings
after Consecration ceremony, November 1994

When it came to the episcopal assignment, I was willing to go anywhere. However, I was amazed to hear the Committee on Ministry recommending my assignment to Delhi and Bareilly Episcopal Areas; assignment to Bareilly Area was an additional responsibility. My work area spread from India-Pakistan Wagah border in Punjab to India-Nepal Kaliganga border in the hills of Pithoragarh in Uttarakhand, covering NCR and five states of Punjab, Haryana, Rajasthan, Utter Pradesh, and Uttarakhand. I joyfully accepted the assignment though did not know why two areas were assigned to me, as I was younger among active bishops, and perhaps other bishops had better exposure to the

Bareilly Episcopal Area than I had. However, neither of them was assigned to the additional area nor any retired bishop was reactivated. The mantles of the area supervision fell on me; they were unhappy and uneasy, but in no way could I smoothen their feeling than to accept the assignments.

Then, I remembered my dream of two rings, which I understood in the simplicity of my faith, not in the complexity of Sigmund Freud's interpretation of dreams, the psychoanalysis – process of recreating lost memories and uncovering the roots of neurosis. That my dream of two rings was symbolical like seven sleek and seven fat Pharaoh's cows and that it was to do with the assignment of the two episcopal areas and sea water was to do with difficulties, which was no way my wish fulfilment[11], but the unasked favour of providence, for which some bishops were envious of me.

Breaking New Grounds

The General Conference's session adjourned sine die, Sharon flew to Bombay and I travelled by train along with ministerial and lay delegates of the Bombay Conference, it was my last travel with them. I recollected the memories of years of working together and living with them while I travelled. I shared with them rooms during the conferences and seminars dined at the same table, sat together in conference sessions, and took up the issues affecting our common concern. Some of them were excited while others were surprised, for they could imagine, I would travel in a sleeper class with them and undertake an uncomfortable long journey by an unpredictable train, which does not keep to its schedule. Actually, I was exhausted, I needed rest and quiet time; however I felt it was time to express my gratitude, oneness, and share my joy.

On December 2, 1994, the train reached Victoria terminus about 8:00 in the evening. I was surprised to see a number of people waiting to welcome me with flowers at a busy hour; office goers were rushing to their homes after a day's hard work. The weather was pleasant and my supporters overflowed with joy. I asked them to celebrate God's marvellous working, not the election winning. On reaching my home, we prayed and thanked God, and the people assembled departed rejoicing.

Then I began to plan to go to Delhi and Bareilly to meet church leaders and start our work. We took several hard decisions; Sharon resigned from St. Anthony's High School where she worked as a teacher. Rayhal was in Sophia College, one of the best-known colleges in south Bombay, and Virtu was in St. Agnes High School, a convent of Jesus and Mary. We were debating whether Rayhal should leave such a good college. At last, we decided, all must move to Delhi. On April 17, 1995, we left Bombay for Delhi. Not long after, struck by unforeseen hurdles, they had to go back to Bombay to continue their education. I was swift in taking hard decisions, I understand, sometimes, they were unwise, too; however, I could not be lukewarm to the call of the hour and then I never knew I would face perils and surprises.

Rayhal, Virtu & I in the front of Bishop's
House, Delhi December 1996

Making things right has never been so easy, it was
challenging like walking on burning coals. As the time
passed by, I realized I inherited problems like dormant
volcanoes; the actual realities were far more disturbing
than I could have imagined, as most church leaders
tended to be like organizational leaders. Nevertheless,
in the midst of inherent obstacles, there were signs
of hope for the church's mission to the world. I had a
limited exposure to the church working until then, the
way things are handled; now I was to be fully involved
in it. I was to deal with volcanic issues, evaluate and
understand them without bias and prejudice, and set
them right. I did not spend more than necessary time
to weigh pros and cons, but made honest efforts. In
good faith and faithfulness to my calling, I ventured
to break new grounds and set things right, which my
predecessors could have done as well, as they were
more experienced, compromising, and seasoned

church politicians than I was; I say this, not in the sense of inflated selfworth. I could not overlook the need to do things for the church, thus I took bold steps, what it may cost. My inner voice was saying, 'I should not be contented with doing stereotype things.' I ventured to make things right and do things right, not as management *mantra* (formula), but as response to my calling to serve people and spiritually uplift the church. The struggle of the past, courage to face challenges, and willingness to walk the thorny path propelled me to do so. Above all, people prayed for me, for God to guide and help me; I was ready to undertake risky adventures.

I was not scared to deal with stormy issues and manage people who looked things differently in anger, frustration, jealously, and selfishness. Making things right was necessary, but sensitive, it was like opening the Pandora's Box, bringing history alive that bounced on me like a trapped spring, forcing its way in an uncontrollable and unpredictable direction. By the end of 100 days in my episcopal office, I was depressed, dejected, and I contemplated over my becoming bishop. I asked God, why have you called me to be a bishop to face such hostile situations, did I not serve you in my faithfulness as a pastor. The words of the Bible pierced my doubts, reminded me, God had a purpose for me, a plan for my welfare, not to harm me and to give me future with hope; my face glowed and restlessness vanished. I recomposed, gathered strength, courage, and braved fiery issues.

There were some pastors and laypersons curious and suspicious about my ability to handle things and unwilling to take fair view of my sincere efforts, for their perception was coloured by politics. Anyway, I strived to find solutions, overcame situations, and led people to expected role performance, at the same time I felt if I do not succeed, it would be disastrous for me, it would leave the indelible imprint of amateurish and incompetency on my leadership; thinking about it, I felt discouraged and it drained out my energy and depleted my hope. Nevertheless, in the midst of it, I also felt the warmth of God's love that undergirded and gave me courage and strength to serve him.

Stationary Trends

The idea of itinerant ministry is challenging. A pastor is also an itinerant or traveling preacher, moving from place to place; it is a great tradition started by John Wesley and continued by his followers and inspired by his life and teachings, preachers reached different parts of the world with the gospel message and holiness of life. But I observed, today pastors or preachers have propensity to become stationary or live in one place rather than work like a missionary, moving from place to place to preach and teach the gospel. I recognized it was an obstacle to the church growth, as it tended to perceive the ministry like an occupation, having no missionary zeal to keep alive and carry forward the mission of the church.

My first encounter to acrimonious situation was that a few pastors in the Delhi Conference did not like to retire though they had reached the age of superannuation. I realized, they were politically exploiting the provision of the church's rule, which said, when a pastor attains the age of superannuation at the seat of the Regional Conference, a formal action taken, to place him in the retired category, or may be voted to continue in active relation on a yearly basis depending on the need. It was not binding, however, and the Delhi Conference made it as rule that was undesirable, and not compatible with the practice in other conferences. Once, a pastor reached the age of superannuation and placed in the retired relation, and then he was not eligible either to preside over an administrative meeting or contest an election. I was amazed, the Delhi Conference without any valid reason or urgency, continued some pastors even after reaching the age of superannuation in active relation. There seemed to be self-serving tendency because as mentioned, there was no dire need or compelling reason to do so; the continuation of the practice for the sake of a few chosen affluent and politically influential pastors was not justified, as there was no dearth of elders in active relation. I did not appreciate the practice that deprived other pastors, and those who did not fall in my line of my thinking were unhappy. One of them was my good friend who came to speak to me in the favour of the pastors who were to retire. After patiently hearing him, I said, I was not convinced of continuing them in active relation even after their superannuation. However, out of sympathy, I assured him, I would continue them in the same assignment, but it did not satisfy them, for they craved nothing less than to continue in active relation.

I was convinced they were unreasonable in imposing their wishes on me for their continuation as active pastors, which was neither necessary nor forcible. I believed, in all fairness, all should retire after reaching the age of superannuation, as in the rest of the conferences of the church. They became stiff, demonstrated tough postures, and made it a prestige issue. They organized pastors and laypersons to pressurize and protest against me, a lorry full of diehard horde was at my doorstep with intent to bend me to their wishes; however, the more they pressurized me, the more I became decisive on the principle of parity.

I planned to hold the first session of the Delhi Regional Conference. The Regional Conference session was an important annual event in the life of the church. Prior to 1981, the Regional Conference was called Annual Conference. I believe the use of word *annual* was more appropriate than *regional*, as the latter tended to spread regional feelings and breeds divisive politics. I felt that it was an unwise change and drawing conferences' boundaries on linguistic geographical areas was like Sir Cyril Radcliffe tracing partition boundary lines on the imperial Indian map, based on religions, which tended to give rise to separatist feelings.

The Regional Conference sessions were anxiously waited for and ritually attended. All pastors and deaconesses – they are like nuns; however, celibacy is a personal choice, and church workers attend it along with their lay delegates from local churches. It was a wonderful time of meeting and sharing work experience, once in a year for three to four days. It was a time when some pastors were anxious to hearing the announcement of their next appointment, in other words, annual assignment, and not accepting the bishop's appointment was serious and invited disciplinary action. So some worried, if transferred, what would happen to their children's education or spouse's work; would they move alone, leaving behind their family? Would they find a house for them to stay back? All these thoughts gave creepy feelings. Some worried about the passing of their character; the committee on ministry examined if a pastor had a clean report card for the preceding year and blameless in the personal and official relation. I recognize, it is a unique feature of great value however, with the passage of time, it has reduced to a mere administrative ritual, a meaningless and time-squandering exercise, not worth its name. Some pastors with questionable conduct barely had difficulty in getting their characters passed swiftly with political consideration; it was painful, nothing better I could expect. Likewise, it seemed that it was difficult for those with similar conduct to become judgmental of their colleagues. Nevertheless, it made them anxious until the time the annual ritual of the passing of character was over, while other canvassed for their election ambition. The ministerial candidates who completed their theological qualification and fulfilled necessary requirements eagerly looked forward to be ordained; it is an initiation into priesthood, it entitles them to use 'Reverend' as title to their name. Only a bishop has the authority to ordain priests and consecrate deaconesses. There were some ordained woman ministers in the church; however, the church had no specific theological affirmation on women's ordination. In the ordination ceremony, candidates take a vow to serve Christ and his church. The bishop lays his hand on them along with Elders, gives them authority on the behalf of the church to preach, teach and lead the flock of Christ into a mature Christian faith. An itinerate preacher desiring to work in full-time ministry of the church and fulfils eligibility criteria qualifies to the conference's full membership and bishop's appointment, right to vote, contest an election, and entitled to chair official meetings. The preachers who do not fulfil all requirements but have calling for the full-time ministry and have requisite minimum theological training are taken into the local category; such preachers are not itinerate, they may get local assignment and are free to do secular work without rights and privileges of a full member. Besides, to become a full member, completing 4 years of course of study was very important, and failing to complete it would cause one to lose the chance of becoming a full member. I remember a young intelligent professor of theology was denied the conference's membership, as he failed to complete it. Candidates were required to write a synopsis of prescribed books or its substitute. I remember, I was asked to write synopsis of one of the books, *The Imitation of Christ* by Thomas a Kempis, translated into fifty languages and for more than 500 years touched millions of lives around the world.

A Regional Conference session was the time of excitement and anxiety; members and delegates sang, prayed and listened to the Bible messages, met each other, moved in cliques, debated, and voted. I tried to lessen their anxiety by instilling the value of good health and by taking them to morning walk. I was happy to see them excited and bounding. I understand, in the past, the Annual Conference was primarily for pastors and church workers who spent time in prayer,

Bible study and sharing of the work experiences of the preceding year before they could make changes in their assignments for the following year. Then, there was protest over lay representation in Annual Conferences; however, it was not conceded. Long after, churches with the Wesleyan tradition united into the United Methodist Church, and the long-standing demand was met[1]. As the years passed by, the original purpose of conference session began to change; the conferences tended to become administrative and election oriented, the spiritual content was missing. Perhaps there was a need to get used to the changing times and seek new ways to satisfy spiritual hunger. The swift was the latent function of administrative mundane affairs that required completing the agenda within a conference's session, as the cost of conducting a conference session was increasing by each passing year.

I felt it was appropriate to discourage the practice of continuing pastors in active relation after reaching the age of superannuation at the time of the conference session and no matter who they were; no one is above or below the rule of law and there was no exigency. I thought it was the moment of decision, the house must be set right, and I did it with overwhelming support of pastors. The aftershocks of the decision were felt for years, and it strained my relations and perhaps it gave them the idea that I was a tough disciplinarian; however, the principle of equality was recognized in the life of the church.

There was a tendency among some pastors to hang on to the same local church for years, to which they were once assigned, although annual appointments were need based, the rule was seldom invoked in some cases. They were appointed year after year in the same church under redundant missionary rule, allowing them to have firm grips, indulge in inappropriate activities, and make the parish their world, while some pastors shunted from one local church to another without any valid need. Besides, it was complex to make appointments for couples who were either pastors or pastor-deaconess; it was an intricate dilemma to resolve, assess the need, and make meaningful assignments. I found some pastors had strong tendency to either continue in the same urban area or not move from the location in cities where their spouse worked or children were studying; they disliked any change in their appointment. I recognized, there was a need to overcome such stationary trends and defy the spirit if the church was to move forward. Had there been comprehensive guidelines in making annual assignments, perhaps such conflicts of interest and complexities of pastors and church workers could have been less acrimonious.

One of the responsibilities of a Bishop was to make the appointment or assignment of pastors and church workers. I did my best with a great sense of responsibility towards the church and sensitivity to their needs. I do not claim, all my appointments were flawless; however, they were fair enough. I remember there was commotion when I changed the appointment of the pastor of the Central Methodist Church, Agra. He was a good and competent pastor, I wanted him to move to another church to solve their problem, but he was resentful, not willing to leave the church. As per model agenda, conference session adjourns sine die with the presiding bishop reading annual appointments. No sooner had I read out annual appointments than he mobilized an unruly horde that bounced on me, swiftly surrounded, immobilized, and pressurized me not to change his appointment. I felt, it was a challenge and struggle that lasted hours, for he made stronghold in the congregation. They locked even the main gate of Holman Institute, the conference venue, and tarried around for hours, hoping I would change my decision; however, I did not yield to his pressure tactics, which could have been disastrous to the church's interest.

Some pastors and lay delegates made a security circle around me to stop anyone hurting me. The misguided horde tried to thrush through the circle, Darshan P. Lal, an ordained minister, was hurt, fainted, and needed immediate medical care. After hours of drama, I managed to come out of it safely, even without committing to retaining the pastor in the church. It was disgraceful on the part of the pastor to use the congregation members to achieve his self-serving goals. Not long after, I said to him that he could have approached me before if he had any genuine difficulty moving to another church. I always gave patient hearing to pastors and church workers who came with their problems; after all, I was their pastor. I was flexible in genuine cases, considered them without any hesitation; however, I could not satisfy all. There were push and pull when making an appointment. I did my homework and tried to visualize practical difficulties in making assignments long before the conference session. I realized it was impractical and even imprudent to burn a midnight lamp and come out with a perfect appointment list, satisfying all. I was careful not to use my prerogatives as a tool to punish those who were critical of my decisions and administrative style; the interest of the church was my utmost concern.

There was a pastor in the Bombay Conference who stayed in the same church for more than twenty-five years. A few members of his congregation complained against him about the Women's Society of Christian Service (WSCS) Nursery school, established in 1944. They alleged, he alienated the church's school funds to another independent Trust, run as his private enterprise with the help of his henchmen. They prayed, pastor be asked to restore funds to the congregation. I supported them, without a doubt, the school belonged to the church. Historically, the school was run by the local church's WSCS for the poor and needy children, members of the congregation were on the school board. The pastor of the church was appointed as the manager of the school; however, by scheming, the pastor's men controlled the school. I could not imagine how it was possible without his blessings. By unconvincing and bizarre logic, they argued the school project did not belong to the church and the church property was given to run the school. The findings of the inquiry committee did not sustain their claim. Piles of documents and the age-old signboard of the school showed, their contention was hallow; conclusively, the school project was of the church. The pastor's explanation was deficient and contrary to the historical facts; however, I desired to solve the issue peacefully. I went out of the way to give him opportunities and asked him to trust me, but he was stubborn, even after my constant efforts. It seemed his wife and his sycophants pressurized him not to give any heed to me. If he was sensitive to the truth, we could have avoided a lot of unpleasantness. It was a stupendous task to get back the control of the school, but I did not think it was right to leave it to its own destiny either. He was asked to reconcile with the truth, he refused; the conference, at the most, could take the disciplinary action against him, but failed to take over the control of the school and reclaim its funds. There was an acrimonious reaction from his relatives, friends, some pastors, and even some bishops rallied behind him politically, overlooking bare facts, it seemed the church's interests did not charm them.

I was clear and confident and acted on convincing facts. It was true, at times, in spite of my honest efforts, some critical information could have escaped or concealed, and decisions so taken could have been faulty; however, it was not so in the case. I was appalled, despite the plain truth, people till supported him. I was willing to give him a patient hearing if there was a reciprocal sensitivity and desire to restore back the school project to the church; the committee, too, was ready to rescind its action if he was to mend his ways. He did not blink, we did not think wise to betray the interest of the church.

A bishop assigns pastors to local churches, who were required to pay them pastoral support or salary. I other words, the conference appointments were centralized and pastoral support was decentralized. It appeared as if it was some kind of imbalance or contradiction in the episcopal administrative system of the church – it was not; it worked well everywhere in the church. In the past, some debated and advocated to centralize pastoral support as well like in other church denominations. I recognized, the decentralization of pastoral support is a unique feature of the Methodist Church, successfully practiced for centuries. I observed that some pastors, with the help of some local church key members, either used pastoral support or Home Mission apportionment as means to pressurize the bishop to continue their favourite pastor in the church or some members themselves used, as means to have another pastor of their choice to perpetuate their hegemony. Although few, such were the source of potential tension. They agitated to either retain or remove those pastors or church workers who either facilitated or became obstacle to their property or commercial interests or social ties, others had no issue and the rest cozily sat on the fence. I found, despite seeming contradiction, the system worked well; however, some tried to misuse it.

As per the church rule, a bishop's appointments were order. However, I tried to inspire politically motivated pastors and church workers, not to defy them, and I encouraged them to bring to me their difficulty if any through proper channels or even personally, but not to try to use congregations like a pressure group. There was such tendency among some pastors who succeeded in the past; now it seemed they realized I was different stuff. It took some time to change their attitude, and then things began to move in a positive direction.

Stewardship of Institutions

With some exception, most the church's institutions lacked managerial expertise and stewardship. The management of the institutions was in hands of the persons who did not have specialized training, it was top-bottom situation. Actually, bishops, pastors, and deaconesses were trained to preach and teach the gospel, not to manage educational, medical, or social institutions, and managerial work was like an enlarged role. Nevertheless, some were naturally endowed with managerial ability. It was pathetic to observe the falling standard of the church's institutions over a period. I felt the deficiency in management skill could be overcome to some extent by giving on-job training. So I planned management seminars to teach basic skills and techniques of management, although I was aware, a mere bag full of skills, techniques, and emphasis on transparency would not work miracles if the honesty that flows from within oneself and which is resilient and sustainable did not become the way of life.

Once, I had an awful experience. My predecessor appointed the spouse of a politically heavy weight pastor as a manager to one of the hostels in the Delhi Conference. Long after I learnt, the appointment was made under duress. I understand, sometimes, there was need to appoint a layperson when no one among the church workers or pastors was available. There was concern over excess spending by the manager that did not improve the hostel's living condition.

On March 21, 1995, a few days before the Regional Conference session, I took along with me R. M.

Basharat, a senior ordained minister, to verify what I heard; not realizing I was not like Nehemiah of the Bible, my good intention backfired and caused me a great ordeal. We tried to reach the place early, but traffic conditions did not favour us; we reached at about 9:30 in the evening, and the manager of the hostel was not around. I inspected the hostel along with other leaders; it was in a pathetic condition. Then came the manager; she behaved as if we were nobody and lacked courtesy and decency. I felt she was rude to her core and in arrogance, she raised her voice and eyebrows over my surprise visit. I could see hatred in her eyes, and arrogance and deceptiveness on her face, she persuaded me to stay back that night, I declined; my sixth sense cautioned: there could be some sinister design in her mind to put me in trouble. On my refusal, she was even more furious, exploded in rage, and before she could calm down, we left for Delhi. I heard, after we left, she dressed well, decked with jewellery, went to the local police station to file a complaint against me, and quarrelled with the local police officer. It seemed she was desperate to hang on to the post by blackmailing me; however, I discontinued her ad hoc services in the conference session. In her place, the deaconess who was given an ordinary work was appointed. Then she filed fake court cases against me; the church won them. There was even the prohibitory court order against her, restricting her entry into Haryana State. I was not personal or revengeful, I was just trying to make things right. Actually, I had good relation with the family and even I supported her husband for Episcopacy, believing he had a good spiritual standard; however, what stood between us was the interest of the church. They tried to harm me, as I could not support their unreasonable demand. I never could imagine, they would use such pressure tactics as I tried to safeguard the church's interest.

There were other few exceptional cases like her; however, there were also talented and committed laywomen in the church who desired to serve the church. Sadly, then the church rules barred their entry into the ministry of Deaconess Conference. I observed there was dearth of competent and committed deaconesses, so it was even more fit and proper to consider committed and talented laywomen for associate membership of Deaconess' Conference. I was aware, prior to becoming the affiliated autonomous church, the Women's Conference, now Deaconess Conference, had associate members, the women of the church who desired to serve the church in a meaningful way, associate membership was open to them; I recognize, its discontinuation was a politically motivated move. If it was not for rule, the talented and committed women of the church should have been appointed to manage the church's institutions effectively.

The Centenary English Church, 24, Lodi Road, New Delhi, invited me to preach. A bishop's visit to local churches is usually announced in advanced. I did not know what was in store for me. On May 12, 1996, Sunday, 8:30 in the morning, I preached in the church, met the congregation members at the tea fellowship in the church's basement. After the tea, I asked my chauffeur to bring out the car from the parking lot to return home. I sat in the car, no sooner did the car start than the pastor's wife, who was hefty, muscular built, and discontinued as the manager ran towards the car along with her son, reared in her own likeness. She said she wanted to talk to me and asked me to come out of the car, but knowing her arrogance, I refused. Then she swiftly twisted the chauffeur's hand and took away the car's key; by chance, the car did not stop, it was in neutral gear. Then she inserted her hand in the car's window where I sat, she firmly held my hair and pulled them with all her strength like deep-rooted grass. Some people who were watching rushed to my rescue and questioned her violent behaviour. I was amazed, the pastor hid in the parsonage and peeped through the window's aperture while she lavishly spilled venom. With much struggle, I ejected her wrestler's hand and the chauffeur moved the car out of the church compound. Some church members pressurized me to lodge a police complaint and others condemned the pastor, it was an ugly affair. I did not quite understand why some bishops were pampering such elements who were harming the church's interest. Some church members continued to press on me to file a criminal case; however, I swallowed the insult, left it to the divine justice like most people do in the church. Their deeds were not in conformity with the holiness of life and such elements thought, if bishops did not bend to their wishes, then they would be treated like this. I was sad; no bishop came forward to condemn it, it appeared, as if they were indifferent to all that was going on in the church, if they were safe.

I grieved by it and wondered why they fell short of spiritual standard being the first family of the local church and reacting in such a shameful manner, which was black spot in the name of pastors, who were expected to live an exemplary Christian life, not a shoddy life style. I perceived, the zeal for power and position blinded them and worldliness was paralyzing the church's spirituality. I could not reconcile with it, I thought, how could the pastor who claimed he was a shepherd of sheep, a spiritual leader, and a man of God under religious vows could so easily got lost in worldly ambition and run out of his calling. I recognized that the church was indifferent to the deficient ministerial standard of pastors and deaconesses. There were some church leaders who, instead of taking corrective steps, even secretly supported them, and the rest were indifferent. In a paradoxical situation, the church workers who were competent and principled were rarely picked up for managerial positions, but those who were soft on integrity and showed flexibility to inappropriate adjustments were in great demand.

I had to face a similar situation in another conference under my charge. The principal of a prestigious high school acted like an autocrat, she barely cared about the manager appointed by bishop, and my predecessors, too, neglected to clarifying duties and functions of the manager. I was curious to know why were they silent on her arbitrary administrative style, though under the bishop's appointment and accountable to him and the school management committee. Not long before, I learnt that she started to have a firm grief on the school administration from the time of the school extension project. It seemed that she had a final say on it, no approval from competent church authorities was taken, and the school admission to the church community children, and fee concession of them was left solely to her discretion. The school administration lacked transparency; she run the school, as if it was her private enterprise, the church practically lost the control of the school. What was shocking, she was even secretly registering the school as an independent entity under the Parent-Teacher Association. I had to take some hard decisions to check her delinquent working, she protested against my corrective steps, resigned in protest to avoid disclosures and surprises. Not long after I accepted her resignation, there was outcry; eventually, the dirty dust settled. I was amazed, there was a bishop who believed, it was an Anglo-Indian, so it enjoyed exclusive right to function without any interference from the church and he was even secretly mentoring her. I recall, she used to dramatically descend in the Regional Conference's session with the cheque of about ₹ 50,000/– for Home Mission with much pomp show to hand over it to the conference's benevolence treasurer. Not long after she left, there was overall significant improvement in the school, academically it became stronger and the Home Mission giving increased tenfold close to (Indian Rupee symbol). 5,00,000/– per annum and for the first time it began to support other schools with substantial grants.

I was keen to appoint competent persons in the church's institutions on merit and carefully avoided the tendency of ascriptive criteria, nepotism, and abuse of prerogatives that deprived deserving persons. However, I recognize, at times bishops could have faced genuine difficulty to make objective assessment of persons under consideration, as they were assigned to other than their home conferences on their election or thereafter. I relied on the candidates' qualification and a good recommendation from conference's leaders; however, I recognized, these were inadequate. Once, I appointed a person with good degrees and recommendations. When I first saw him, he looked simple and sober, dressed in ordinary clothes and wore Hawaii slippers. There was a broad smile on his face, as he walked towards me, greeted me with folded hands like an Indian politician, touched my feet and spoke politely; his pleasing disposition misled me. Not long after, he invited me to his family function; it was an impressive gathering of fine gentry. During the course of our conversation, he said, his wife was the daughter of a vice-chancellor, born with a silver spoon, and they lacked nothing in life. I appointed him as the director of a technical institute when there was need. He did well as long as I was there. No sooner had I left the conference than he indulged in unacceptable deeds and misused his official position for self-gain. He disguised to get the covetous post and became a political force to be reckoned with; a little had I imagined then, he would do such things and fall short of the church's expectation. I gave him term appointment; however, an influential pastor who was a good church leader pleaded persistently, so I changed retirement age to 60. I was swayed by his pressure, but not long after, people came out with secret stories, and then they were scared to be a prophetic deterrent to his phenomenal political growth. People criticized me for sowing the bad seed; however, they barely recognized, they were the source of his nutrients. Regardless, I made the colossal mistake and wished, they exposed him before I appointed him or left the conference. Long after, he met me; I exhorted him to mend his ways; he was defensive and adamant. He could no longer inspire me whereas some bishops used his brain and bravado, supporting and promoting him to achieve their own political ambition. Then I was convinced, qualification and good recommendations per se mean nothing if honesty were missing; whenever I remember, I grieve over my error of judgment.

I realized, my overemphasis on management excellence led me sometimes to overvalue managerial skills and techniques; although these are important, I believed, it was honesty that mattered the most; the values of honesty and hard work could not be inculcated or internalized overnight. I strived to pick up right persons on my team – then I thought, they were right people for work; however, I confess, in some cases, I failed awfully in my judgments. I could not perceive the dark side of vested interests of my men and doing things but differently, it was tough to digest by pastors and the church workers and absorbed by the system, to which they were used to.

Mindset, Affinities and Pressure Groups

There were people who did things joyfully without expecting a reward or recognition. I remember one of my church members was punctual for Sunday worship and rarely late, expect for some exigencies. He was always ready to assist me in whatever he could do. He did it year after year, from the time he joined the church. There were such people in other local churches as well who did one thing or other; however, the rest were curious to know what the church could do for them. I felt they were unrealistic and unsupportive to the advancement of the mission of the church; the time had changed, but their mission mindset did not, as though they were living in the bygone foreign missionary era, overshadowing the present realities, in utter neglect of the church's mission to the world. I believe that if the mission of the church was to move forward in the changing world, such captive thinking should change, which was an obstacle to fulfilling the missionary mandate.

Bishop's House, Mumbai

As said, we lived on the 21, YMCA Road, Bombay, when I was pastor of the church. It was a small house like a small apartment, allotted to us after marathon efforts, unlike Bishop's House, which was like a mansion on other side of the road. Then I never knew one day we would occupy it nearly for fifteen years, more than any other bishop did – when financial support was withdrawn, we could not maintain it, for leaks and cracks appeared all over and turned worse as years passed by. An unmarried old lady was our immediate neighbour who lived by herself. At times, she had someone to live with her. She was a Methodist by birth, and it appeared she reaped the benefits of the missionary era. Rayhal used to go to her school by school bus; in mornings, we used to escort her to the bus and on returning, she came on her own. One day, when she was returning from the school, the lady called and asked her, 'Do you know? We are born Methodists, we have a right to live in the church property,' Rayhal could not comprehend her parabolic expression; she was just 14 and not brought up with the church politics. She repeated the same three to four times. Then I told her, 'If she tells you again, then tell her, 'Good, we are born Methodists, however it will be better if we are born again Methodists as well.'

It seemed that most Christian had same or similar mindset, what they could do for the church was irrelevant, what the church could do for them was of a great value. I recognized such thinking was prevailing everywhere from the time of foreign missionaries who built churches, schools, hostels, and hospitals. They settled around the Christian community like Robert Redfield's little community, relatively simple or less differentiated[2]. They gave them work to do, a place to live, a church to worship; they helped them on the occasions of marriages, festivals, and unforeseen needs. I recognize, it was the need of the hour and a commendable foreign missionary endeavour; however, it also made some of them parasite on the church for their needs, the time had changed, but the tendency to expect something from the church did not, especially those who were under the influence of bygone foreign missionary era. They came to church for worship, gave very little, and expected more. In the past, foreign missionaries had zeal and funds, now both are lacking. As I thought over it, I was convinced, it could be better if people saw the difference between the *church* and *mission*. In my public speaking, I demonstrated the difference between these two familiar and powerful words. For easy understanding, I said *mission* means what the church could do for Christians and *church* means what Christians could do for the church's mission to the world. I tried to convince them that they were at the threshold of a new missionary age, they were no longer someone's mission, but they had their own mission to the world. There was need to change their set thinking; however, I recognized that any change from familiar to unfamiliar was not so easy. I am convinced the old mission paradigm served its purpose; perhaps, in that historical context, it was inevitable, now the time is calling on us to change it, what Christians could do for the church's mission for the world was vital for effectively witnessing.

I observed connectional relation was not shared value and did not transcend social affinities, which tended to be like Berlin wall. In one of the conferences under my charge, the director of the Methodist Technical Institute was a retired military lieutenant commander. Some local leaders pampered him a lot, as he acted pious and evangelical; actually, he was contrary to prevailing perception. He was successful in making people believe him although neither had he belonged to the church community nor he spoke the language of the people, but his good rapport with church leaders did miracles. It seemed he was autocratic; barely anyone knew what went on in the institute. Not long after he left, we found the institute was financially weak; it was at the brink of losing government's recognition and grant, as he run the institute like his private enterprise and kept the governing body in the dark. He painted a rosy picture, everyone in the board believed him, but the actual story was just the opposite. I had to take corrective steps to streamline the administration. In the beginning, he was willing to cooperate, and then he resisted and became uncooperative. Eventually, the governing body wrestled to make him resign to save the institute.

Then I appointed another person as director, a Methodist from another Regional Conference. The bishop, who looked after the conference for an interim period in my place, did not want him to continue. He stirred regional feelings; some conference leaders and their followers insisted, the director must be from their own language. In tactical move, the bishop first took away financial control from him and the hostel management and then he created a situation for him to resign. He shared with me his agonizing, humiliating, and painful experiences. I consoled him to have patience and obey the bishop. I said the situation would change, but it did not happen, on contrary, the language agitation coupled with other issues rendered him miserable and he resigned in frustration. A retired wing commander was appointed as director from their language community. His initial euphoria faded, it seemed his rising expectations did not materialize, so he resigned. It was pathetic, the Methodist connectional relation was of no consequence, but language affinity was, even social change in India could not bend significantly the parochial attitude when it came to settling political scores.

There was a similar scene again in the conference; the director of the Methodist Hospital was a highly respected cardio-thoracic surgeon. He was a successful surgeon and a Methodist by heart and mind who served the church for many years. The hospital was incurring losses, he wanted to discipline the hospital staff and workers, mostly local Methodists, and pull out the hospital from financial crisis. I was appalled to know some conference leaders with a parochial mindset, and although of evangelical conviction, secretly supported the staff and workers to chase him out. On March 8, 2005, I was in the Heart Hospital for a meeting, another medical institution run by the church in partnership with an influential local Hindu family. They descended like a horde, demonstrated and demanded his immediate removal, did not let me move, until I agreed to his removal. They pressurized me to appoint the director from their own language stock. Love for one's language was understandable; however, its being a means to achieve goals was not. I felt they were actually pursuing the 'sons of soil' ideology. They were unreasonable and levelled baseless and malicious allegations against him; everyone knew he was a senior, seasoned, honest, and committed doctor. I stood by him; however, he got tired of opponents spewing venom on him and lack of cooperation from the hospital staff, and he left the hospital. Not long after, the local conference leaders were repentant for their short sightedness, but it was too late, the hospital services deteriorated and the hospital's liabilities galloped. Then I learnt out of desperation, they tried to lease out the hospital.

The Methodist connectional relation did not rise above petty politics of language affinity in the church, and what they believed, they did not practice. These events gave me the bigger picture of the reality that existed in the church. It was disappointing, the Council of Bishops did not find time to deal with such destructive trends; however, they had enough time to engage in the cutthroat politics of revenge and greed. People forgot that these great institutions were the gift from the dedicated souls who were neither Indians nor regionalists. I recognized it was, but the clash of the interest of little communities within the Christian community. Methodists in India were tending to make petty borders for their own little communities, while claiming themselves to be part of worldwide Methodism.

The Christian community in India, generally perceived as a social community, actually is an imagined community, for it lacks homogeneous social and cultural traits. I think it can best be described as a religious or faith community, which somewhat binds Christians together on some core Christian beliefs in India's mosaic sociocultural realities. With European and American Christian missionaries, Westernization influenced Christians' life style; however, it could not uproot them from the Indian tradition; there is change with continuity. I perceived there are social groups in the church that are like little communities, each having its own social and cultural traits. Christianity could not bind them together, making them a social or cultural melting pot; the elements of language, regionalism, and people's group were as real as faith. Christian faith is yet to emerge as the single most unifying factor integrating social, cultural, and regional latent tendencies into a complex whole. I found the little communities played a significant role in the church's working. People tend to segregate by language or region or people's groups and sometime were driven to separatist introspection. Each of the little communities tried to exert its influence over each other, either to gain or control ecclesiastical power and position. The socio-political reality was an obstacle to Christian unity and connectional relation.

The sociopolitical push and pull were active in the church. I read Salig Harrison's *'The Two Most Dangerous Decades,'* and I found similar forces at work in the church, as described by him; at one end the Discipline of the church tended to bind people together, on other end the affinity to little communities pulling them apart[3]. I recognized if the Discipline ceased to act as a unifying force, people would be likely to be inclined to act in the support of their little community than in the general good of the church. I felt sad for the play of such trends in the working of the church. I did nothing radical by appointing qualified people from other conferences, when no competent person was available in the conference to run the church's institutions; however, they were euphuistic over their language affinity[4]. The regional or linguistic feelings and social affinities were obstacles to cohesiveness; it restricted mobilization and distribution of the church talents and assets and effectively serving the poor and needy. I perceived the rising expectation was promoting the politics of little communities, which had wider and deeper ramification on the life and ministry of the church.

There were pressure groups in the church like the Methodist Lay Association in Gujarat, the Methodist Organization for the Protection of Property in Hyderabad, and the Christian Welfare Association in Bareilly Conferences. It seemed they sprang up as reactionary groups to oppose certain decisions of the church leadership; perhaps, local people felt their interests impinged. I faced the tempest of such informal pressure groups, exerting pressures on me to achieve their parochial and personal goals; sometimes, they were enthused by local leaders and even some bishops used their political clout against me. I recognize the freedom of expression is essential for democracy to thrive; however, the pressure groups were not constructive contributors to democratic process. Bishops, officer bearers, and members used such pressure groups to either win election or oppose certain candidates' election. The informal pressure groups were unlike nongovernment organizations, which have specific interest to support candidates to influence government's policies at national or states or local levels, on certain issues like environment conservation, right to information, and rights issues, etc.[5]. Their roles at the government level were understandable. However, then I was not convinced, if there was any justification for such informal pressure groups in the church, for they seemed merely the engine of self-serving interest, taking advantage out of disinformation on the alienation of church properties or misappropriation of funds or misuse of authority or denial of executive positions to locals. In the past, such voices were wisely and effectively dealt with, but now it appeared, the administrative working style of church leaders was the fertile ground for pressure groups. As a bishop, I had to deal with them and I did it with courage and conviction. I was melancholic, some bishops stirred them to settle their score with their colleague bishops and others escaped from them by not living in episcopal residence or by not visiting sensitive places in their episcopal areas. This tendency stimulated inferior episcopal supervision that deprived free access to the church workers, seeking administrative and spiritual guidance. The burning issues were turning volcanic because of inaction and perhaps the anxiety of unveiling of murky intentions. Paradoxically, the Council of Bishops sumptuously feasted on trivialities but showed apathy to serious problems and put the seal of their approval on things that did not invoke the holiness of life.

On July 13, 1995, Monday 4:30 in the evening, the management committee of Titus Elementary School, Moradabad, was held in the manager's bungalow. I reached the venue well on time. No sooner had I began to chair the meeting after tea than the group of twenty to twenty-five people was forcing their way inside; they were angry and violent. The manager shut the door; they started hitting the door, shouted slogans against the manager, and demanded her immediate transfer. The manager was inexperienced, and she recently did her church workers' training and joined the deaconess' ministry. I felt perhaps she could not deal with the local tactfully. However, I thought, it was no way to raise the issue and solve the problem. They were desperate to force me to transfer her immediately or at least give the undertaking in writing to do so. I turned down their demand, they turned hostile and threw stones at the door and windows to disturb the meeting. With the commotion outside, I could hardly take up some important items, it became dark, it was time to push off for Bareilly or else, I thought, it would be too late. The manager and her husband urged me to stay back, however I declined as next day, I had to preside over another meeting. I was hurrying, as I had to cover the distance of about 100 kilometers. I stepped out of the Bungalow with great difficulty, as the horde blocked my way, I sat in the car, the chauffer started the car, but the car could not move an inch, as they lie in front of the car. Some of them were boozed; others expressed their disgust, the way the manager worked. At the end, the district superintendent gave them assurance in writing to look into the problem to end the impasse.

I looked at my watch, it was 11:25 in the night, some from the horde were still around, though voices mellowed down and some of them left. I thought I would push off soon. The scenario changed, one of them who was boozed, when sobered up, said, 'I know you are a bishop, you will not come to my house.' He moved me, I accepted his invitation, went to his house to have tea although it was late in the evening. I entered his home, he was calm, tea was served, and I was asked to pray. After the prayer, he knelt down, apologized for his behaviour, and asked me to pray for him. As I sat in the car than, he quickly rushed with a pair of giraffes, made up of brass, about three feet tall and weighing about seven to eight kilos each. I was reluctant to accept them, but he pleaded like a child and kept them in the boot. I learnt that Moradabad was very famous for brass work and brass items are exported to several counties. The pair of giraffes is kept in my living room, and when I look at them, I often remember the incident.

From February 1 to 3, 1996, the Moradabad Regional Conference's session was held in Bijnor, Uttar Pradesh, a highly instigated pressure group planned to obstruct me from conducting the conference until I concede to their unreasonable demand. They wanted me to restore the pastor to the full membership of the conference who voluntarily resigned and not willing to give up school teaching. The church laws did not allow me to do so unless he resigned from his secular job. However, I was willing to take him back in into the local category, but the pressure group was fierce, unwilling to settle for less. They sat in front of the conference's dais to stall proceedings like those who protest in a General Conference's session or State Assembly or Indian Parliament. I could not accede to their unlawful demand, as I was no stronger than the church's laws. After they made much ruffle, delegates of the conference came to my rescue and cleared them from the scene.

From May 29 to 31, 1996, the Regional Executive Board Meeting was held in Moradabad. All was fine on the first day, but the next day, the local Methodist horde intruded the meeting, profusely abused the executive secretary for his suspicious role in some imagined property deal. I remember, board members were whispering that some insider was misleading them that they would be vacated from the mission property. They were highly charged and misguided, started breaking windowpanes and water glasses and throwing tables and chairs. By chance, no one was hurt; however, vandalism shattered me. I felt, it was the insane act, not compatible with the Christian character, even if they had some genuine grievances. Absolutely, it was no way to deal with the matter. I never saw anything like this before in the church and wondered if I was getting the glimpse of the bigger picture of the church. There were rival political groups in each Regional Conference who wrestled politically against each other; however, I never could imagine, they would stoop so low. I did not get up from my chair or move a bit, but speechless, well composed, however, in a contemplating mode. I mulled over the affairs of the church while I gazed at the spilled water, scattered pieces of glasses, and broken tables and chairs, except the one on which I sat, and wondered if the broken pieces could be fixed. It was a planned move, not the sudden outburst. I learnt it was not the first time; such was the political life style in the conference. It seemed, in the past, some bishops tried to tame such uncontrolled expressions, but it did not change the situation. However, they assured me of my safety and said, no harm would be done to me; their prey was the executive secretary. Nevertheless, I was grieved over what they did and barely had they realized it was not a Christian way to settle one's grievances. The entire situation turned ugly and chaotic, I adjourned the board meeting sine die.

There was an annual convention of the Gujarat Regional Conference's WSCS at Vadodara. They invited me to give the Bible massage in its concluding session on Sunday. A pressure group was blocking my way to the church because of some false propaganda and at instigation of one bishop who was envy of my acceptability in his home conference. Not long after, they rejected his unpredictable politics and tactics and withdrew from him, and he could not make over his image, which he created for himself. I was amazed some bishops love to indulge in vengeful and ridiculous activities against their colleagues, used pressure tactics, and spent time and money of the church to prevent others coming to power to secure their own position. It seemed that partiality and protectionism overshadowed the church's mission, seldom had they heeded the Bible dictum; vengeance is mine[6]. It affected the life and witness of the church, but who-cares attitude flourished like weeds among good seeds. Bishops who sporadically immobilized by such pressure groups burst into anger, others were cozy with the self-serving mission that did not take forward the mission of the church. I observed, in the Council of Bishops, active and retired bishops lacked prophetic disposition; they were indifferent to the burning issues that impinged the general oversight and injured spiritual and temporal interests of the church[7].

I was focused and persuasive to do things, as I was clear in my vision and faithful to my calling. I tried to do my best, as expected of me. I kept church before me and self behind me, and God gave me courage and zeal to break new grounds for the growth of the church. I was neither flexible nor indifferent to my responsibilities and did not avoid risky issues under the pretext of unreasonable outburst or protests. I do not claim I was always wise, calculative, and cautious, but tried to solve thorny issues with courage and conviction. I did not feel any psycho phobia of the people or issues or lay them dormant to be aggravated or pass on into the lap of the incoming bishop and under pious pretension did not spend my ministerial God-given time in leisure and peace.

I was faithful to my episcopal duties and did not waver or remain lukewarm to demanding situations. With great care and concern, I moved forward. I felt speed was essential, as time does not wait for none, it flies, you cannot catch it, once it is gone, and neither can you bring it back. So I struggled to do more in less time, I spoke essential, listened sympathetically to their problems, and got back to my work. Some misconstrued me; they did not take in right spirit. I heard some said, 'In the past, bishops used to spend time with us over cup of tea, talked for hours, now we sip tea without much chats.' I wished they appreciated the fact that I was short on time and did not feel wise in faffing around. Perhaps, my living in a mega city influenced my life style. Barely had I time for leisure talk, I had much to do and to supervise two episcopal areas. I was not used to being prodigious on time; time was precious like gold, so I was cautious not to squander but to use it profitably for the church and I had no intention to undermine the value of social relations. I simply liked to avoid lazy talk, for it was my intrinsic nature. I could not do otherwise; neither was there any genuine occasion for it. My focus was on my specific goals; the responsibilities and challenges of church growth, institutional and social work, and ticklish property issues occupied me. I barely spent quality time even with my family. I remember, at times,

I received intercom calls or notes through my secretary to seek my appointment. I was workaholic and do not remember if I had ever taken an annual leave. I felt guilty about it and my anxiety to justify my negligence did not satisfy anyone in the family.

As said, bishops do theology and generally do not have specific training in management and administration. However, by the nature of their duties and responsibilities, they are the spiritual and temporal general superintendent of the church. I observed some bishops were naturally endowed with managerial ingenuity and prudence than others. I felt if newly elected bishops were given some crash course on general orientation to the episcopal work, elucidating pros and cons of administrative hazards, challenges and risks involved in dealing critical issues, and some guidance on property management, it could be of immense help. Moreover, learning from the experiences of bishops and experts in the field should be of great value to effective episcopal leadership. Regardless, there was a difference between knowing what bishops do and actually doing it. Bishops were free to do work, as they liked, however, within rules; but overnight, some assumed themselves as all wise, powerful, and craved for public recognition like a worldly leader. I remember a young worker said he did not listen to the wife of a bishop despite her insistence to call her husband as Bishop Doctor, as he did not earn a doctorate or even an academic excellence. On another occasion, a senior pastor shared with me his agony, how his bishop ill-treated him. He gave him an appointment but made him wait throughout the day in his office's corridor without any hope of meeting him. I was puzzled, why some bishops loved to leave behind the air of their importance and longed to get adoration from their subordinates. I felt persuaded to think, as if they were showing their selfworth and failed to learn the Bible lesson of humility.

I felt most bishops were happy with stereotype work, did minimum requisite to avoiding taking hard decisions; often, they were contextual and reluctant to face challenges in the changing world; the difference between seeing and believing was real, but the situation in the church was not stagnant, it was fast changing and necessitated the ability to take prompt and wise decisions. My family members and well-wishers prayed for me to get wisdom. I confess, I was not having wisdom like that of Solomon; however, whatever little understanding I had, I was amazed, I could quickly perceive what people were thinking, as they deliberated on various committees and personal meetings. Before they could speak, I almost knew what they were to speak; it helped me to take quick decisions in the larger interest of the church. I concede, sometimes, I had greater propensity to go astray from my prayer warriors than my political advisors for temporary strategic gain.

I was aware that I, too, had no specialized training in church management; however, my education came to my aid, and more importantly, my clear goals, unwavering decisions, unbroken devotion and zeal held the key. I could break new grounds, take new initiatives and handle volcanic issues; my staying power and the fire in my heart did amazing things, but not impossible ones like dividing a zero.

Church Growth

I was melancholic to see the church work, once flourished, and then barely had church activities; most bishops were occupied with minimum routine church governance, and new initiatives in evangelism and church growth were seldom seen. The church's precious scare resources were spent prodigiously in creating and maintaining the episcopal paraphernalia that did not facilitate the church and institutional growth. A great deal of time and energy were spent only on discussing property matters to raise funds to keep greasing the administrative machinery of the church. Not many were passionate soul winners; others were armchair evangelists, thus the circuit work, a small group, attached to a main congregation, dwindled in many places. Evangelism and missionary activities did not inspire like power politics and the pathetic state of the holiness of life was pushing out the church members to charismatic churches, it was a truly disappointing scenario. However, in the midst of gloom, there were some signs of hope, new centres of preaching or church extension activities sprang up in some parts that tended to sustain fading cheers. In Moradabad and Agra Conferences, it was alarming. The church growth was visible and vibrant in some places in Delhi, Gujarat, Bombay, and South Indian Conferences. It was a joy to learn that some local churches in Delhi, Punjab, Rajasthan, Bombay, and South Conferences were actively engaged in missionary endeavours; in the Gujarat Conference, it was amazing. In some conferences, Methodist congregations were mission oriented, they generously supported the missionary work and adopted missionaries, but evangelism and church growth concern did not get prime attention of the apex bodies of the church, perhaps due to pre-occupation and over occupation with the church administrative humdrum, despite everyone unwaveringly vouched for the urgency of missionary mandate. Once in a quadrennium, a seminar on missional priority was held symbolically at astronomical cost, in some scenic resort without any follow up to measure the achievement of projected goals. I felt the seminars were like an evangelism showpiece: it did not conjure the imagination of the church to save perishing souls or rekindle the spirit to do the work of an evangelist.

There were some local congregations that did praiseworthy evangelistic work and churches grew. I realized, it all depended on pastors, if they were motivated, then congregations were enthusiastic to do its best, laypersons came forward in a big way to evangelize unreached areas. I made some feeble efforts to sensitize pastors and laypersons towards evangelism and church growth. A number of new churches, parsonages, and institutions were built as part of evangelism and church growth endeavours. I value, some of those experiences, which were amazing and exciting that manifested God's power in the midst of impossibilities and scarcity.

It was rare experience to baptize 465 adults in the village called Dholwal, Rajasthan. I invited my colleague bishops and church officers to participate in it. It was a wonderful experience. I remember, people sang, read the Bible with a great zeal and devotion. It was possible due to India Every Home Crusade, a missionary organization that worked among them for several years. None induced new converts or gave any monetary or other incentives to accept the Christian faith; it was wholly their personal choice and decision to accept Jesus Christ as their Lord and saviour. I remember, when the proposal came, I agreed to receive them into the church. We were overwhelmed and our hearts overflowed with joy when they donated a piece of land to build a church. Four of them were chosen and appointed as local preachers to nurture the rest spiritually, and it was decided to send them for Bible training.

There was happiness over the starting of the new mission field. Delhi Conference purchased a piece of land in Udaipur, a city of lakes in Rajasthan at the cost of ₹ 38,00,000/-. It was a very beautiful site, close to Fateh Sagar Lake and an adjoining mountain. We were planning to build church and Conference Centre for Retreat and Meditation. On August 28, 1998, the foundation stone for the Lake Methodist Church was laid in the presence of my colleague and the select gathering. It was a joyous and a memorable experience. Bishops were sanguine, except one who looked scornful, his gestures spew jealousy and disapproval; not long after, he raised mischievous objections on the property title and conspired to damage me, although unsuccessful, as there was no deficiency in it and it was a transparent deal in the best interest of the church.

The organizing Udaipur District, an ecclesiastical jurisdiction, was one of the milestones in the church growth efforts and the Delhi Conference's congregations contributed joyfully their mite for the work. The building plans for the church and the

Conference Centre in Udaipur were drawn and finalized while I was still the bishop of the Delhi Episcopal Area. By the change in my episcopal assignment, the project vision changed; the area bishop was not serious about it, he was toying with the idea to sell the property to raise money to build another episcopal residence, as the present historical one was to be acquired by the Delhi Metro. Just before and after independence, Jawaharlal Nehru, the first prime minister of India, was a visitor at the time of J. W. Pickett, an American bishop, and Indira Gandhi in her teenage attended student Bible study and rose to ask questions. From here at the time of the partition of India, untiring efforts were made to get medical relief supplies from America for the victims of Hindu-Muslim riots on the request of the prime minister. The church enjoyed good rapport with political leadership at Raisina hill and then kept aloof from it. I was dismayed to learn the mission and the church growth interests were not prime concerns, but comfort was. Eventually, the Methodist guesthouse on 17, Boulevard Road was converted into Bishop's residence. Then, the direction and goals of the project swiftly changed, the good work was not pursued with right earnest, but on the contrary, shelved. I felt there was need for some kind of institutional deterrence to protect and continue the work in new areas, if it was left to the wills and fancy of an incoming bishop, it might suffer setback.

We travelled from Udaipur to Abu Road to lay the foundation stone for a new church building and then to Jaipur. On August 30, 1998, the Pink City Methodist Church was built on the piece of land purchased by my predecessor. There was joy and excitement among the local church members, we shared their happiness, participated and dedicated the new church building, and by the construction and dedication of the new church building in Jaipur city, the Methodist presence was firmly established.

There was another amazing experience. Way back in 1997, a piece of land for a church building at Nerul, New Mumbai, was purchased at the discount rate from the City and Industrial Development Corporation. I was aware, but there were no funds with the conference for the church building project and no serious efforts made to build the church. I had never seen the plot and had some vague idea about it. One day, the district superintendent invited me to see the plot and meet congregations. I agreed to visit the place in the evening of April 18, 2002. It was incredible, the plot was beautiful, and it was an ideal location for the church. Until then, the Methodist Church did have any church building in New Bombay, now New Mumbai. I felt it was good to build the church there. After prayer, I gave a big push to the four congregations to raise funds by giving my personal donation first; they were motivated and inspired. The people assembled spontaneously reciprocated by their generous giving, it was beyond my expectation. I was thrilled by the way people were eager to have a church building, and the amount collected on the day was ₹ 2,30,000/-. We praised God, it was a step closer to achieving the goal and the sign of their determination and pledge that they would never look back in building the church.

The approved building plans lay idle for a long time for want of funds, but we pulled them out of dusted drawer to start the work. On May 22, 2002, the foundation stone was laid for the Epworth Methodist Church. The congregations raised more funds and the conference gave the grant of ₹ 17,00,000/-, the ground and the church sanctuary on the first floor were completed, and on May 1, 2005, the church was dedicated and declared open for worship.

The work of the church planting ministry in Gujarat Conference was already going on; the Bombay Conference did not have such work. I felt, it would be good to start the church planting ministry, to revive the old circuits work and start new growth centres. I appointed a director and some missionaries to do the work. A considerable fund spent, but no church growth work, worth its name done, director's post was abused for petty politics and boosting election prospects.

Sharon, Rayhal, Virtu & I during Pastors'
Seminar at Pahalgam, Kashmir, May 1998

It was necessary to lead pastors for the evangelism and church growth activities, so to motivate them,

I planned pastors' prayer breakfast meetings and seminars; prayer breakfast meetings were held once in a month and seminars occasionally. The meetings were to pray for the church work, encourage one another, and develop personal bonds of friendship. First, I did it in Delhi Conference and then in Bombay and Gujarat Conferences; it acted like a stimulus.

I remember the church leaders were inconsistent, contradictory, and presumptive on the church membership statistics; attendance on Sunday worship and the migration of members to other churches did not support their statistical claim. I looked at the statistics with skeptic curiosity. In 1965, it was said that there were little more than 500,000 members; in 1980, the same number was claimed. Contrary, in 1981, it was claimed that there were 600,000 members in the church. However, some were sanguine and heroic, although for fifteen years, the church membership did not increase significantly, and in 2007, then, an imaginary 648,000 membership was claimed[8]. Actually, the figures are inconsistent, presumptive and unconvincing, unsupported by reliable statistics and empty pews. It seems that the church membership, for fifteen years, was more or less static, and from 1981, more than twenty-five years, there was barely increase in the overall church membership. It suggested spiritual stagnation, feeble efforts for evangelism, and church growth or absorption of the church leaders in malicious politics. If the current Indian annual population growth rate of 1.93 per cent was taken into account, it was not even proportionate to natural increase – thinking like Malthusian's geometric ratio was mere imagination. I am constrained to think that there was an overall decline in the church membership, while huge funds were spent, the episcopal offices increased and the institutional work decreased.

Social Concerns

There arose emergency in Urlana and Joshi villages in the Delhi Conference. Emergency relief was needed for these villages; the villages were in a close proximity to each other and near the famous Panipat town in Haryana, where three decisive battles were fought that established Mughals in India. In 1996, the flood severely affected villages; most families in the villages were Methodist Christians, primarily engaged in agricultural activities. One day in the early morning, I was surprised to greet the pastor and the people of the villages at my doorsteps; they narrated awesome miseries of the families in the villages caused by the floodwater and pleaded for the relief. The conference had no funds for relief work and by now, the CORAR was inactive. Anyway, I comforted and assured them that something would be done. As I spoke, I perceived the spark of hope on their worried faces. No sooner had they left than I asked my district superintendents and pastors to request local congregations in Delhi to contribute towards relief; the local churches compassionately raised the relief.

I also asked their district superintendent and pastor to prepare the list of affected people in the villages, mentioning names of families and income. After a few weeks, they came with the list. I did not know whom to approach for help. After much thinking, I decided to ask the Bread for the World, a German agency for the relief through one of my German acquaintances. After months of anxious waiting, I received affirmative reply that ₹ 25,00,000/- for rehabilitation was on the way. In the beginning, we thought of giving buffalos to the affected people, but others in the villages, too, asked for the same and the fund received was insufficient to meet everyone's needs. Then I discussed the matter with the director of the CASA, New Delhi. After several initiatives and meetings, it was decided to launch a rural development project in these villages. I handed over the grant to the CASA, assured them our participation, and urged them to start the project. The CASA took keen interest in the project and walked a second mile by supplementing funds from their resources for the rehabilitation project. Health care and clean drinking water facilities were provided and the cooperative handloom industry started, as a self-reliance programme in Joshi village. The conference renovated the church and parsonage in Urlana village.

May 16, 1997, was a great day, when these facilities were declared open to the people of Urlana and Joshi villages. The handloom centre was dedicated in Joshi village, people assembled applauded when the director of the CASA handed over the key of the centre to the village headman, people smiled and the village looked like Manchester. Amazing things happened contrary to what I expected; my experience in the relief and rehabilitation would be a boon to me – the life of people changed for good, turning despair into hope.

I believe when people are motivated rightly and kept focused on goals, they do incredible. I remember the fascinating story of Shantijai Khristimurti, an ordained minister in the Gujarat Conference who was the director of Bartimai Centre for Blind, Ahmedabad. We were no strangers; we were students in the same seminary and in same years. He invited me to visit the centre. It was a great joy to see him working on the project. I understand that blindness is one of the biggest problems in India, where there were over 15 million blinds, more than Mumbai city's population and 37 million globally. Shantijai was committed to eradicating blindness, for he said, 'Sight is life.' He was devoted to the work and perhaps he drew inspiration from his father who was a Methodist missionary in South Rhodesia in 1938.

I was amazed by his good work among blind children. He explained his goals; they were twofold viz. eradicate blindness at birth and provide shelter and treatment to blind children. It was interesting that he chose the name for the centre after a legendary the Bible character Bartimae'us, a blind beggar of Jericho who pleaded Jesus Christ to have mercy on him and instantly regained his eyesight.

As we walked around, there was excitement and glow on his face, he introduced me to his work, took me from one side to another. He said that here is Braille, over there, we come and pray, and look at the little children, and the way they live and play, with the sense of concern and anxiety said, 'But the place is not sufficient.' By his simplicity, sincerity, and devotion to the work, I was immensely touched. The work began in 1997, in a rented place, at the time of my predecessor. I could see that the place was not enough for the programme and free movement of children. Then I kindled his imagination, encouraged him to buy a piece of land to build the centre, he was taken aback, puzzled and perhaps thought it would be impossible; yes it was, as he did not have resources at his disposal. However, I could sway him in my imagination and jogged his motivation. He sprang into action, began to locate an ideal place, and there he found a piece of property of a Christian who wanted to sell it. Then I organized a local committee to assist him in his endeavour. They met several times, burnt midnight lamp to finalize the property deal and raise money, by untiring efforts, persuasion, and hard work, the money was raised and the property deal signed, sealed, and delivered.

I kept him dreaming and the zeal inflamed him. The building plans were drawn, local congregations supported the project with financial grants and loans, friends from aboard sent donations and I assured the Gujarat Conference would boost the financial support. Unbelievably, the centre with ground plus two levels was constructed. I felt if it was not for the divine providence and unquenchable zeal of Shantijai and others, the project could have been shelved. On September 21, 2003, I dedicated and declared the centre open. I was overwhelmed to see smiles on Shantijai's face and excitement among those who were present, uncertainty vanished and impossible was made possible. He looked relaxed and cheerful, looking at the future with hope, forgetting the despair of the past, children were joyous, moved freely and thanked God, and local Methodist Christians appreciated the good work done. Then, I never could think, it would be internationally known.

On January 26, 2001, I was at the Republic Day function at the Methodist Centre, Mumbai. We assembled on the terrace of the building at 8:00 in the morning for flag hoisting. We felt mild shaking sensation; one of the church officials said that he thought he felt giddy because of rise in his blood pressure and was diabetic, too. However, it was not so; not long after, we were shocked to know it was tremors. An earthquake measuring 8.00 on Richter scale hit western Gujarat; its epicentre was Bhuj, several national and international relief agencies rushed with relief and begun to do rehabilitation work. One of the organizations was Good People World Family from South Korea, who mobilized relief fund, but due to an unforeseen situation, they could not do the rehabilitation work over there. Thus, they were looking for an alternative project to use the funds for humanitarian purposes. They approached me with the offer of rebuilding the school and the hostel at Talegaon, a town close to Pune. I was aware the school and hostel buildings were old and dilapidated, but I was not inclined to go for it. However, Vasant Raiborde knew what makes me melt; persuasively urged by saying it would benefit the poor and needy children; it aroused my kind instinct and I agreed to accept the offer to serve humanity. Rebuilding the school and the hostel was needed, inasmuch as the funds offered was insufficient and yet I signed 'the Letter of Understanding'.

On February 5, 2002, David Yonggi Cho, the South Korean pastor of Good People's Church, Seoul, South Korea, and I inaugurated somewhat an ambitious school, hostel, and auditorium building project; some psychopathic critics could not digest the project vision, and they were quick to react and condemn me. Then the initial school building plans were not compatible to the mandatory requirement of the government education department, and therefore, the plans were redrawn, it exceeded the original estimates. I was sad; donors did not appreciate our compliance. They wanted us to reduce the size of the schoolrooms, and if not so, then perform a miracle to reduce cost to the level of the donation's purse; I differed. I felt such once-in-lifetime project should have long-range perspective, thus, There was the need for a long-term intelligent planning, taking into consideration both cost and future needs. There was genuine need for more funds, but they thought we were inflating figures. Since, the donors were inflexible, the trust began to vanish, and after several discussions and initiatives, the donors assured additional funds, but they flawed and funds never came while the work progressed. I was hard pressed, I had to raise loan from the Hutching High School, Pune, to pay the contractor's bills and complete the classrooms, which were urgently needed. Despite repeated promises, donors were short on their words that frustrated the project and me, the work could not progress. Meantime, I was victimised, the project lay dormant and eventually the project vision severely bruised and changed.

It was amazing, by my humble initiative, a number of churches, parsonages, and education and social institutions were built. I believed they were stepping stones to church growth. Many appreciated these humble endeavours, but those who were political, vitiated the atmosphere. Among them were even some of my colleague bishops who seemed to look politically, not appreciating how people were benefitting; driven by envious mode, they could not appreciate the work and the speed, however perhaps wishing if they did the same.

Jealousy

If it was not for politics, I could have done evangelistic and church growth work in the Bareilly Episcopal Area as well. I could not do so, as one of the bishops conspired to remove me from the area, for he could not bear to see me being younger than him assigned to two episcopal areas by the General Conference and I felt, although he pretended as pious bishop, I perceived he was a bit scornful in a very scuttle manner. He instigated local leaders against me and his claim of seniority was without any basis – there was no seniority system among the bishops in the church, only the order of election followed, and his works, too, did not match his claim. His faithful political flock in the North India Conference felt the heat of my administrative decisions, for they felt, I was hurting their interests, as my work style was not compatible to their old-hat tactics of magical performance.

Karriappa Samuel's issue was still lingering. Sampath Kumar desired to bring him back into the Council of Bishops' fold and I supported his move. I felt, it was good to heal sore wounds, despite my knowing, he was still nurturing bitterness against me. Then, it was decided that he should give an unconditional apology and affidavit to recover the Baldwin school money. He agreed, rendered the unconditional apology, and he was given retired status; however, he neither gave an affidavit nor cooperated in the recovery of ₹ 94,00,000/–from A. G. Hoover, the Baldwin school's contractor despite his promise and reminders. The Council of Bishops could not make any headway in the recovery matter, so they shifted the buck on the South India Regional Conference. However, Karriappa Samuel's entry paved the way for the episcopal vacancy. Then the bishop, who acted as a pious man bounced in action with vengeance to dislocate me from the Bareilly Episcopal Area, spearheaded the campaign of assigning the area to a retired bishop; I opposed, as the General Conference assigned it to me. Then I never imagined that he would propose to call a special session of the General Conference. I remember, once he took my permission to stay in the Bareilly episcopal residence for few days. I thought he may be having some genuine personal work, oh no! He was busy with his political kith, conspiring against me. I could not figure out his subsequent political game plan, but he was miserable, burdened by the thought that I held two episcopal areas and he held one, being a senior. He and his political disciples swarm on me with conspiracy sting to safeguard their positions. Other bishops seized the opportunity, supported him, as they too were not so comfortable with my success and, perhaps, felt that I, being the youngest bishop, was effectively heading four regional conferences, and this was denting their leadership image.

Then he turned aggressive, hatched the plan to fill the vacancy; it was vigorously supported by his political fraternity from the North India Conference, as some of them were also members of the Executive Council. Anyway, they succeeded in it and then it was decided to call the Special Session of the General Conference from February 17 to 23, 1997, in Kolkata. There was no seriousness to fill the episcopal vacancy and the election ballot begun only on the fourth day of the conference and in all, only twelve effective ballots were cast, the brutal intention was to dislodge me from the Bareilly Episcopal Area. There was no election of bishop; a huge expenditure was no deterrent. It was inferior politics to varnish vicious desire. For namesake, the conference's session was called; the secret strategy was to empower the Council of Bishops to reactive a retired bishop of his own choice[9]. While in Kolkata, television channels flashed breaking news, the name of Bombay city was changed to Mumbai; it was a familiar name though not in prominent use. I perceived no real change, only the Bombay name was dropped, burying the reminiscence of the bygone Colonial era. Some felt that the politics of name would not change the historical reality of the city, as it was never an exclusive preserve of any one language. Anyway, I liked the Bombay name like others who were nostalgic about it, and still liked to call the city by its old nametag.

Then, Stanley Downes was reactivated for six months. When his term was about to end, Sampath Kumar came up with the proposal to reactivate Elliot D. Clive. I felt, it was a good move although Elliot D. Clive was not comfortable with my voice. I believed the Council of Bishops ill-treated him. On September 19, 1997, we met Elliot D. Clive in Inder Lok Hotel, Dehradun. We took his consent for his reactivation and encouraged him to attend the Council of Bishops' meeting. He looked frail and weak; however, he was still having usual smile, well composed and spoke with wisdom. On October 27, 1997, the Council of Bishops meeting was held in Delhi and I presided over the meeting. The names of retired bishops Stanley Downes and Elliot D. Clive were proposed; it was like a strong and hefty anxious to wrestle with shrunk and frail, contrast complexions were added deciphering feature. There was voting; Stanley Downes was desperate to cast his vote in his own favour, but the rule of natural justice did not allow him, as he himself was one of the contesting parties. There was a tie; the presiding bishop had right to cast the tie-breaking vote, so I voted in the favour of Elliot D. Clive. He was winner and reactivated until the next Regular Session of the General Conference. Stanley Downes frowned at me in unrighteous indignation, his sideburns looked brave while in the deep sense of defeat, his countenance fell; I felt he was true to human emotion. Bishops who voted for him were dismayed over his election loss, not mortified for sordid politics. I was amazed at the loss of human insensibility and suffering, and yet they did not hesitate to give pious glances. I felt, it could have been gracious on the part of Stanley Downes to withdraw from the race in his favour to heal the hurt than inflict injury. I recognized, Elliot D. Clive needed healing touch, as he was unjustly and unkindly treated.

While supervising the Bareilly Area, I learnt some leaders of the North India Conference pressurized him to sign some property documents, which he seemed to have resisted. Not long after, he fell ill and died on February 4, 1998. The local church members in Bareilly were angry with the conference leaders and did not allow them to conduct his funeral service. The Council of Bishops asked Nimrod Christian and me to go to Bareilly to participate in the funeral service. When we reached the place, people were anxiously waiting; we conducted the funeral service, local pastors joined us and the rest of the things were smooth and solemn.

As no other retired bishop was willing to be reactivated, the active bishops were asked to supervise the Bareilly Area. Sampath Kumar was given the additional charge of the area. In 2001, a similar situation arose after the retirement of Victor Raja. When my name was suggested, the bishop who claimed seniority tried to show me in poor ethical standard. His political rant hinted that the convener of the Inquiry Committee on Haldwani Property was close to me, suggesting I would influence findings, overlooking the fact that other members of the committee were close to him as well. In the church setup, bishops' men were everywhere on some committees or other. Anyway, I did not press on it, as I was occupied with my work. No concerted efforts were made to improve the work in Bareilly Area; the focus was to elect delegates of their choice to the next General Conference's session. The work suffered in the episcopal area because of bishops' power politics. After I left, it never shined, as bishops were interested in the election politics than work, busy satisfying their opportunist political fraternity, it was their greatest concern.

I remember, Sunday C. Mbang, the Bishop Chairperson of the Executive Committee of the World Methodist Council held in September 2002, Oslo, Norway, in his opening address he said, 'No matter what you do, still people criticize you.' I recognized, it was same everywhere; in the church around the world, some people could not bear to see my work and speed and some of my brother bishops did not hesitate to act like Cain.

The bishops seldom recognized and appreciated the good work of their colleagues; on contrary, they were quick to find faults. It seemed professional jealousy and inferiority complex tended to mire the bishops' image in one way or another and I wondered if it was the symptom of appreciation deficiency syndrome? Some bishops looked down on the work of their predecessors to boost their own image and express inner feelings, if they were to do it; they would do the same and even better. Thus, some of them indulged in erasing the memory of the good work of their predecessors either by neglecting or stopping or destroying the work rather than building or improving on it. It was easier to spoil the work than to further it, as bishops were invisibly engaged in fierce competition, the spirit of cooperation barely cheered. I felt that good work, prudent proposals, and wise decisions did not conjure the imagination and sparingly received the applause it deserved, silently and systematically sterilized by the political perception of the bishops. Then, the prevailing work culture was not coherent and conducive and it needed rethinking; however, no serious efforts were made.

There was a general feeling that bishops lived as lord, unlike apostles did; it was not so with the bishops who were faithful to their calling and walked on thorny path without roses. For days, I was away from my family, and even if I was at home, I was glued to my work, some people often without any genuine work kept me occupied and wasted my precious time.

In the early years of my episcopal ministry, I barely stayed at home, it was not pleasant to live in the Delhi episcopal residence, for we felt, it was a haunted one; to that matter, I felt all mission houses were. We had some strange experiences from the time we entered the church house. We lived in the house on the 21, YMCA Road, below the rear side, there were water taps, and We used to hear water sounds in the middle of the night, as if some women were filling water jars, we could not see them, and sometimes we heard footsteps like soldiers' boot. We learnt the building was built for widows and single women, some of the women's husbands died in war; it was said that they came to see them. We felt that hundreds of demons occupied the Delhi episcopal residence. My domestic help who came from Bombay to live with me used to tell us, at times in the night a girl used to sit next to him and played with his hair while he was asleep. There was a story of the girl who was a daughter of a worker in the episcopal residence. I heard some people saw the girl eating mud before her death. A gardener of the Bishop's House died in the outhouse; he used to peep inside through the eastside bathroom window, asking for his salary. My family members could see them suddenly appear and disappear, but I could not. The unseen guests occupied the Bishop's House in Mumbai, too. In the episcopal residence at Mumbai, one of the bishops' cook died of unnatural death, we used to hear strange sounds and seen strange figures appear and disappear that disturbed us. Actually, bishops come and go, but the unseen guests were its permanent occupants. These were unpleasant experiences and the source of anxiety.

I know some do not believe in spooky stuff; however, they exist. I heard many stories like these from those who had such life experiences. In Budaun, a town close to Bareilly in Uttar Pradesh, there was a spine-shivering demonic disturbance. The manager of the hostel, a deaconess, narrated the horror story. She said that as children used to return to their hostel dormitory after school hours, they used to see their cots lifted, 'It could have been a hair-raising sight', I heard it for the first time. The demonic disturbance continued for almost a month, and after earnest prayers, it stopped. I understand, all cannot see demons or feel their presence; some can see them, others can only feel their presence. I believe they trouble those who follow God, but those who are in their camp have a jolly good time. I cannot see them; I can only feel their presence, my hair on hands and ears erect at their presence like a magnet pulling a needle. Often I spent stressful nights in Delhi episcopal residence, despite that I got up at dawn to do my work, forgot all about it, and again at the sunset, it's thought was stressful. My episcopal ministry was the mixture of joy and struggle; nevertheless, the latter was far more dominant than the former.

I could break new grounds as much I could and do more in less time with speed. I believe God helped me to make things right, do things right, and take new initiatives, no matter how difficult they were, or how poor was the living condition, it did not blur my vision or dissipate my zeal. I faced challenges, complexities, and overcame them by divine grace.

FRIENDS OF CONVENIENCE

After the consecration ceremony, I felt I should have good working relations with Sampath Kumar and Nimrod Christian, as my episcopal colleagues although I barely knew them, as they were from different Regional Conferences than I was and all I had but a few brief encounters with them during my episcopal election tours. Sampath Kumar was suave looking and had a modern life style, whereas Nimrod Christian appeared coarse and claimed, he was a strict vegetarian and proudly invoked traditional remedies; however, their power ambition was alike that made good grouping. As for me, the church's connection relation was the only commonality between them and me. As years passed by, camaraderie was diminishing and the cords of affinity were breaking, which were essential for genuine and enduring working relationship and the corporate leadership. However, having clear vision for the church, I began to cooperate with them regardless of their subtle intrinsic nature. Our episcopal election swayed me, it conjured my thinking, the time, the place, and the last election ballot was magnetic. I felt, perhaps, there was some divine purpose in it, but I could not see anything tangible, it was my waking state wish. I spent strenuous long working hours for years without knowing the virility of our friendship ties. When I realized their scornful instincts, I felt tormented, but by then, it was of no use. I wished I had some chance to do the acid testing of their trustworthiness, as they did mine and felt satisfied. I read Charles Warner's wise words; with all his wisdom and expertise in human relations, he said 'One discovers a friend by chance and later feels regret that twenty or thirty years of life might have spent without the least knowledge of him'[1]. It was so true in my case, I spent more than ten years, never had I the wind of what they were actually made of, only to discover they were anything but the Friends of Convenience. Long after I realized, they treated me like a matchstick, cheered me, so long as I could be of any use to their self-serving ambition.

Growing Relations

As years passed by, our friendly working relations reached a new height. I was proactive on issues that concerned the church and acted for the good of the church with speed and without analyzing political consequences. I did not tremble when interests of the church was at stake or when it came to supporting my episcopal friends in their bad times; however, while doing so, I was careful not to scorch my prophetic voice. Some situations and happenings gave me clue to their intrinsic nature. I remember Sampath Kumar hired a professional to take the video shooting of our consecration ceremony. I was glad to join him and shared its expenses, but he was focused throughout, while a scanty coverage was on my side, it sucked the joy and excitement of my supporters. They were skeptical from the beginning about the spark of gentleness, and his urbane look could not mislead them. His moves were puzzling and annoying. I tried to specify; however, I could not satisfy them. Then I did not appreciate that it was unwise to ignore their warning massage. I expected him to have a large heart, as he was set to occupy the highest office in the church, but I was dismayed, he could not see beyond himself. I tried to sort out misunderstandings, knotty disagreements, and clashes over thorny issues. I was not closed to their cravings to keep alive good working relations. I remember Sampath Kumar was coveting the chair of the programme council assigned to me. He urged me to exchange the chairmanship; I was glad to do it without an excuse, although some retired bishops made fuss over the process. Not long after, I learnt he was in the habit of coveting best things and would go to any level to get what charmed him and if anyone came on his way, he would devour with tyranny and conspiracy. I observed, the leaders driven by power avariciousness could do and undo things by using unacceptable means to achieve their political ambition, as for them, ends were everything and means nothing; I could not absorb their way of thinking.

He was craving to go to Bangalore Episcopal Area by the next episcopal assignment. There was nothing bad about it, but he secretly schemed to achieve his goal, which was rather shocking. Then he cornered B. James, the then bishop of Bangalore Area, for nonrecovery of ₹ 94,00,000 from A. G. Hoover, the Baldwin school contractor. In 1994, Karriappa Samuel gave him the amount to buy land on Sarjapur Road, Bangalore, and nonfiling criminal case against him, paying a hefty income tax penalty of ₹ 20,00,000/- for using the Baldwin school funds for building churches and failing to occupy the designated episcopal residence. In the Council of Bishops meeting held on May 15, 1998, in Bangalore, he was furious against B. James and coerced him to proceed on leave until the next session of the General Conference. Not long after, I perceived, he was not actually serious about the recovery, but he was preparing ground to move to Bangalore Area. If B. James was appeasing A. G. Hoover, then Karriappa Samuel, too, evaded giving the affidavit as promised, and when Sampath Kumar's turn came, he was curiously soft on him. It fired my imagination; he almost acted as de facto bishop of Bangalore Episcopal Area, long before the area was assigned to him. I perceived there was lack of transparency in the working of the Bangalore Area. I regretted; I supported him without realizing that he would be like venom for me.

There was perception that his administrative style was despotic and contemptuous. He suspended an employee of the Calcutta Girls School from the church membership on the unlawful ground that he approached the court of law against the church authority. In the contempt petition, the employee challenged his suspension before the Calcutta High Court. On June 2, 1998, when the court passed the order, he was rebuked for taking disciplinary action against the employee. The court asked him to tender an unconditional apology and give the undertaking to delete the rule from the Discipline that restricted employees going to the court of law for their grievances or face consequences. The court also directed the church not to give effect to any such rule or take disciplinary action against anyone moving the court of law for grievances in the exercise of constitutional right. He concealed his iniquitous act and not even disclosed it to me that the court directed him to expunge the contemptuous rule from the Discipline. I was aghast when the episode surfaced in the meeting of the Council of Bishops held from April 25 to 26, 2000, in Ghaziabad. In the meeting, I had no clue, so I kept quiet, it was actually a serious issue, as he had no right to give undertaking or hide it from the competent body of the church. Obviously, he was not transparent, kept the church in dark on the issue, and secretly acted and never placed the matter either before the competent body or before the General Conference Session 1998, for deleting the rule from the Discipline was serious misconduct. As an afterthought, solely to mislead the Council of Bishops and escape disciplinary action, he made a misleading claim that he filed the petition for amendment but it was not found in the book of petitions, or circulated during the General Conference session. I was amazed at his audacity and manoeuvring trick to dodge the vital issue with the help of his supporters in the Executive Council. His unacceptable conduct and defying the Discipline were no deterrents, he triumphed over the mess without any harm and scratch and our silence signalled as approval. I realized fending him gave the cue; he could do anything in the church if he had the political backing, so he was not hesitant to celebrate such things with sumptuous feasts of rage and revenge.

Denying constitutional rights of an Indian citizen was a serious matter; no one appreciated it, as it would mirror the church as an undemocratic and imperialistic institution, tarnish its image and spread defying spirit. In the meeting of the Executive Council held in Mumbai from July 27 to 30, 2000, the Calcutta High Court order was revisited and the resolution was approved, asking the church authorities not to give effect to the rule that restricted an employee of the church to move the court of law for grievances. It was published in the month of March 2001 issue of the *Indian Witness,* an official monthly newspaper of the church. But, in absolute insensitivity, subsequent steps were not taken to expunge such rules from the Discipline which restricted the fundamental right of Indian citizens, perhaps with oblique motive and with still lurking desire to embalm it. The church is in continuous contempt of the court; the rule still exists in the Discipline and invoked to punish political opponents[2]. I wrote letters to Elia Pradeep Samuel, the then general secretary of the church, to know if it was in force; long after, on August 10, 2004, he replied evasively and in duplicity, his answer was in a riddle. It seemed that the church leaders had two faces: in public, they blew a trumpet to honour the Judiciary of the land and the church, and in private, they were anything but contemptuous, they ignored truth, justice, and equity.

It was obvious that some of the church leaders did not adore fundamental rights; on the contrary trampled it when they become inconvenient to their power ambition.

There was a stinking scandal, Nimrod Christian's son-in-law, T. Henry Charles, was at the helm of the affair of the Mother Teresa Urban Co-operative Bank, Hyderabad. I felt that Mother Teresa, the Saint of Gutters, as the prefix to bank's name was inappropriate. However, I was exuberant that Christians were migrating to nontraditional professions. I happened visit Nimrod Christian in Delhi around the same time. As I entered the episcopal office, I felt, as if I was in a bank. He was engrossed facilitating the bank's work, however, welcomed me by making head and hand gestures, and asked me to sit. When he was free, he apologized to keep me waiting. We conversed, tea and snacks came, I sipped the tea, it was a bit sweet, I munched snack to change the taste. I could not hold back my feelings too long. I hinted at him to skip the bank's business, as it was the act of nepotism; he vociferously reacted. He said, 'If I do not help my son-in-law, then who will help.' I was stunned. I realized I would be making a futile effort to budge him, so I left him to his obsession. Then I turned to casual chats, but its thoughts hovered in my mind. I had no iota of doubt that he was alienating valuable working hours of his sacred calling and his fallen countenance and gave out energy were the signs of his guilt feelings. Helping relatives without abuse of the bishopric was not a bad idea, although not so simple, as it appeared to be, as the church leaders barely drew inerasable line between public and private domains and the rest had a great propensity to cross over its boundaries. I believe, gaining riches by hard work, not by dishonest gain, is a highly admirable adventure, for rich are not necessarily damned to the fire of sulphur and brimstones, if they did not defile themselves with perishable riches or used it to destroy others. Bishop, a man of God expected to serve God, not Mammon, for avariciousness is one of the deadly sins. He lured the church institutions under his charge to deposit money in the bank by the influence of his office, an attractive rate of interest, as an incentive assured, but there was neither the guarantee of safety nor liquidity. Like missionary zeal, no stone he left unturned to mobilize deposits and surprisingly succeeded despite mounting concerns.

In February 1999, Victor Raja and James Nathan were elected as bishops. With the election of Victor Raja and James Nathan, S. R. Thomas was hilarious, a short-lived political clique was formed, and the balance of power tilted in their favour in the Council of Bishops. Thus, they were tempted to flex their political muscles, first against Nimrod Christian, then Sampath Kumar, and me. I heard, even one of them was announcing in soprano voice in the Methodist Home, Mumbai that S.R. Thomas was their *guru* (teacher), and they would listen to his time-tested political wisdom. I perceived they were of one mind to crush us all; however, only by turn. It so happened that the opportunity to do so fell in their lap, they smiled and bounced when the situation in the Hyderabad Conference was anything but serious. There was the complaint filed against Nimrod Christian before the Council of Bishops on serious charges of finance and property matters. He was asked to reply, but prima facie, his reply was deficient to prove his innocence. In the Council of Bishops meeting, the newly elected bishops with the inspiration from their seasoned political teacher and retired bishops were set to suspend him. I watched Sampath Kumar; he was indifferent and silent with the loss of expression on his face. I felt it would be the saddest day in the church if he was to be suspended. I was convinced that inquiring into the serious charges was unavoidable, suspension was. I was desperately convincing and persuading the bishops, trying to gather more 'aye' than 'no' against his suspension, as he was then not the bishop of the Hyderabad Episcopal Area. After fiery debate and persuasion, a two-member inquiry committee was appointed and sent him on leave until the inquiry was over. Nimrod Christian came to see me in the evening. He asked me to get him an apartment in the proposed development project at Fateganj, Vadodara, Gujarat. I consoled and encouraged him, not to be so pessimistic. Then in my wild imagination, I never knew, he was not a kind of person who deserved any sympathy.

In his place, Victor Raja was given additional charge of the Delhi Episcopal Area. I was appalled, even for a few months he could not conduct himself well. Nimrod Christian and his family had to undergo unimagined miseries and humiliation due to excess committed by him. He toured places in his new jurisdiction like a lord with his followers, known for their doubtful integrity who were his advisors and bodyguards. He subjected managers and directors to unreasonable demands. Then, the Executive Council of the church declared the action of the Council of Bishops sending

Nimrod Christian on the leave as unconstitutional, but did not exonerate him for it was contended that he himself could have proceeded on the leave or be suspended. After he resumed his episcopal office, on August 5, 2000, I received a personal letter from Vatsala Christian, Nimrod Christian's wife. She wrote in her letter, 'From this trial God showed our great treasure "YOU" for which we are proud.' She profusely thanked me, but he misconstrued my genuine efforts to pull him out of the indictment and for my helpful tips on his property developments proposals. He did not appreciate in the volcanic rage; leave was a better option than suspension. Then everyone knew I stood behind him like a solid rock during the time of his crises and barely had I realized that he would act contrary to my expectation. I felt deeply hurt; never had I expected that like a paranoid, he would have obsessive distrust on me to go against me.

The inquiry report found him embezzling the church funds and illegally leased the church property; no one raised an iota of doubt about the credible findings. He leased out farmland in Zaheerabad, Andhra Pradesh, without any authorization and raised deposits from the church institutions, inappropriately handled finances, and in collusion, authorized the Life Society to raise donation from the church's institutions[3]. He deserved a severe disciplinary action; however, he escaped unpunished, as he gained huge sympathy due to the vindictive acts of Victor Raja. Then the Council of Bishops curiously turned soft on him after the Executive Council found them wrong, for sending him on leave. They merely asked him to submit clearance certificates from all Regional Conferences on deposits held by the Mother Teresa Bank and the recover the donation collected by the Life organization. He neither cared to comply with any of these, nor were the bishops as vigorous as before to take disciplinary action against him, and thereafter he acted as if he was exonerated. I felt, it did not help him overcome his materialistic tendency that had bearing on the church finances and institutions under his charge.

In October 2002, under the public outcry, the lid of the bank's scam was blown up. The bank's deposits disappeared due to dubious lending practices; depositors could not withdraw money as the bank was in liquidation. It became the talk of the church and town. Nimrod Christian's son-in-law was chairman and his elder daughter manager. They were arrested, sent to jail, and after frantic efforts, bailed out. At that time, I was in the Unites States on the invitation of Wes Griffin, the president of the International Leadership Institute, Atlanta, Georgia, to be on the faculty. I first met him in 2000, at the Haggai Institute, Maui, Hawaii. He held his earned D. Min. degree from the Asbury Theological Seminary, Wilmore, Kentucky. He is a wonderful and loving person with passion for evangelism; he shared with me his life-changing experience of his healing from cancer that inspired him to serve the worldwide church. While I was in Atlanta, I received numerous calls from India on the bank's scam. Then I called Sampath Kumar to ascertain it; he said that he was trying to get an anticipatory bail and advised me to do so, as there was the grapevine that a big chunk of the bank's money was given to us. I did not go for anticipatory bail, as it was not true;

however, I felt, it was a wakeup call to take precautions in our working relations.

By then, Sampath Kumar fortified his political position; he came up with the proposal to redevelop the Montgomery hall of the Baldwin Girl's school, one of the prestigious schools in Bangalore. The Executive Council approved the project with the rider that he would not demolish the front portion of the hall, as it was a historical monument; however, he tore it down. One of the members of the council who was a pastor then close to me voiced his concern against its pulling down. I felt that Sampath Kumar was not under the influence of the virtue of meekness, lacked tolerance, and became vindictive. He could not bear anyone dare him, shrewdly thwart all challenges. He kept it in his mind and long after he had audacity to barter with me his support for me in lieu of disciplinary action against the pastor. I felt it was an impious bargain, as he did nothing wrong deserving punishment, everyone has right to ventilate feelings and opinions in a business meeting, and for that one cannot abuse one's position to take revenge. I tried to calm his nerves; however, he refused to forget and forgive and victimized him when he became the in-charge of the Bombay Conference.

Francis Sunderraj was a close-knit friend of Sampath Kumar. He was his chief episcopal election campaigner who tirelessly canvassed for his successful election. He filed a complaint against him with the Council of Bishops. I was perplexed at the sudden turn of events. I remember, he did all he could under his reign to see that Sampath Kumar was elected as bishop. I could not imagine that one day their friendship would be so fragile, and as human, I failed to draw the lesson from it. I was curious, wanted to know the reason for the rift; I asked Sampath Kumar, and he was being evasive and perhaps he suspected me of instigating him, so I made no efforts to probe into it. It so happened that then I was the president of the Council of Bishops (the president was elected on yearly rotation). I dealt with the complaint in a fair and just manner, as per procedure. I asked the complainant and Sampath Kumar to reconcile. It was a sensitive matter to handle; allegations levelled against him were very serious, relating to mismanagement, misuse of institutional funds, and property matter. The reconciliation reached the dead end. His and others' petitions against Sampath Kumar lifted up in the Council of Bishops meeting held in Igatpuri. A small committee of active bishops was appointed to scrutinize and bring report. He softened some active bishops, and then they came up with manoeuvred opinion that documentary evidences were insufficient to substantiate the allegations. On hearing the report and its adoption, retired bishops were resentful, especially about Francis Sunderraj's petition. They felt like smitten by its grief; however, Sampath Kumar was full of smile and high in the spirit. I felt mortified for supporting him, then I never could imagine, one day he would be a snare to me. A number of leaders from the Bangalore Episcopal Area clamoured over it, some of them were on national committees, but could not brave him. I heard, they felt he would blackmail them and harass or even fire their relatives working in the institutions under his charge. On May 19, 2007, I was in Kolkata. I was sitting by myself in the hotel lobby where bishops were lodged to attend the General

Conference Session 2007. S. R. Thomas and Taranath Sagar passed by me; S. R. Thomas said they were going to inspect the conference venue. Then the treasurer came, I casually asked him, if there was no solution to my problem; he said there was, and whisked away. Then came an elderly bishop from Bangalore, a good man, who said, 'We like you, but you did wrong thing in shielding Sampath Kumar in Francis Sunderraj's matter.' I recognized he was right, however I politely said, the Bible teaches us to forgive, for I knew, although, he was genuine, he did not use his wisdom to guide Bishops in my matter, for he too, was swayed by the wind of injustice. The malicious power politics was suffocating and reconciliation looked remote. I was dismayed; I returned to Mumbai on the same day. I brood over the words of the bishop throughout my journey to Mumbai, as he was right on the matter. I perceived Sampath Kumar's sober look and enigmatic smile were anything but misleading and his tactical sweet words were like honey, it made me think, as if he sparingly practiced Dale Carnegie's advice.

There were also other serious complaints against Sampath Kumar relating to finance and mal-administration of the Baldwin Institutions, Ellen Thoburn Cowen Memorial Hospital and Nursing College, Kolar, Karnataka, and abuse of authority. He registered the Baldwin Education Society without getting its Constitution approved by the church and made his wife as one of the directors. Also, an open letter was in circulation against him, voicing rampant malpractices, neither inquiry ordered nor explanation asked. By then, the political and property development interests of Taranath Sagar, Nimrod Christian, and others merged, they compromised with Sampath Kumar in the exchange of his support; they shielded him and barely was there one's best efforts to preserve the dignity of the bishopric. I was amazed, he was praying to God, not for forgiveness and to love and comfort people, but for a Harley Davidson, an American iconic bike. He said, 'It was like a child asking his father for a toy'[4]. Nimrod Christian in duplicity and in camera condemned him; he said, 'Sampath Kumar was unfit to hold the office of bishop', and then collaborated with him in the conspiracy, for the sake of his own survival in the bishopric and fear of pending inquiry report against him. The words of his prayer spread like a wild fire in the inner circle and called him jokingly Harley; bishops made empty noises and the Council of Bishops eluded to reprimand him or impose a disciplinary action on him for his unministerial conduct.

Sampath Kumar undertook the building project of the Christ Methodist Church, Khursi Road, Lucknow. The Lucknow Regional Conference had the financial crunch to complete the church building. He requested me to lend some money from the conferences under my charge. I rose to the occasion and agreed to help, as it was the worthy cause. I placed the request for a loan of ₹ 1,00,000/– before the Board of Methodist Hospital, Mathura, Uttar Pradesh. The board approved the loan and released the money to the Lucknow Regional Conference for the project. I was glad to see the church building completed and dedicated. However, I was dismayed, the conference did not keep its words to return the loan, some tricky leaders escaped from their responsibility and on the contrary argued that it was the deal between the bishops, and the conference was no way responsible for it. I felt melancholic over such tendency prevailing in the church. I recognized it was the barrier to working as a team in advancing the church's mission to the world. It seemed the church leaders were not open to 'connection relation' whereas the United Methodist Church's Annual Conferences were eager to have covenant relations with the Methodist Conferences in India to support programmes, projects, and develop personal friendship ties. I felt sad that some of the church leaders were not even keen to have the connection relation among the conferences in the church. I recognized it was not money; leaders' attitude was an obstacle.

Presiding over General Conference, Bangalore, October 1998 by rotation. (L-R) I, Bishops Samuel R. Thomas, Sampath Kumar & Nimrod Christian

Sampath Kumar and Nimrod Christian were bitter to each other because of the Bangalore Episcopal Area assignment, for it was their greatest craving! From

October 12 to 18, 1998, the General Conference Session was held in Bangalore. One day, during the break, while we were returning to the hotel in a car, they fired words on each other. In rage, Nimrod Christian stopped the car and stepped out. I tried to reconcile them; however, I failed, as they were fierce and unwilling to unlock horns. The Bangalore Area assignment was the cause of disagreements, tension, and misunderstanding. Prior to the General Conference Session, we met several times to sort out the differences; however, it was a hard and delicate task like trying to open a rose bud. Nimrod Christian was aware that I preferred Sampath Kumar to the Bangalore Area, for by then I realized, he would not hesitate to do anything to achieve his goal, for there was perception that he was ruled by the force of his cravings than sacrifices and I felt if by chance he was unsuccessful, he would make Nimrod Christian's life miserable. The affluent Baldwin schools were mesmerizing. I remember, once Sampath Kumar stayed with me when I was Delhi. We leisurely conversed while we strolled in the garden of Bishop's House in the delighting moonlight. I was surprised, he suddenly pulled orange and scarlet bracts of bougainvillea and in excitement exclaimed, 'Dinesh the Baldwin institutions are like a honeycomb, you can simply suck it!' It seemed that his vision of sucking the Baldwin honeycomb was not in conformity with the vision of advancing the mission of the church. In Bangalore session, episcopal assignments were unchanged, we returned to our respective episcopal areas. From February 8 to 14, 1999, then Adjourned Session of the General Conference was held in Ghaziabad. Sampath Kumar was assigned to the Bangalore Area, Nimrod Christian to the Delhi

Area and I was assigned to the Bombay Area, but S. R. Thomas grieved over my assignment to Bombay Area, as he, too, was craving to continue in the area. There was nothing unrighteous about my opting for Bombay Area, for episcopal assignments were voted, he mobilized support to continue in the Bombay Area and I did mine to move to Bombay Area, I was voted for the Bombay Area[5]. That was how bishops were assigned to different episcopal areas, but S. R. Thomas did not take it in good spirit, perhaps influenced by the city's comfort and symbolism. I recognized missionary spirit and nobler side were dormant. Then he waited for an opportunity to settle score with me on this count, and not long before my assignment to the Bombay Episcopal Area, in prejudice, much malicious information was diffused against me, this was difficult to sponge.

As years passed by, Sampath Kumar restrain himself; as expected of an episcopal leader, he acted more like an organizational boss. In his power ambition, stretched to undesirable level, he achieved what he coveted, used inappropriate means, and expected others to relinquish their rights and privileges in his favour. If anyone refused, he would act in scuttle manners, held grudges, and prepared evidences to revenge. A number of church leaders and workers became his victims; inconsistent conduct lowered the image of bishops. However, I was cautious to avoid curves in our working relations without hurting the church interests; but things did not work in that way.

Breaking Relations

Our working relations did not grow as a tree planted by streams of water, for the conflict of interest, lack of mature understanding, and trust deficit were not conducive to its growth. As for me, I was genuine in cooperating with them to advancing the work of the church, and although my ties with them were limited to the church work, I was alive to their personal and family welfare. Our working relations had limit to growth, as I did not absorb their intrinsic nature nor did they mine like oil and water. They seemed to be indifferent to the vows of their office, and abiding by the rule of law of the church was not priority to achieve their political ambition. It seemed reasonability and saintliness were not held high – power obsession, cutthroat competition, and alienation were. I was not averse to their power ambition, except for surging inappropriate means. Our friendly ties began to crack, not being resilient and as for me, the church's growth was priority.

Nimrod Christian was unfazed to teach lesson to Victor Raja. He was nurturing the memory of his hurt and humiliation like a man sitting in a moving bullock cart with bundles of straw on his head. I recognized that he was deeply hurt during a short kingly reign of Victor Raja. Sampath Kumar was replenishing his energy and sharpening his vengeful weapon against him, as he, too, had stored revenge and belonged to the same home conference and were antagonist to each other. In the meantime, Nimrod Christian was also bouncing to frame James Nathan for defamation. I dissuaded him, for I knew, it would barely serve any purpose;

on contrary, it would lead to ugly in-fights and mire brotherly relations. Anyway, he reluctantly shelved his plan. Then Sampath Kumar and Nimrod Christian joined hands against Victor Raja in Hammurabi's code balance, vowed to sickle him politically and repay him by the same measure or even more. They prepared few people to write complaints against him on the noncompliance of the Judicial Council's Decisions[6], financial and property matters and Tapegate scandal – his ridiculous comments on some bishops and church leaders. Two separate inquiries were set up and he satisfactorily replied some of their allegations. The telephone conversation was in Kannada, but it was genuine and so its authorized English translation was obtained from Hyderabad lab; however, the charge against him was not pressed as complainants failed to produce the original tapes. There was believable hint that Sampath Kumar's invisible hand was in the Tapegate scandal, he managed Ebenezer Shivapur, a lay member from his episcopal area to engage Victor Raja in the telephone conversation with intention to record and prepare evidence against him, which is often criminal offence. The church politics was getting indecent, as bishops did not show leaning towards holiness of life.

I was dismayed by the way they chased Victor Raja, a good man, though at times, he hurled impetuous temper, jealousy and hatred blinded them. Nimrod Christian was vocal, but Sampath Kumar was strategic. After much reluctance, I came out in open to support Victor Raja on many counts, as they framed him out of dislike. I was amazed, Nimrod Christian, no sooner had he managed to come out of the crisis than he forgot that he was found guilty in the financial and property matters that deserved him disciplinary action. There were altercations between Nimrod Christian and me on several occasions on Victor Raja's issues. I felt in-fights among bishops would vitiate church's working and none of them was like an angel, living in a glass house and throwing stones at him. In the meantime, Victor Raja attained his 65th birthday, and then rule required to put him in retired relations. He protested against the action and challenged it in the court of law. By the demonstration effect, James Nathan, too, filed a civil suit; however, both could not succeed, perhaps their opponents knew how to handle it. After some resistance and protest, Victor Raja acceded to retire. S. R. Thomas was their close friend; however, curiously, he was silent on Victor Raja, as it seemed he was unhappy, Victor Raja opposing his episcopal candidate who was close to his heart. I conceived that when the holiness of life ceases to be the aim in life, sordid politics thrive.

Taranath Sagar was perennially antagonist to me; he misconstrued, unless a thorn like me was removed, he would not easily ascend in the church leadership, and perhaps, his political kith, too, had the same thinking, so they worked against me to help him achieve his goal. It seemed Taranath Sagar had the knack of influencing people in power and came close to Sampath Kumar; the position of the general secretary of the church and the ability to speak Kannada language were very useful in achieving his power ambition. It seemed, he first sown the seed of distrust in Sampath Kumar's fertile vengeful attitude, other bishops barely thinking about the Bangalore

Area assignment made him fume, as if it was his birthright. I remember, I was chairing the committee meeting from August 29 to 30, 2002, in Chennai on the proposed Constitution of Regional Executive Board. I was amazed; Sampath Kumar's henchman asked me if I was interested in the Bangalore Area assignment. I said, no, then he asked me to tell him, for he said that there was misgiving and whispering. I was persuaded by then political circumstances to believe that Taranath Sagar led him to believe that I was trying to snatch his Baldwin honeycomb while he still desired to relish it (and perhaps stirred Karrippa Samuel to worry about to his younger son, Who was the then principal of Baldwin Boys School). I do not remember if any bishop hailing from the north was assigned to Bangalore Area at any time until then and did not know why there was so much craze about it. However, in good spirit and with sole desire to maintain cordial relation, I said I was not interested in the Bangalore Area assignment; however, his doubt grew like the mustard seed of the Bible parable. He kept it in his mind and not long after stirred others to join his revenge expedition to reduce me to nothing.

In September 2002, Sampath Kumar invited Nimrod Christian and me to attend the North India Regional Conference Session in Almora, Uttarakhand. After much prompting, I accepted the invitation. I was watching Sampath Kumar presiding over the Regional Conference's session, he struggled to organize the house; if he were not helped, it could have been a clumsy failure. During the conference session, the bitterness between Nimrod Christian and me brewed up, as he was keen to regularize the appointment of the principal of Ramsay Intermediate College, Almora, which he made while he was caretaker bishop of the conference for an interim period, I advised Sampath Kumar to announce his appointment as supplied by, meaning temporarily, but Nimrod Christian thundered and said, 'I should not interfere in his appointment.' I replied, 'It was not yours, any longer!' As I felt it was improper to regularize in haste the appointment made by bypassing the managing committee and without dealing with the queries raised on his eligibility to the post. People raised the questions about his eligibility to the post and the curious purpose of the sale of his land. No sooner has he taken the charge of the principal than he entangled in the litigation that made him find himself in a bed of thorns. I remember a similar incident I faced. The District Superintendent of Pauri Garhwal, who was also the manager of the Messmore Inter College, came to Delhi episcopal office, daringly sneaked in my bedroom – traditionally the episcopal office was in the bishop's residence, offered me money to appoint his person as principal who was not a satisfactory candidate. I declined, sternly warned, and did not appoint him. Then he manipulated selection papers and secretly got approval from the Government Education Department, resulting in legal suit. On fierce exchange of words, I skipped the rest of the session. I returned from the conference with a heavy heart and strained relations. I pondered over it more than before, how human relations are complex and fragile; they are like a web of actions and interactions, resulting in either cooperation or conflict. I read David Bidney, a celebrated Ukrainian-American theoretical anthropologist; his words echoed in my ears, a man is a problem to himself, because he alone has ability to reflect on himself and his experiences[7]. It seemed, the conflict of interest sprouts when moral values are least internalized and self-propelling ambition is accentuated. I found in more than one way, the well-spoken words were true and even in my case, as I mulled over what I experienced.

The negative energy of egotism, hatred, and fear eventually paralyzed our friendly ties. The Friends of Convenience were far apart in their hearts, and yet by incurable political ambition, were mutually inclusive in their goal like natural selection. Then they started to distance from me, church leaders curiously watched, as they were anxious to scourge my prophetic voice. They pursued their power ambition more than anything else did. As I said, I was not averse to their rightful authority and power ambition, but I wished they valued means as well. At any rate, I chose the path they did not adore. They viewed differences seriously and acted differently; until then, I never knew, they can go the way they chose. Not long after November 2007, one of them said John Hanchinmani and Taranath Sagar were close knit and like siblings, the latter addressed the former as *Anna* (an elder brother) secretly scheming to make me vanish from the leadership scene of the church. Perhaps taking the cue from Christ's words, the house divided against itself cannot stand, they masterly used the time-tested divide and rule policy. Taranath Sagar captivated the mind of the Friends of Convenience and stirred their dormant ambition to hold on to their episcopal chairs beyond their tenure with aim to ascend to bishopric and then to sickle me with their support, as my prophetic voice was becoming an obstacle to their goal. John Hanchinmani too maliciously contemplated to cleanse the conflicting voice to safeguard his self-interest and to have hassle-free hegemony, which he was enjoying to some extent without any manifest opposition. The hostess of the Methodist Home, Mumbai, was John Hanchinmani's first wife, she was unhappy for my being the chairman. Taranath Sagar came to live in the Methodist Centre after his election as general secretary of the church; they concretized their efforts and plotted against me, their political champion from the north India used to share with me, their reaction to my work and relations. Taranath Sagar was aspiring to bishopric and they stood solidly behind him, so to satisfy their own thirst for supremacy. It seemed it was his political game plan. Then I also learnt that the church's treasury office secretly used as an 'Election Strategy Centre' to facilitate the election of the episcopal candidates who would be his anchor and act as a shield to him, it was close-guarded secret in the church. The treasurer's position gave him immense political advantage and influence, bishops came and gone, but he remained and ruled.

Then, the inquiry report on the Haldwani property in Uttarahkand was out despite Taranath Sagar's massive efforts to scuttle it by the abuse of his office. He tried to throttle it and vainly contended that the deadline to complete the inquiry was lapsed. His letter of November 13, 2002, showed his great anxiety. He was hurrying to hold the General Conference Session 2003, as he was worried if it was delayed, he would not lead in the episcopal election or even he might not win, as his part in the property deal was haunting him. it was intriguing, why he issued thirteen power of attorneys in haste and at the time, when he himself did not have physical possession of the power of attorney from the church's Trust. He was neither asked to explain his illegal act nor inferior authority and the sale proceed was not deposited into the church's treasury. Besides, it appeared, the property was sold at much lower rate than its market value. The church's treasurer said he did not receive money, but even then, took no initiative, kept silent, and took no steps to recover it[8]. What's more, Taranath Sagar and John Hanchinmani were seized with the fact that the sale proceed was deposited in the fictitious bank account, opened for the purpose and yet they acted as if they had nothing to do with it like Pilate did. I felt, it was a farcical situation, persons involved in such scams held high offices and I was amazed, no one dared John Hanchinmani, the omnipresent member of Sale and Development Committee, whose words prevailed over others. The report was submitted to Sampath Kumar, the then president of the Council of Bishops and the co-chairman of the Executive Council, but for curious reasons, he kept silent, perhaps because of political secret understanding and compromise. However, the key findings of the inquiry report spewed, Taranath Sagar was panicky over its far-reaching danger to his episcopal ambition, so he was worrying and pressing desperately to hold the General Conference 2003.

On December 2, 2002, John Hanchinmani and I were travelling to Delhi for the meeting of the Executive Committee of one of the Programme Councils, of which I was chairman. I casually asked him if he knew about the Judicial Council declaring the conduct of the South

India and North India Regional Conferences null and void. On hearing me, it seemed he misconstrued my simple and sincere query and fired Sampath Kumar's imagination of my political interest in the Decisions with aim to divide us, it ignited Sampath Kumar's pride and prejudice, changed his perception of me that I could have influenced some key members of the church Judiciary who were close to me. The seed of doubt sowed in his mind turned him against me, my years of cooperation and unwavering support engulfed in the flames of his skepticism. Instead of gracefully considering a review petition, he chose to dismiss the Decisions per se with the help of some political like-minded church leaders. In the political situationism, Nimrod Christian and S.R. Thomas backed him. I was dismayed on their iniquitous move although not averse to their personal interests; however, I expected them to follow the judicial process to salvage the crises. I felt, desecrating the church Judiciary's decisions, which were final and binding, would sink the church's image, but they were in no way inclined to any such sane advice, unwilling to take chance with their cherished power ambition than to commit the historical blunder; they could have avoided if they had not chosen rebellious remedy.

In the situation, Nimrod Christian and S.R. Thomas did nothing to uphold the sanctity of the Discipline and Judiciary. Shaped by the same political mould, strongly supported the Sampath Kumar's egoist adventure for the sake of continuing in bishopric. They were resolute to override the church Judiciary, it was not a gracious move by the bishops of the church, Taranath Sagar cheered them. They raised two members of the Executive

Council who lacked objectivity in the matter. One of them was their spokesman, who was like a demagogue, not an ideologue, was the champion of their cause. The other one was not so successful medical practitioner, a distant relative of Sampath Kumar and a close confident of Nimrod Christian was chivalrous to play the role of Performer. Other close-knit aspirants joined them, galvanized by their power ambition, and merging election interests. Their mutually inclusive political interests appalled me, tied political knot, conspired and profaned their sacred calling. I recognized they were anything but Collusive Clique who was set to thrash the Discipline, conceal the truth, deny justice, and strangle prophetic voice for the sake of power ambition. I was agog at Sampath Kumar's ferocious mode, could not imagine that he by the surge of inferior politics would be gnawing at his conscience, become law to himself, and throttle the church's Judiciary. On January 4, 2003, morning, he called me to the Methodist Centre, Mumbai, just before the special meeting of the Executive Council to solicit my support to render the church Judiciary's Decisions 575 and 576 ineffectual that declared the conduct of the South India and North India Conferences null and void presided by him, but I was melancholic at his move (Vide Appendix). He believed it was his personal defeat, could not rein his ego, and gave to it the political face. I patiently heard him while I looked at his anxious face without uttering a word. I was dismayed by the way in which he was conspiring to scourge the church's Judiciary. I chose to be silent, for I realized, any sane advice given would be futile. I believed destabilizing and ridiculing the church Judiciary would be obstacles to the free flow of justice, but the Collusive Clique was surreal, unrestrained and unhesitant to chisel the church Judiciary, for the sake of survival in Bishopric and election interests. They seemed to believe, abiding by their vows to enforce rule of law of the church at that critical hour would jeopardize their priceless political ambition, defying it was painless. My silence displeased Sampath Kumar, but for me, it was the call of the hour to be like a silent prophet. In the presence of the Performer and in the tide of his displeasure, he said that my attitude was not right, for he realized, I was not dared enough to nourish his defying instinct, I meekly gulped his fallacious notion. I stood by him when I was convinced he was right, but on this matter, it seemed he was swayed by his egotism than wisdom. I was sad about the political episode; nevertheless, I chose to go by my natural instinct and by the voice of my conscience.

As rule, active bishops were co-chairmen and its meetings called in consultation with all active bishops; however, curiously, they ignored me. As human, I felt hurt by the divisive politics of Taranath Sagar. By my letter of December 26, 2002, I raised objection to the way in which he sidelined me; however, it was of no consequences in the politically charged atmosphere. Anyway, I signed the roll call subject to receiving an explanation to stop fuelling the political fire. Law-abiding members, though not vocal, were unhappy in the way in which the constitutional matters were dealt. Long before the schedule meeting, B.P. Singh and few others wrote letters on the violation of rules for calling the meeting. Namdeo Karkare, B.P. Singh, and Vasant Raiborde, the then Executive Council members, voiced their concern on the violation and illegality. They knew the Discipline and needed no one's coaching. They argued with passion and conviction that the meeting was called in the violation of rules and declaring the Decisions noncognizable and ineffectual would be illegal and imprudent, the Collusive Clique, although they knew what they said was right, they persisted in defying it. The time was the gigantic obstacle to achieving their political ambition and satisfying inflated egos, it became a political challenge that tempted them not to abandon their chosen path, let what may come. Election stakes were high to remain in power and position to attain their ultimate political goal like *Nirvana*. The covetous souls were ready to forsake the holiness of life, bend, and defy the church rules for the sake of power ambition; concern expressed on the way the serious issue was dealt did not appeal to their volcanic mind and exaggerated self.

Those who opposed the Decisions contended that the president and secretary of the Judicial Council did not sign them and there was no provision for a pro-tem-chairmanship, despite knowing the Discipline and precedent that the elected members are to elect one among them, as president. I recognized they were in order and in the absence of any rule, the *Robert Rules of Order* was to be followed that provides for a pro-tem chair. Having realized that it would not serve their purpose, gone by different rules, made the form as an issue, and its substance was dismissed. There was the suggestion to ask the church Judiciary either to review the Decisions or clarify so-called anomalies. I perceived, there was wisdom in it to put to the end all controversies and illegalities and it was prudent to call an emergency meeting of the Judiciary without postponing the General Conference Session 2003. Sampath Kumar was stiff and skeptical of the proposal and was aware of his administrative misconduct and perhaps recognized that neither a review nor the clarification on anomalies would help him varnish his administrative misconduct. After mustering political support, he became stubborn and made it as his prestige issue to dismiss the Decisions per se. It pleased Nimrod Christian and S. R. Thomas as they, too, did not like to gamble with the schedule dates, for they had incurable ambition to continue as active bishops for an extra quadrennium and Taranath Sagar was anxious to occupy the episcopal office by taking advantage of the constitutional crises, differences among us and exploiting horde's feelings. Perhaps he felt if he did not actualize his dream then, it would be a political watershed for him. They thrived to actualize their power ambition by their hierarchical superiority and lawlessness, never I tried to frustrate anyone's political ambition; however, I was committed to lawful means and the sanctity of the church Judiciary; it was a decisive departure. They could not appreciate my views, as it did not support their perceived and construed political goals; I was not one with them, but not personally against them. Thus, they became all the more defiant, indulged in give-and-take politics to muster support to defy Judiciary, conduct the General Conference 2003, and achieve their mutually inclusive political ambition. Those who thought bishops were next to God and the Discipline, the sacred document next to the Bible, were shaken awfully, as they had never seen anything like that happening. I was amazed, S. R. Thomas, a staunch believer of it throughout his ministry, fell flat when his continuation as active bishop was at stake. It seemed the message was clear and bold; rules do not matter, if they become inconvenient to achieving the self-satisfying desires and goals of those who rule.

Thirty seven days were left for the General Conference 2003; the dates were from February 10–17, 2003, and the place was Jabalpur, Madhya Pradesh. It seemed to them like hours, and faced with the choice between time and law like Eden's apple and obedience, they dared not risk the golden opportunity, for their political stakes were the deciding factor. There was a perception that they coerced their subordinates and inspired supporters to defy the sanctity of the church Judiciary to satisfy shared ambition; egotism was a driving force, like Alexander the Great's conquests. Mustering support and the force of number rendered the Decisions noncognizable and ineffectual. It was disgusting; the Executive Council paralyzed the church Judiciary and overstepped its jurisdiction and authority. I felt it was a dark day in the history of the church; all conventions and precedents defied the vows of their office and, even worse, aroused others to imitate them, and the tyranny of majoritarianism could not be justified by the right-thinking people.

They approved the resolution in the midst of protest and walkout. I watched the audacious Collusive Clique was full of defying spirit and the boundary line between right and wrong dissipated. They frown against those who opposed the resolution and spearheaded to cleanse the voice of dissent in the flourishing shadow democracy in the church; it was a black spot on the church. They made much ado about trivial issues to accuse me falsely, for failing to arrange

General Conference apportionment – the Regional Conference's share toward the General Conference delegates' expenses. Until then, other bishops, too, did not pay the apportionment from their conferences, but nothing against them. They were aware that the Bombay Conference did not have money, only fund available with the church treasurer was on the account of the Civil Line property sale-cum-development project, Nagpur. They politically coerced me to give my consent to debit the fund account and the Gujarat Conference raised the apportionment locally. Some Regional Conferences never paid for their delegates on time; however, delay in paying apportionment from my conferences had blown out of proportion. In malice, a trivial issue of not signing the certificates of election of delegates to the General Conference 2003 was amplified, twisting the context and facts and yet claiming the Wesleyan spiritual heritage. They spread rumours that I was trying to stall the General Conference 2003 and to stir emotionally and politically naive delegates and make them act like a herd and to varnish their wrongdoing.

I do not regret that I did not go with the flow of the iniquitous power politics. If I did, I could have escaped sufferings, but not held in honour the Discipline. Amazingly, such persuasion was characterized as anti-church. I watched them; they were hilarious to wear the crown of their contemptuous politics; however, the glow on their faces that comes out of the holiness of life was missing. I felt, the church Judiciary was fair and just than the Collusive Clique. By ochlocracy, the prophetic voice throttled when the truth became inconvenient. Such inferior political ambition was sprouting like weeds that tended to tarnish the church's image and rendered the Christian witness ineffectual.

The reaction to the resolution of making the church Judiciary's Decisions ineffectual and noncognizable had vibrating effects; it agitated many in the church, especially those from the South India Regional Conference. There were political convulsions and court cases and in the beginning retired bishops, too, perceived it in disdain. It was pathetic; the bishops of the church did not guide members to act appropriately for the sake of their personal stakes. In sadness, I watched lawlessness, shoddy politics, collusions, compromises, unchristian principle and practices; these were norms of the day, and it was anything but normlessness. I did not waver in my stand, for I felt going by the Discipline was good for the church than self-satisfying ambition since politics was not my guiding star, I was isolated and defamed, for refusing to walk on their political footprints.

They marginalized me, kept in the dark on all vital information and in camera took decisions. I learnt, there was an order from the Mumbai court; however, then I had no order copy or was aware of the text. The court directed both the parties in the lawsuit to place the church Judiciary's Decisions before the General Conference and conduct elections only after they were considered. The order was wrapped, neither they placed the Decisions before the house, nor called the plaintiff in the suit to do so. A legal opinion of inferior substance and value from an advocate of unknown repute was selectively read to mislead the house, and the maneuvered legal opinion on the court order was nothing but the dilution of justice. For namesake, there was a discussion on the participation of delegates whose elections were under dispute. It was mockery of democracy; before voting on the issue, whether they should participate in the General Conference 2003, they were already sitting in the conference's bar, debated on their own participation, and voted in their own favour. A number of the Bombay Conference's delegates voted against their participation that fumed Sampath Kumar. Those who were in favour of the resolution acted like a horde. There was also ad interim injunction order of February 10, 2003, from the City Civil Court, Hyderabad, against the holding the General Conference 2003. It was neither cared nor was any attempt made to vacate it. Sampath Kumar, the then president of the Council of Bishops, and Taranath Sagar, the then general secretary, having secured political backing, became arrogant, refused to accept and recognize the court's injunction order. On March 6, 2010, I was surprised to find the affidavit of Chanchal Sharma, an advocate from Jabalpur in my mail. I was shocked after reading it, they despicably said, they did not bother for such orders and refused to accept it. I felt, it was an act of inflated ego. In the past, such court cases were often filed and stay orders obtained against the holding of a General Conference's Session, it was a routine feature; however, stay orders were promptly vacated. It seemed power craze and rage caused the chaotic situation. The bishops were impetus to causing litigations, and conducting the General Conference 2003 without resolving its legality was spreading lawlessness in the church. Sampath Kumar's hurt ego was driving the Collusive Clique to achieving their inclusive political ambition, so they stirred delegates, but its legality was nonissue. The composition of the house was not in order, a slightly more than one-third (35.48 %) of the delegates illegally participated in the shadow-democratic process. There is no iota of doubt that the election of Taranath Sagar and S. S. Singh as bishops was a forced one and legally untenable, inasmuch as the Executive Council and other elections. There were rumors that they hired local ruffians at hefty cost to ensure the smooth conduct of all elections and played with delegates' emotion by saying, my supporters and I were engaged in the anti-church activities to camouflage their defying of the Discipline, invalidating the church Judiciary and veiling the contempt of court. By emotional appeal, they aroused the horde's feelings and inflamed them in the absence of the fair play of democratic process, and logical reasoning was limited to intellectual delegates only; in malfunctional democracy, the horde was ready to vote on anything in their favour and at their call. Taranath Sagar was elected by voice-vote, John Hanchinmani, as if an avowed parliamentarian swiftly proposed to cast secret a ballot, which was no more secret and to legalize his illegal election, it was the beginning of a worse episcopal election scenario. I observed most delegates had a herd mindset and the bishops could influence voters by the power of their office. In despondency, I watched the great political drama. I thought the devil should be cheering over the eclipse of the truth and justice and the church started by the men of God was facing the crises of conscience. The shift in spiritual thinking and holiness of life was clearly visible. I expected someone among the bishops to act like a prophet or give direction or spiritual guidance; however, none came forward and the retired bishops seemed too glad to say 'Amen' in silent conspiracy, putting the seal of their approval.

In the General Conference 2003, the situation was gloomy; it was soaked with bitterness and revenge, and the bishops seemed defiant about the rule of law. Never before had such things happened in the history of the church. I wished in vain, there were enough apolitical and committed members on the various church bodies to uphold the Discipline than people with narrow ambition. The church Judiciary, too, was in turmoil; division and party spirit was visible. On February 13, 2003, the Judiciary at the seat of the General Conference wrote the letter challenging the resolution of January 4, 2003. The Judiciary contended that the president and secretary signed the minutes of their meeting and authenticated the Decisions by its seal and forwarded with the cover letter, signed by the secretary. They said it was precedent, not new practice, followed in the past and accepted by the church. Some juries avoided signing; however, the majority of juries signed the letter. James C. Lal resigned from the pro-tem chair, Komal Masih gave dissent vote, and G. R. Singh absented (Vide Appendix). The letter was sent to the executive secretary of the Executive Council and copies to active bishops, which they did not place before the house.

Bitterness between the Executive Council and Judiciary did not vanish; it was inflamed. As I reflected on the church in the South Asia's geo-political context, I recognized, the experience with democracy has been disappointing; it did not yet come of age. There were sporadic conflicts between legislators and Judiciary. Everyone knows it is settled law that Judiciary expected to give decisions within the framework of law in force and Legislative body makes laws, and once it did, any decision taken by Judiciary based on those laws, Legislative body cannot trample it. Likewise, the authority of Executive body is subordinate to General body; it can execute decisions and actions, but cannot override decisions and policy guidelines of General body. Judiciary cannot make or break laws; only Legislative body can amend or make laws. The Collusive Clique was anomic, set-aside the Judiciary's Decisions, as it becomes inconvenient to achieving their shared political ambition, the bishops and some heavy weight church leaders acted like colonial masters. Sometimes, such tendency is seen in South Asia; the former president of Pakistan, Pervez Musharraf, by using emergency power, declared a state of emergency in November 2007, suspended the Constitution and arrested the Supreme Court judges to remain in power. I understand such manifestations are not unknown in South Asia. The church, too sadly, tended to slip into such tendency as experience with democracy was disappointing, for democracy was yet to be matured, so was the case in the church.

As I stood by myself near the dinning tent of the conference, an office bearer of the church Judiciary came to me, he was resentful, and he expressed his feelings at shoddy affairs in the church. He was disturbed, for the church Judiciary dealt with contempt and said that no arrangement for juries' accommodation and meeting was made, as if the institution of Judiciary had no room in the administrative scheme of the church. There was conflict between those who were under the influence of the Collusive Clique and those who supported the church's Judiciary. I recognized it was an appreciable justice system; however, its functioning was mired by prejudice and favour, not free from bias and pressure. Some juries who were under bishops' appointments often tutored and the rest were susceptible to influences, except a few. It seemed, there was lack of willpower to deliver flawless justice, and at times, there was miscarriage of justice for the sake of powerful and mighty ones. What was worse, the church Judiciary was rendered dormant; it became a recurring event, and the budgetary provision was withdrawn to hold its meetings. However, having realized that they could not do so too long, perhaps for the fear of outburst in the church, on July 21, 2005, the consultation between select members of the Executive Council and juries was held in New Delhi, as a face-saving devise. There was fierce debate; members of the church Judiciary took position against the arbitrary and unlawful interferences of the Executive council. After ventilating anger, the money was released to hold meetings, however, by then; it became like a lame duck, faint in spirit and suffered with anxiety. I supported the Judiciary to protect the institution of justice, so long, it did not indulge in judicial activism, but it did not please my colleagues. I felt, the membership of church Judiciary was crucial for fair and speedy delivery of justice, for the members employed in the church or under some obligations tended to defeat the end of justice. They lacked judicial integrity and formed cliques to either support or oppose certain decisions under pressure from influential ones. Justice did not even trickle; flowing like streams of water was inconceivable in such political scenario. In the midst of despair, there was a feeling of joy, as some did not yield to such political manoeuvrings and were willing to pay the cost, what it may come. It was truly frustrating; instead of advancing the mission of the church, bishops seemed to be involved in such undesirable acts and power ambition. Truly, no matter who you are, if driven by self-serving pursuits, such things do happen; however, I could not imagine it would be so in the case of the bishops – it was a disturbing discovery! I was at loss at the bishops who preached on self-sacrifice and self-denial but did just the opposite; it was unbelievable! I wondered if I was like a utopian, seeking the spiritual warmth in the church.

I was unwavering to walk on the right path, and never had I realized that one day I would have to pay a heavy cost. Anyway, barely, there was a hurdle to the smooth conducting of the General Conference 2003 on the scheduled dates; they were triumphant. The delegates from my episcopal jurisdiction participated and I presided over it by rotation.

General Conference 2003 delegates, Bishops & I

When I think about it, the entire episode stands before my eyes like a motion picture. When the time for episcopal assignment came, in strategic shrewdness, the active bishops were asked to give just one choice. Sampath Kumar was sitting next to me on the conference's dais. He was watching and observing me with great anxiety; restless as he was, he could not resist inquiring if I was opting for the Bangalore Area. I said no, and yet he acted like doubting Thomas. It was not the end of my troubles, but the beginning. He was scheming to harm me, as I could sense, while I watched him forcefully scribbled on his writing pad. I needed no great wisdom to comprehend that our relation is going to take an unpleasant turn. I was seeking the holiness of life and believed in vain that there was no peril to those who walk on the right path, sadly, my twin expectations were far from true and wondered if it was my presumptuous sin. Anyway, no sooner had the episcopal assignments been announced than Sampath Kumar was politically ferocious; he said to his supporters from the Bombay Conference that he would take it over within two months.

Our working relations tottered; it was unbelievable. They were victorious in achieving their cherished political ambition and buried principles and the Discipline. It was the moment of decision for me to keep myself away from them, as I valued the possession of my conscience. I knew it was a painful choice that would separate us and the divide would please those who were keen to break our ties to attain their political ambition and reign unopposed in the church. I was convinced beyond iota of doubt that Sampath Kumar and Nimrod Christian were anything but the Friends of Convenience, intolerant to others' voice, principles, and shared values, for it was obvious that they cared more about their chair than the church.

Then they became intolerant, pursued me like their prized prey with the blind curb in their spiritual foresight, and the rest rejoiced over our broken ties and yet skeptical about its tenacity, as in the church politics, generally principles, values, and the rule of law are conveniently adhered. I observed, in political situationism, no one is a friend or a foe forever; so those who politically toiled to pursue, divide and rule policy were worried. I felt satisfied, I played my role in the situation in joining the devote men of God who rose to safeguard the church's good, even at the cost of their life.

I was broken and torn by the political storm, and yet I held close to my heart the church's mission to the world. I drew inspiration from the bishops who put church before friendship, even at the risk of losing their high offices and life. My experience with the prophetic voice was small as compared to them, inasmuch as it was neither the first nor the last. The story of Thomas 'a Becket, an archbishop of Canterbury, inspired me and it replenished my depleting energy. He was a trusted friend of Henry II, a king of England in the eighteenth century. The king wanted him to be an archbishop of Canterbury; however, he was reluctant, for he said, if he ascended to the post, then he would lose a friend in him. However, the king prevailed on him, made him the Archbishop of Canterbury with desire to use his friendship to establish the king's supremacy over the ecclesiastical jurisdiction. Thomas'a Becket balked with the king, for he valued principles over friendship. Then, the king was very upset and in hasty expression of anger, arranged to assassinate him. In 1172, they canonized and continued him as one of the most popular English saints until the Reformation. The situation forced Henry to abandon the features which Thomas 'a Becket objectionable in the Constitution of Clarendon and did penance at his grave[9]. It seemed stoning saints and erecting memorials in their names have been the tradition in the church; however, such men of God like him are rare. I was melancholic to observe that the church leaders were not even contrite for defying and bending the church's laws and neglecting to practice the holiness of life. They were focused either to continue to stay high on the power ladder or to climb it, as if they set apart themselves to be served by the church than to serve the Christ; indeed, it did not speak for continuing the apostolic succession inasmuch as the spiritual inheritance.

MASSIVE CONSPIRACY

The General Conference Session 2003 adjourned sine die. I thought worse was behind me; however, its agonizing memory kept haunting me. The Collusive Clique was triumphant over achieving personal ambition, however, by eschewing rules and inappropriate means. I consoled myself for a while, only to face the worse. The ancient weapon of revenge was sharpened by sinister designs to rule brutal with political rod, not by the shepherd's staff of comfort and love. By unimaginable magnitude and speed, both evangelicals and liberals alike among them throttled the prophetic voice and scornfully demolished the right to expression, a cornerstone of freedom in democracy. I recognize that dissent and disagreement are virtues of democracy and not the cause for hatred and revenge, but nay, there was lack of understanding and edifying spirit. Even after more than half a century of freedom in India, in the church, the right to expression was shackled, eagerly waiting for someone among the bishops to rekindle it like John Stuart Mill, an English philosopher who said that the freedom of expression is the essence of discovering the truth. I felt the throes of struggle for democratic norms and holiness of life was worth pursuing. The bishops, the men of God, were absorbed in power ambition and became the engine of negative energy, despised the creative energy of love, compassion, and forgiveness. Even in my wild imagination, I did not expect the church leaders to emit hatred that enslaved them in impious pursuits.

I felt, they were idyllic over their grand political alliance; S. R. Thomas acted as if he was apolitical; actually deep, Taranath Sagar felt insecure, and lived in imagined fear, but was cheerful. Nevertheless he profusely complimented himself the way he swung the episcopal election in his favour. However I perceived, he was awfully smitten by the anxiety of his uncertain political future. He was aware, he could lose his windfall election gains if it was challenged, and his questionable role in the Haldwani property scam was good-enough ground to disgown him. Therefore, he was brooding over losing his bishopric, which he always dreamt of, as these issues were alive and hanging over his head like a sword, and if pressed to its logical end, he would be in a miry situation. Sampath Kumar's obsession with the Bangalore Episcopal Area, self-absorption, and revenge and Nimrod Christian's temporal ambition to hold on to power were driving forces; what was inside was seen outside. I perceived that if Taranath Sagar did not enthuse them, then perhaps they should have not pursued their vengeful expedition.

I did not support cut-throat politics, which was incompatible to my nature. After the General Conference 2003, power politics, took an ugly turn. I recognize, from the time immemorial, some church leaders were obsessed with power. I read Harry Johnson's *'Sociology'* that described power as the general ability to get one's wishes carried out, despite opposition. Power is largely used to influence the actions of others by influencing people with ideas and sentiments or goals or by distortion of facts or one's invention[1]. The Collusive Clique did not cease to arouse malevolent feelings and the pro-Constitutionalists were labelled as anti-church. It seemed that Nimrod Christian believed like Joseph Goebbels, closest to Adolf Hitler, for he used to say that if you tell a lie a thousand times, it becomes the truth, and being affluent in venomous tales, he lavishly fed his listeners' mind with the intention to stir them against me. I felt sad for such a sorry state of spirituality of the bishops of the church, who were supposed to lead the flock of Christ in the changing world. At times, I was inclined to think that the bishops who had such a great calling needed more spiritual enlightenment than to whom they were leading. I was aghast at the audacity of the bishops and the extent of the leaven of falsehood that varnished the truth. There were some in the church who dared to experiment with the truth as Mahatma Gandhi did. However, I believed that one-day truth would tear off the smokescreen of falsehood and shine like a lamp on the hilltop[2].

The vengeful church politics and conspiracy grieved me. I reflected on the thought-provoking teaching of St. Augustine, the bishop of Hippo in Roman Africa

(396–430), who penned down his Christian political thinking in his work, '*The City of God*'. He said that a hierarchical organized church, which was of elect ones, whom God chose for salvation, should rule the world to preserve peace[3]. Unbelievably, such potential fertile thinking seldom ploughed. The Friends of Convenience were of one mind to rule the church by overriding the rule of law and Taranath Sagar; a canny politician was keeping alive their dream and exhorted them to retain their episcopal throne. Barely realized, they were no more than a tool in his hand and a stepping stone to his rising temporal ambition. I was surprised that they could not measure the size of the man and there was none who could appeal to their reason or warn them of the danger of falling into power trap. In the political mirage, the power hungry, as they were seen, rode joyfully with their self-accentuating instincts, contrary to the Christian teachings, as if practicing the holiness of life was the sign of weakness.

They ignored the voice of their conscience, an inborn gift to decipher between good and bad, as if it was wrapped with the warning of expiry date, leaving aside conducting the General Conference 2003 in the absence of changeless light. Driven by the force of selfish ambition and defying the rule of law, its business was concluded with one go; this never happened in the past when order ruled over disorder. There was virtual democratic fiasco – everyone was ready either to gain or retain chair and be on the top of the church hierarchy. I observed in doing so, they unreasonably acted and were set to victimize those whom they perceived as snare to their political ambition. Such tendency dominated the life and ministry of the church; it was dawn of the dark quadrennium like dark ages.

By collusion, impropriety, and emotionally vitiated political atmosphere, the election of bishops and other elections were conducted; the legality was nonissue. Taranath Sagar kept alive Sampath Kumar's wrath against me, and being soft on Nimrod Christian's property sale and development proposals kept me alienated. I was amazed, I did not perpetually wait to hear one of the Friends of Convenience say that he was like a shrewd political manoeuver in the living memory of the church, who knew how to cut Gordian knot to establish his reign in the church. After his election as bishop, although questionable, rising expectation increased. He craved to hear people call him Doctor and put the Doctor's title to his name. I was curious about it and learnt Doctors' titles were mushrooming in the church; anyone could buy it like a commodity without any laudable contribution in the field of their work or academic excellence. It seemed some church leaders craved to have such intellectual tags and were absorbed with the delusion of self-greatness. It was amusing; they addressed each other as Doctor and exhibited Doctor's title on their office stationary to claim intellectual status. Those who genuinely earned a doctorate degree felt ridiculed at the flourishing honorary degree market in the church. I recognize universities around the world confirm honorary doctorate in the recognition of one's outstanding contribution or performance in the field of his specialization; however, by no way are such genuine achievers obsessed as those in the church with negligible achievement or intellectual output, craving for social recognition and adulation.

Taranath Sagar was in the rival political camp in the Bombay Conference, our home conference. It seemed that certain developments prior to his episcopal election deepened his prejudice against me that made him severely oppose and perceive me, as his greatest foe. I was not aware if he was known as an intellectual or spiritual man; however, I knew his colleague pastors perceived him as mediocre though he was a good pastor and highly ambitious young man in a hurry to climb the church's leadership ladder. As an aspiring politician, he always was on the ruling side, seldom on the right side, and it was perceived that he barely cared for the credibility of those to whom he showed affinity, likewise there were others as well. Then I never knew he was a master in political manoeuvring, although I was cautioned from the time he became general secretary of the church and came to live in the Methodist Centre; however, by my do-not-care attitude, I ignored the warning, and I wished I heeded it. Nevertheless, I felt he was worried about the Haldwani property scam, for he knew he was yet to prove his innocence by going through the acid test. When the new general secretary took over the charge from him, he listed the inquiry report on the agenda of the church's Trust meeting, but he misled members by calling it sub-judice. He did not lay any evidence on table to support his claim and the bishops in collusion covered and shielded him without verifying it. There was perception that by tactical move, he might have even asked his close confidant to challenge the inquiry report in the court of law to escape disciplinary action.

There was barely discussion on it and then curiously the item vanished from the agenda, perhaps due to collaborative politics. I remember, sub-judice matters were discussed and acted upon at various church bodies under the chairmanship of bishops when it suited their political motives and daringly and vociferously said, 'We will cross the bridge when we come to it', rather than building bridges like peacemakers with those who balked. By absolutism, the church's interests were sacrificed and there was lack of desire to root out corruption in the church.

What's more, record shows that he did not even restrain his wife claiming money from the church's Trust for years, while she was still on the payroll of a primary school, Municipal Corporation, Mumbai. There was settled practice in the church that the bishop's wife resigns from her work if employed to take active part in the ministry of the church. By virtue of being, the bishop's wife holds the constitutional position of the president of the Deaconesses' Conference, for which the church pays honorarium, office, and travel expenses. I remember, I signed cheques as co-signatory, unaware that she was drawing salary at the same time from the civics' institution. It was intriguing, Elia M. Peter, a retired bishop, not so controversial, bounced with impetuous to sustain his cupidity. In inquisitive pretension asked if the bishop's wife could not pursue her secular career although he held answer in its fullness close to his heart. I remember, most of the bishops of the church were short on prophetic disposition and failed to exhort him to ask his wife to be transparent with civic authority, inasmuch as to avoid breach of trust imposed on him by the church.

Ironically, they covered him, but for others, whose voice differed than their own, used different standard. By antipathy, impiety, and impropriety, bishops pulled blindfold to tilt the justice balance and were exuberant to exult him.

Prem Sagar, younger brother of Taranath Sagar, worked as host of the Jagruti Centre at Lonavala from the time it was under the management of Inter Mission Business Office (IMBO), a separate unit, of which the church was a major partner. The IMBO paid him full compensation when relinquished, the management of the Centre and Bombay Conference continued him in service, perhaps with nepotistic impetus. It all happened before I took over Bombay Area. Then, the Centre was incurring losses, the Bombay Conference invested good money to improve facilities and make good for losses; however, Prem Sagar did not give his best to work, he handled funds imprudently and arbitrarily raised loan for the Centre. He was often found absent and negligent in his duty, so the management took action to fire him from services by giving him notice and compensation. Not satisfied with even a second time compensation and having an unrepentant attitude for recurring losses, he filed a lawsuit against the church in labour court. It was perceived, he could not have been so avaricious and audacious if Taranath Sagar did not prompt him, and not long after, and he began instigate disgruntle people against me.

My predecessor initiated the Civil Line sale-cum development project, Nagpur; however, he could not complete it, as he moved to another Episcopal Area. After I took over the Bombay Area, I put the project on move with the approval of the Trust; however, Taranath Sagar seemed unhappy over the choice of the developer for some curious reason, decided by the sale-cum-development committee. The committee was composed of elect members from the Trust and the Bombay Conference and it did spadework, followed tender guidelines, and placed the developers' offers before the committee. Then the church's Trust and statutory approvals were obtained. A systematic and transparent way of handling the project was lauded as model for other property developments, but there were people like Moses Yangard, a committed Methodist member did not agree to selling church property, as it was a means to dishonest gains. In contrast, I felt there was nothing wrong in putting to use nonperforming assets of the church, so long as it benefits the church and I hit the hole and showed it was not always the case. However, a new church building could not be built, as I envisaged, and the project vision was not achieved because of hostility, stirred up by massive canards. Nevertheless, out of the Bombay Conference's half of the share of the sale proceeds, a permanent endowment of ₹ 2,00,00,000/- was made, and interest from it was to be used for pastors' salary and the church work operation and ₹ 50,00,000/- was kept aside for the development work in Nagpur District. All active bishops were party to the sale-cum-development, and yet by vengeful politics, they maligned my name through their local followings and others in the church. I faced tough times and tensions, including an income tax inquiry; however, I came out clean from the malicious fire.

By taking the advantage of vicious political atmosphere, Taranath Sagar swung sympathy wave in his favour and like a snivelling hypocrite said all kinds of malicious things against me before the church leaders, especially those from the South to give me a hard punch. In 2005 summer, Pradeep Samuel and I had a lunch meeting in the Copper Chimney Hotel, Worli, Mumbai, arranged by Vasant Raiborde, a common person. In the course of our talk, he penitently said that Taranath Sagar used to visit them before becoming bishop and lamented that I would ruin his election prospects and career. He felt contrite and said they did mistake by elevating such kind of man to Episcopacy. It seemed he was constantly spreading ill feelings about me like heart pumping blood. He took the full advantage of my strained relations with Sampath Kumar. I was shocked; Sampath Kumar could be so gullible, lose the balance of his reason, and act on concocted tales. I recognized that the language affinity or familiar spoken words had magical influence on him and transformed him into an absorbed intolerant. Of course, it is a social reality that languages or regions and people's groups either bind or break political ties like nuclei.

Made Me a Scapegoat

Sampath Kumar was eager to celebrate his disapproval of me, as I did not appreciate his scornful adventure against the church Judiciary's Decisions. My conscience and the vows of my office held me back, for they are my valuable possession. Then I could not think, even in my wild imagination, that he would expect me to act on his impious inclination. I perceived no sound reason and simply because of one man's pride and prejudice many led astray. Had he the slightest concern and respect for others' feelings, perhaps he could not have expected others and me to bow down to his gnawing desires. Like a naive, he was imposing and was unkind to the church's juries, mocked at them, and called them jokers. Sampath Kumar, Taranth Sagar, and Nimrod Christian – Priests of Vengeance – were invoking nemesis and refusing to be contrite and offer the sacrifice of their ego to propitiate the Alpha and Omega. Clinging to power was one thing, but continuing as active bishops beyond superannuation was their greatest craving, and ensuring Taranath Sagar's Episcopal destiny was the act of compromise, for they felt that it could not be so smooth for him until a thorn like me is removed from their broad path, so he was living under the shadow of its scary thoughts. Taranath Sagar acted as if he was their great benefactor; it was pity, they never realized, one day they would meet their waterloo and their pursuit for power would be crushed, which would be perhaps the saddest day in their life. It appeared, initially Sampath Kumar and Nimrod Christian contemplated to subdue me, but Taranath Sagar enthused them to oust me from the bishopric to secure himself. Sampath Kumar was fierce to settle his score against those who did not vote in favour of illegally elected delegates to participate in the General Conference 2003 and Nimrod Christian was gloating the idea to retaliate, as he believed, I supported the action of sending him on leave with some ulterior motive; actually, I rescued him from suspension trauma. Had I not stood for him, he could have been in my place forever without any hope of resuming episcopal office; so, soaked by the prejudices, he conspired against me. Sampath Kumar conceived the conspiracy and had sown in the south Indian vengeful fertile soil, and unbelievably, it did not wither; it bloomed like congress grass, abundant in Bangalore. First, false and fabricated evidences were prepared, and then they seduced venal witnesses to achieve their covetous ambition.

On March 29, 2003, the Council of Bishops met in Mumbai and in premeditated strategy, they asked Taranath Sagar to present an oral report of court cases against the conduct of the General Conference 2003. Nimrod Christian, the secretary, scripted his concocted reporting in minutes in a great length by his habitual style; it was the malicious move to prepare mounting evidences against me. I grieved; the bishops were anything but hostile. They isolated and blamed me for Sampath Kumar's administrative misconduct; the minutes of the meeting amply show the nauseas of the conspiracy and the deeds of inferior ambition. I felt it was pathetic, how the bishops lived in pretension and practiced impiety than social holiness. Then, in a calculative move, they referred the matter of court cases to the Executive Council with the aim to investigate and authenticate their a priori findings. The focus of the searchlight of the conspiracy was on others and me, who voted against the resolution of making the Judicial Council's Decisions noncognizable and ineffectual. Obviously, it was ill conceived, oppressive, and an act of a vengeful mind. Bishops who were supposed to do no evil, contrary engrossed in it. Going to court of law is the constitutional right of every Indian citizen. I was appalled, the bishops and other leaders knew that Sampath Kumar was the root of the problem, thrusting people to the court of law and scuffling justice; however, they never reproached him. The investigation into the court cases was just a symbolical act to make me a scapegoat and subject me to further inquiry and disciplinary action. It was an unjust move being intolerant to others' views and defying the church laws to disguise their vengeful attitude. They chased me like medieval crusaders with their political vigour and revengeful stamina, sensitizing the church was their least concern. The Executive Council appointed an inquiry committee to identify persons behind court cases and delaying the General Conference, overriding their own action in compliance to the Calcutta High Court order, not to stop people from going to court of law to seek justice in the exercise of their constitutional right. A few prejudicious stalwarts were appointed from the Collusive Clique on the committee and the Performer was its Convener. The choice fell on him, for he was the best bet, and he was spiteful to me as well. In 2001, some local churches in Hyderabad obstructed their pastors going to pulpit in protest against the school property development and to overcome the impasse, the Executive Council appointed the special committee on the Hyderabad Conference's matters under my chair. One of the recommendations of the committee was to transfer him and his relative who was a pastor. I chaired the meetings, there were other active bishops too, on the committee, but in prejudice, he chose to target me. Then, I declined to chair subsequent meetings in such a politically hostile atmosphere, Sampath Kumar chaired it, he tilted and buried the remedial measures. I failed to read the writing on wall that they were conspiring with premeditated findings. It was iniquitous to punish members of the church for going to court of law just because they protested against them for going by different rules and not holding the church Judiciary in honour. I believed it was but a just and right cause. He sent me the questionnaire of five open-ended questions relating to going to court of law and delaying General Conference Session. No sooner had I received it than I asked him to send me documentary evidence against me if any and objected to Joseph Massey being on the inquiry committee since he was a co-complainant against me. He evasively replied by saying that he sent the questionnaire to all bishops, but he said nothing about my objection to Joseph Massey and documentary evidence. There was perception that the symbolical methodology of inquiry was the brainchild of Joseph Massey to prepare evidence against others and me who did not support their breaking of the rule of law of the church, and to catch me like a big fish in their vengeful political net. Anyway, since I did nothing wrong, I answered the questions, but not all bishops did. My answers were plain, simple, and short; however, they conspired, treated dry bones as meaty and the Priests of Vengeance mentored their men who were on the committee, principle of natural justice and equity sacrificed in the presence of spiritual emptiness. I was amazed, the undiscerning bishops even had no fringe regret to impinge the church Judiciary and canonize Sampath Kumar's administrative misconduct, and self-propelling instincts were not conducive to the holiness of life, but by tyranny and lack of integrity run hither and thither to victimize me to varnish their act of not abiding by the rule of law.

Again, from August 8 to 9, 2003, the Council of Bishops met in Mumbai. I was shocked; Sampath Kumar and Taranath Sagar managed to make Ebenezer Shivapur, the layman who they earlier declared as the man without any locus standi, to appear before the Council of Bishops and to bring pressure to take action against me. However, they did not allow him to appear before the council, for the sake of outward decency. Sampath Kumar was disgusted by delays and the blink prospect of disciplinary action, so he in want of norms sprang up to hurl at me the copies of prepared affidavits of Ebenezer Shivapur and George Edward, another layman, and their prepared affidavits were claimed as genuine, when actually it was an act of conspiracy. My protest voice was lost in the intolerance, revenge, and seditious applause. Then Stanley Downes and Karriappa Samuel, retired bishops and old-timer antagonists to each other, were authorized to talk to him and bring report; it was an unusual step, not in conformity with either procedure or precedence. I never could imagine they would sink so low and place unfair and unjust report of his tutored averments. I refuted all allegations, however, in vain. They asked me to give my written response. By chance, I escaped the wrath of their vengeful axe on the first day of the meeting; the meeting was adjourned to facilitate the bishops to attend the funeral service of James B. Satyavrata, a former executive secretary of the church. He was a wonderful man and a mature Christian leader who contributed a lot to the life and ministry of the church. He was supportive and kind to me. Sampath Kumar was funnelling bitterness and fuming venom, so on the following day, he lifted the tabled matter and authorized Nimrod Christian, the then president of the Council of Bishops to appoint a committee of two bishops to inquire into the prepared affidavits. By collusion, he then appointed Taranath Sagar and Karriappa Samuel; the duo was bias towards me.

The bishops were fully seized of the fact that Sampah Kumar strip off Ebenezer Shivapur from the church membership for filing court case against the misconduct of the South India Conference presided by him. It was sad; he did not care for the Calcutta High Court order, the rest of the bishops once antagonist to him, however, were now thriving to glue to him on the contemptuous issue, which was a hypocritical act. It was paradoxical; Sampath Kumar and Taranath Sagar affirmed by giving affidavits before the court in Belgaum that he was no more the church member and thus had no locus standi, but by conspiracy, they used him against me, who, until then, was not even restored to the church's membership. It was wholly the work of political craft. As said, not long before, Samapth Kumar used him in the Tapegate scandal, implicating Victor Raja. In the south, the church leaders knew pretty well that by force of his habit, Sampath Kumar used venal characters against his political rivals; I grieved over it. Bishops were revengeful, devoid of reason and social holiness; I remember the man was merely an induced tool. Not long after, they made his advocate from Belgaum, a non-Christian to depose against me. He made wild allegation that I promised to pay his legal fee – baseless and brazen allegation under inducement.

I knew neither Ebenezer Shivapur nor his advocate, nor did I ever meet them, and he could not prove his mischievous allegations.

Taranath Sagar and Karriappa Samuel, a retired bishop, despite their manifest bias against me, conducted inquiry, which they did with stubborn malice. Sampath Kumar terminated Sheila John Wesley, a deaconess; she filed the lawsuit challenging her termination; however, she could not succeed. She was desperate to be restored, and perhaps, they assured her restoration. Thus, they induced her to give affidavit in lieu of it, and she gladly did it. By taking a cue out of their frustration and perceived feeble life style, they pressurized them to give false affidavits against me; she, too, was called to Bangalore for recording her statements. Lured by their tempting promises and anxiety to end their own woes, they were ready to do anything at their call, inasmuch as not known for upholding ethical and moral values. In secrecy, they held the inquiry in Bangalore and the report was prepared and signed in Mumbai. Without giving me an opportunity to present my side, they vengefully and unfairly framed me. The report amply mirrored their malicious attitude than my wrongdoings; it was an outpouring of their hatred and revenge, which I did not expect. They stooped down so low to the level of malicious allegations and tried to build the spurious case against me. By the reward of position and pressure tactics, they maneuvered everything and everyone; it was the result of the prevailing low state of spirituality and the mockery of truth and justice in the church.

In the meantime, the report of the inquiry committee was placed before the Executive Council meeting held in Mumbai from September 11 to 12, 2003. I was not surprised by its findings, for during the inquiry, Sampath Kumar curiously given an unsolicited donation of ₹ 10,00,000/– from his episcopal area to Crawford Hospital, Vikarabad, of which the Performer was the Director; it deepened prejudice and prompted premeditated findings. I grieved over their collective revengeful endeavours. By scheming, they referred the report back to the Council of Bishops to take an appropriate disciplinary action against others and me, for which the Collusive Clique was exuberant to get the seal of its approval. Anyway, it was a foregone conclusion and a step closer to achieving their conspiracy against me.

There was a perception that none of the Priests of Vengeance was a fiddler, but differently. I perceived if Sampath Kumar was skilled schemer, Taranath Sagar was a master executor in preparing evidences and influencing witnesses, whereas Nimrod Christian was untamed and unmatched in twisting things. I could not imagine they would stretch too far, stoop so low, and not feel contrite about their malicious pursuit. I was like an idealist, for the actual situation was not like the Garden of Eden and Sampath Kumar was scornful and closed to the truth. Bishops knew he was plotting, and yet out of grudges against me, for some reason, they refused to embrace the truth. However, I did not say 'Amen' over his injudicious and imprudent conducts; but, they adored him as the champion of their cause. I could not believe they would victimize me for upholding the Discipline and make me languish in pain and agony for my prophetic voice.

Ebenezer Shivapur and George Edward were led to sign the affidavits, alleging that I instigated and financed them to file court cases against the holding of General Conference 2003. It was intriguing to know the reason for the change of heart on the matter, for they vociferously litigated against Sampath Kumar, for misconducting the South India Conference. Ebenezer Shivapur filed suit in the court of law. George Edward filed petition before the Judicial Council and the Decision No. 575 came in his favour, which the Executive Council rendered noncognizable and ineffectual, so he challenged it in the court of law. Sampath Kumar greatly misconstrued me for not supporting his defying mode and twisted the truth that I was behind the court case and thrust blame on me, of which I was innocent. His aim was to varnish the collusion and conspiracy; I was in the situation like one against many. They damned others and me by calling us anti-church although we were no Luciferians and deserved no such eulogizing. It was unreasonable; although the bishops were cogent of the truth and context in which the court cases sprang up, they pretended as if they knew nothing – shielding, supporting, and becoming like him. It was no evil to go to the court of law, to enforce the rule of the law of the church when the bishops, protectors, and preservers ruthlessly defied the Discipline to survive in power. Ebenezer Shivapur also alleged that M. Elia Peter, a retired bishop, instigated him; however, curiously, they shielded him, and in malice, I was isolated and made a scapegoat. I was at loss; they passed the blame on me as Adam did. Barely, there was doubt that Samapth Kumar used Ebenezer Shivapur against other bishops. The bishops were aware that Sampath Kumar and Taranath Sagar induced them to sign the prepared affidavits by golden carrot and iron stick, such seductive and pressure tactics often used in the church to either bless or punish their helpless victims. There was an overwhelming perception that Ebenezer Shivapur and George Edward were intimidated by the threat of firing their relatives from the church institutions if they did not cooperate with them in their close guarded conspiracy and lured them with lavish rewards if they did. It worked out well, in fear and greed; they laid down their arms, ceased their cock-like fight with Sampath Kumar, and began to facilitate their conspiracy. I was disturbed and shattered. Taranath Sagar took active part, did a magical performance, and made them sign on the dotted lines of the prepared affidavits. The bishops, being hibernated to holiness of life, indulged in deplorable things to victimize me, they lost sensitivity to their calling, and their pitiable piety did not edify the holy office of the church, which they held. Then I never realized that the bishops would go astray, take revenge, and at the same time, claim to follow the Bible; it did not match their deeds. I felt it was nothing less than discrediting Christianity and bruising Methodism.

It was unbelievable that George Edward, a resident of Bidar, Karnataka, could take a strenuous long journey of about 300 kilometers to Raichur, Karnataka, to buy stamp paper, type the content, and sign and affirm it before the notary public there, which he could have easily done in his hometown. By turn of events, he confessed that he was called to Bangalore, not to Raichur, to sign the affidavit; it made huge sense. Anyway, after he signed it on July 27, 2003, under allurement and threat, he returned home on the same day, perhaps with gifts and promises and mixed feelings of joy and guilt. On the following day, the prepared affidavit was notarized in Raichur. Likewise, the prepared affidavit from Ebenezer Shivapur was also obtained, and long after, Sampath Kumar confessed that he appointed him as manager of a school in Belgaum on a monthly honorarium of ₹ 5,000/. Beyond doubt, they prepared concocted evidences to cut me to size, otherwise, they felt, I would be like a political hot potato. Seduction and threat tactics were the means to achieving their ends. No sooner the prepared affidavits were signed than George Edward was given the supervisor's post in the Methodist Hospital, Bidar. Ebenezer Shivapur's wife was back to the school in Kadehatti, a village in Karnataka where she was transferred when her husband fought the court case against Sampath Kumar and Sheila John Wesley was restored to the Deaconess' Conference. These were neither natural nor supernatural events, nor was there any sign of repentance or restitution, for it was not an inclusive act, it was anything but the peril of punishment and the promise of reward. Unbelievably, it was perceived that Sampath Kumar believed in profaning compromises and vindictive tactics. By force of habit, he used his venal antagonists at remarkable ease and skill against those whose voices conflicted with his self-interest, and when he achieved his goals, he would bounce back and seek an opportunity not to spare them; I dared not to envy him. I observed, he could easily become amicable with his enemies, when he found himself in a dock. After nearly six years, I was surprised to find in my mailbox the counter affidavit of Edward George. He wrote in it that his conscience was biting him for a long time and agonized by its thoughts could no longer live without confession and persistently said that he was led astray and did not know his prepared affidavit would be used against me, for which he asked my forgiveness. It seemed Sampath Kumar bestowed the appointment on him to keep lid on the conspiracy inasmuch as to have hold on him. He said no sooner did he depose against me before the inquiry than he realized the plot; he grieved and waited to divulge all until the dismissal of the court case filed by Namdeo Karkare in the Aurad court, but did not press, challenging the prepared affidavit. Not long after, Taranath Sagar threw him out of his job like the salt that lost its saltiness. By the storm of conspiracy, he was remorseful for believing and doing things unknowingly, what they asked him to do. He began to unfold the conspiracy and unwaveringly contended that Taranath Sagar made him sign the prepared affidavit without disclosing its purpose and did not allow him to read its content and verify its correctness. He said, in good faith and believing him as a bishop, a religious leader, he signed it. He emphatically said that he neither went to the notary public to affirm it, nor did he sign in the notary's register; Mumbai police did not find both his name and signature in the notary register. He even recorded his evidence statement in the box against accused Taranath Sagar before the Add Chief Metropolitan Magistrate, 46th Court, Mazgaon, Mumbai. It appeared that by impersonating him, the affidavit was notarized and the notary public was either willing or negligent, the former seems to be more plausible than the latter. Believably, Sampath Kumar's scheming attitude, inasmuch as Taranath Sagar's virulent endeavour and the yearning of Joshua Samuel, younger son of Kariappa Samuel, solemnized the ritual of fraud. They attempted to get prepared affidavit from north India as well from Clerence Peter, the petitioner of Judicial Council Decision No. 576; however, then one of the church regional officials confided in me that he dissuaded him not to nourish their malicious desire.

Sampath Kumar's inflamed ego was the driving force to rendering the Decisions noncognizable and ineffectual, which spurted litigations. Taranath Sagar and Sampath Kumar's statements, affidavits, and records in various courts in Bidar, Belgaum, and Mumbai abundantly show that court cases were filed against them to protect the sanctity of the church constitution. Then they argued, the jurisdiction to file a lawsuit against the church rests with courts in Mumbai, so George Edward rushed to the city, filed lawsuit No. 517 of 2003 in the City Civil Court to bring stay order on the illegal holding of the General Conference 2003. I neither knew him nor called him, nor did I know if it was his own doing or, in disguise, someone prompted him in my name, or both. On January 31, 2003, the court passed the order; however, not satisfied with it, George Edward appealed to the Bombay High Court. I came to know about it only after I received the notice as one of the defendants. Namdeo Karkare, one of the defendants in the appeal, chose to support him. No way could I restrict anyone either by enforcing any law of the church or by denying the constitutional right. He was not amenable, inspired by his own reason known to him. He wrestled against the injudicious acts of the Collusive Clique to uphold the rule of the Discipline and Judiciary. However, in the political heat of Sampath Kumar's bruised ego and the Collusive Clique's power ambition, the original issues of misconducting South and North India Conferences by Sampath Kumar and rendering the Decisions 575 and 576 noncognizance and ineffective were lost. They made much ado about court cases against the General Conference than paralysing the Discipline; stalling the General Conference Session 2003 was not the actual focus; however, I was curious to know its outcome and sympathetic to those who were pursuing it, for they were going after those who politically seized the Discipline and the church's Judiciary. Taranath Sagar, the then general secretary, was defending his own action on war footing. However, as resident bishop, I felt I should alert him by sending the copy of the court notice that I received, but he misconstrued my honesty and misled others as if I was behind it. Sampath Kumar, not I, miserably failed to stop George Edward and Ebenezer Shivapur going to the court of law, for they were from his episcopal jurisdiction and in war with him. I was not averse to his winning; anomie was the sole consideration, but his appeal was dismissed; however, the City Civil Court's order was in force. There were no legal deterrents to approach the Judiciary of land, yet the bishops maliciously alleged me that I did not take steps to restrict people going to the court of law. It was a conspiracy, not an act of fairness. The Collusive Clique with a great vigour defied all norms and concealed the truth to victimize those who exercised constitutional right to safeguard the Discipline, as if going to the Judiciary of the land for justice was an abomination act.

I was melancholic to observe that bishops were intolerant and chose to dismiss the Executive Council's action that did not allow any disciplinary action for going to court of law for justice. Regardless, in collusion and conspiracy, they made me a scapegoat. I was perplexed, how pious men in purple shirt had gone astray, acted in conflict with the church's interest, concealed the truth, practiced revenge, and by conspiracy, alleged me of malicious intent. As said, Taranath Sagar chased litigants to courts in Mumbai to frustrate justice and injudiciously argued that the jurisdiction to file cases against the church rested with courts in Mumbai. In malice, they accused me for not stopping to those whom he chased, as my voice was in conflict with their political interest. The Priests of Vengeance concealed the truth of their acts of omission and commission, amplified, and camouflaged the context to victimize me. They were contemptuous without any remorse, stirred by revenge, jealousy, and hatred. Helpless and isolated as I was, I wished a small reasonable sense prevailed on the bishops to save good witness of the church. It did not happen, and the legality of election of the delegates to the General Conference 2003 was shelved. They did not uphold truth and justice, for they lacked prophetic courage and conviction; however, in vain, I waited, expecting them to adore it. It was a pathetic show: members were in litigation for justice and they construed as if I was the force behind them, as I did not sing the litany of their defying attitude. In fact, it was a conspiracy, camouflaging their untamed political ambition in the name of the church and victimizing genuine well-wishers of the church. In malice, they did things, either to gain or survive in positions of power by destroying others because my and others' prophetic voice was hurting their power ambition and I wondered why they did not believe in the divine providence. The active bishops whose stakes were high supported the issue and sensitized delegates, for they realized that if the General Conference 2003 was not held as scheduled, they would retire without getting an extra quadrennium. Therefore, in political aphorism, they stood with Sampath Kumar, who spearheaded the conspiracy, pushing it hard by his inflated ego, as it was the question of their chair, not conscience. The conflict of interest shattered my ministry and life and they misled people in the name of the church's good, to satisfy their personal cravings. However, I felt it was the call of my consecration vows to hold in honour the Discipline, it badly shook them. I was not averse to their rightful claim to remain in power or acquire power. I believed that means were as valuable as ends and essential for the holiness of life. My conscience held me back from walking the Collusive Clique's way; however, they were hilarious to demolish all that was truthful, logical, and legal.

No Written and Signed Complaint

There was no written and signed complaint against me, which was mandatory as per the Discipline for a disciplinary action, except in the case of clear violation. They shirked the rule and ironically alleged as said that I instigated church members from Sampath Kumar's episcopal area to go to court of law and did not stop them and others. Actually neither I knew them nor obstructed the holding of the General Conference 2003. Bishops conveniently ignored the facts that the General Conference passed my character along with them and I presided over it. It was a conspiracy to act on the prepared affidavits. I perceived that Nimrod Christian, the then president of the Council of Bishops, weighed the political opportunism when misfortune smiled at me; bitterness ignited him, and he was bubbling to snub me to satisfy his stored revenge. By collusion and conspiracy, he treated the prepared affidavits as complaints and asked me to give a written reply. In the absence of a written and signed complaint, it was illegal, and he skewed the rule and spilled malice in his letters of August 23 and September 25, 2003. He did not give any cognizance to the affidavit of Namdeo Karkare under the pretext of managed legal opinion and did not verify the authenticity of George Edward's affidavit. I knew Sampath Kumar was pressurizing him to fall in line with him. I remember, one of the bishops who cherished the holier than thou art attitude and parabolically used to say, the South was deceptive; pointing towards him and yet he was one with him without any remorse when his stakes to continue as active bishop were high. Unbelievably, they cared little and paralyzed the great spiritual heritage of the holiness of life for the sake of survival in the Episcopacy.

They selectively victimized me and rewarded those who filed lawsuits. In public, the bishops made tall claim about the freedom of expression; however, secretly they often throttled it with a wall garden approach and iron will. Those who agitated against the violation of the Discipline were tormented by the fusion of negative energy and the cocktail of their political interests, for their wisdom failed and the holiness of life was sacrificed for them to ascend to positions of power. The goals were either to attain or survive in power and take revenge, and allegations were mere excuses. It was ironical that upholding the Discipline was tagged as being anti-church and enslaving it was adored as being pro-church. I perceived that the bishops considered themselves as immaculate and gorgeous democrats, but in true sense and spirit, fair democratic practices were lacking in the church, and ochlocracy was thriving, leaders could do and undo anything even if they stood in aberration.

Intolerance and injustice exceeded, the church's equity equilibrium tilted, and the bishops isolated and targeted me to ruin my ministry and life. Like congenial liars, the bishops conspired to level spurious and flimsy allegations borne out of revenge, whereas serious charges against them lay dormant and buried. I remember, N. John, a lay member from Hyderabad Conference, was grieved and filed a written and signed complaint against Nimrod Christian. I was shocked in the way the bishops shuffled the findings of the Inquiry Report 2000, in which, as said, Nimrod Christian was found implicated, but the bishops in collusion shielded him. Disgusted by the collective cover up, he filed a criminal complaint against the bishops in the Abid Road Police Station, Hyderabad, for abetment of offences. I was stunned to read the letter of March 8, 2007, addressed to the Station House Officer. In guile Sampath Kumar, Taranath Sagar, Sunder Singh, and S. R. Thomas, the end signatory, not as president although then he was, and Nimrod Christian, too, signed the letter in his own favour. I felt that it was no less than political bartering of their souls to survive in episcopal power by concealing the truth and shielding him so to escape abetment charge. It was in public domain that Nimrod Christian was found implicated on serious charges, and yet there was no disciplinary action against him; on the contrary, they rewarded him for his collusion for breaking the Discipline and joining the conspiracy against me. Other bishops were also found implicated in other inquiry reports for serious violation of property or financial matters, but they were smiling, no action was contemplated, not even an exemplary one. However, as for me, such bishops sat on the judgment seat to punish me, the victim of their conspiracy. They ousted me for my prophetic voice, as truth, justice, equity seldom inspired them, and it seemed that the preachers of the gospel became the evangelists of revenge. They devastated the principle 'no man is above law' and abundantly demonstrated that powerful people with powerful allies can commit any crime in high offices without being brought to justice. By the heinous act of treachery, they conspired against me, an episcopal colleague of their equal rank, though I deserve the right to hold a different opinion than theirs in democracy and love, but they treated me like a thorn in their side.

Reconciliation Episode

Sampath Kumar acted as if he was keen to reconcile and bury bitterness. Reconciliation is a Judeo-Christian tradition; it is unknown to other religious faiths. In my theology class, I learnt that the Christian theology of atonement is based on reconciliation, Christ reconciling humans with God by his own sacrifice, which is core to Christian faith and an inevitable process in making peace. I read Michael O. Hardimon's *Hegal's Social Philosophy: The Project of Reconciliation*, he says, reconciliation is like when two parties begin as friends and then are entangled and again become friends; thus, the basic pattern is of unity, division, and reunion. The bishops knew the rule: the reconciliation step was first to be taken, and if it fails, only then was the process of disciplinary action to begin. Reconciliation is central to the Christian faith, the path is shown by Christ to put an end to hostility to restore peace, the world needs it most; however, I waited in vain.

May 2, 2004, was the dedication of Baldwin Methodist Educational Centre, Bangalore. Sampath Kumar persuaded me to attend it. He said when I come, they would ask Ebenezer Shivapur to withdraw his affidavit, and curiously, he said nothing about George Edward. He also said that Nimrod Christian, the then president of the Council of Bishops, would come to reconcile the issue. Then I did not realize it was a calculative and malicious move to hold a symbolic reconciliation and to show that the reconciliation failed, even in the absence of a written and signed complaint, and affidavits per se were not complaints. He schemed: Nimrod Christian would pretend to reconcile, Ebenezer Shivapur would not budge, and then the matter would be placed before the Council of Bishops for constituting an inquiry and suspension. Taranath Sagar knew the plot. Being unaware of it, I decided to attend the function. Not long after, I recognized, he was not sincere in sorting out the issue. In the function, I met Karriappa Samuel and other retired bishops. I watched Karriappa Samuel's scornful face and his younger son glanced at me. I perceived, he had some guilt feelings; their gestures and responses dismayed me and Nimrod Christian did not show up. After the function, I wanted to return to Mumbai, as the following day was Rayhal's birthday. Sampath Kumar urged me to stay back; he said Nimrod Christian would come at any time to reconcile the issue, but he did not come. Things did not go as per his plan, it was a clumsy failure and perhaps he felt that the chance of initiating disciplinary action was blink. Taranath Sagar was already camped in Bangalore. In the evening, he took Taranath Sagar and me for a dinner to some hotel on the M. G. Road to disguise their plan and to give me the impression that he was still my great friend who buried the hatchet; however it was not so. I heard them whisper something fishy, perhaps in Kannada. I do not know the language; however, their body language gave me the cue that they were conspiring against me. I felt uneasy, not at all comfortable in their company, and sensed something stinking about the whole episode. Then, I never knew, these malicious cooks were preparing South Indian conspiracy recipe for me. The next day, Sampath Kumar and his wife came to meet me at the Baldwin girls' guesthouse, where I was lodged. He tried to calm my worrisome feelings and hide his ill intention by taking me around the city. He brought some sweets for me and seen me off at the airport in the evening without having the farcical reconciliation. Then I did not suspect his honesty and never imagined the bishops could be so dramatic and could demonize peacemaking.

His obstinate face beamed anxiety and frustration, as despite his best efforts, neither Nimrod Christian nor Ebenezer Shivapur had shown up. I was not sure if Nimrod Christian knew or was serious about the symbolic reconciliation. As said, there was nothing to reconcile in the absence of a written and signed complaint. However, Sampath Kumar looked miserable over his failure to hold the symbolic reconciliation prior to the Council of Bishops' meeting of May 6, 2004, and in disguise to show that, the attempts to reconcile the matter failed. I thought, if they were genuine, it could have been a great day, it was not even necessary to be a part of the process; however, they lacked will-power to do right things.

I found that adherence to the truth and justice was missing. I had nothing personal against anyone, I was thinking differently, as they were focused to pursue their power ambition by vicious means like spiritual celibates and I failed to comprehend their utter insensitivity. Some people were making efforts to reconcile us, but in arrogance, they snubbed them. They could not escape the negative energy of egotism, hatred, jealousy, and revenge, and I began to lose faith in the piety of the bishops; however, my hope for good things to happen was not lost, I was comforted to know that there were still good Christians who walked a second mile to reconcile and forgive. I remember, Pope John Paul II, one of the great spiritual leaders of the twentieth century, was admired for his act of forgiveness. In 1981, the Turkish terrorist shot him at St. Peter's square. When he recovered, he resumed his work and forgave his would-be assassin. Such Christian spirit of reconciliation, forgiveness, and love was missing in the church and Christian values and virtues then seldom mattered. The bishops even refused to reconcile and settle trivial issues. One of the church members confided with me that he asked Taranath Sagar, the then caretaker bishop of the Bombay Conference during May to November 2007, to put an end to hostility, but he seemed resolute and fumed and bluntly said, 'If it was to be, then why they had to do all these?' Obviously, he was personal and not in the right attitude to sort it out; on the contrary, he was determined to intensify and torment me. I observed the Priests of Vengeance thrived on power ambition, proudly focused to doom me, and there was barely room in their heart for reconciliation; political aggression was the norm of the day to achieve temporal ambition. The church expected them to practice servanthood and become light to nations; however, it seemed that the holy oil in the bishops' lamp was depleting to keep it shining bright, and although dimly shining, it was kept under a lamp stand.

Some complaints against bishops were resolved like a spark of light under some pretext and others stretched to scorch. It seemed that the motive was to make them sub-judice, not to settle in the church, and to drive complainants or victims to the Judiciary of the land to frustrate justice. They abandoned the reconciliation procedure when it was seen as an impediment to achieving political ambition, and sometime symbolical, to victimize or cover delinquent bishops who were loyal to the majority of political lobby of the bishops or had social affinities and without any admonition.

The provision was abused conveniently; those who supported the Collusive Clique were rescued despite serious charges, and for those who did not, although flimsy and trivial, injustice was melted. The symbolism led to a stinking situation in the church, and laissez-faire administration became the norm of the day that vitiated the holiness of life and moral conduct, not to speak of the effective Christian witness. The affairs in the church were not edifying, as the bishops, spiritual and temporal leaders of the church were playing deflective roles and destroying others to stay in power.

Desperate Pursuers

On March 30–31, 2004, the Council of Bishops meeting was held at the YMCA Tourist Hostel, New Delhi, and Taranath Sagar was heroic, foretelling in arithmetic certainty that a very important decision was in store; obviously, hinting at my suspension. I spotted Sampath Kumar and Taranath Sagar in the lounge during the tea break, engaged in sub rosa talk with Nimrod Christian. It seemed that they were convincing and luring him with some reward to get his support, for three votes of active bishops were needed to approve the action, as retired bishops had the privilege of the floor but without the right to vote. No sooner had I walked closer to them than they whisked away. I asked Nimrod Christian about it and he told me of their ploy. In the evening, Sampath Kumar, Nimrod Christian, and I walked down to Connaught Place and tried to clear Sampath Kumar's misunderstanding. We sat in a coffee shop and, as we sipped coffee, discussed the consequences of falling apart. Nimrod Christian cautioned Sampath Kumar how John Hanchinmani was using the spokesman to untie our friendship knot. Then he firmly believed the need was to stay together, not to depart. There was a sign of some change in Sampath Kumar's capricious attitude, as he often used to change his position, especially when sensed danger to his personal cravings. Nimrod Christian in satire used to call him 'colour', for he displayed a chameleon-like character. I felt sanguine to hear him say that if my matter comes, he would say that others misled him on the court cases and he had nothing against Dinesh. I felt relieved for a while. We returned to the YMCA. Sampath Kumar showed a little friendliness, called me to his room, and showed some letters which he obtained from the pastors under his charge against a few pastors of the Bombay Conference. By seeing us together in a cordial relation, Taranath Sagar looked disturbed and showed disdain and displeasure; however, he was determined to harm me after his elevation to episcopacy, thus he did inconceivable things to achieve his personal goals. I perceived that, for the moment, perhaps he felt he would not succeed in his nocuous plan against me at one go; nevertheless, he was resolute and vigorous to pursue it and would overcome the momentary setback. Not broken by his failed attempts, he was anxious to win over their support to fulfil his cherished desire and sharpened his time-tested political weapon of greed.

The position taken by Sampath Kumar and Nimrod Christian in New Delhi was short lived. I perceived Taranath Sagar by political shrewdness and knack sensitized their personal narrow ambition. He tempted them with the idea of dividing the Bombay Episcopal Area between them; elated by the prospect of more power and influence, they held him in high esteem, as their benefactor. Then he stirred Sampath Kumar's somewhat dormant urge to take revenge on me, and those who voted against the resolution of January 4, 2003, and opposed the seating of illegal delegates. Nimrod Christian was overwhelmed by the prospect of ruling the Gujarat Conference, his home conference, and lavishing creamy appointments on his bosom friends.

After I returned from Bangalore, I went to Vododara on May 4, 2006, for a meeting. Some local leaders were in contact with some closest of the Priests of Vengeance, they warned me of their conspiracy and advised strongly not to attend the Council of Bishops' meeting and volunteered to bring stay order if I so desired. I was careful, the days were bad, and I could not trust anyone and I thought they could be spying on me. Until then, I had unshakable faith in the church's justice balance and believed that there was no risk to those who pursue the church's ideals; however, I was broken, lost my faith in it, for realities were far harsher than I could imagine. I said to them I would manage, and then never had I known I would be so coarsely dealt.

On May 6, 2004, the Council of Bishops met in Mumbai. Nimrod Christian called me early in the morning to make sure I attend the meeting. Anyway, I was to attend, as I was the then secretary of the council and although I knew, the situation might be stormy; however, I thought I would come out of the political fire, for my innocence was my strength and the church's social holiness undergirded the Discipline, truth, and justice, so I was firm. I regret I was too presumptuous; I was shattered to experience that the collegium justice system was the fertile ground for vengeful adventure, as though making virtue out of villainess. The bishops were unmoved by truth and justice and were one and the same like beads of same rosary and their craving for power did not edify the church or urge them to do heart searching. Then I realized bishops were not concerned about the holiness of life. Sampath Kumar was fuming, egoistic and malicious as he was, his benevolent gestures a few days ago were nothing but farcical. Regardless, I made the last attempt at the tea break to impasse his misconstruing and offered him an olive leaf. I said to him, not to put me in embarrassing situation, as we were planning Rayhal's marriage. He said, 'I know, what you are saying, I, too, have daughters.' I could not arouse his noble side; it was like counting sand. He was obsessed with his plot against me and safeguarding Taranath Sagar's bishopric, so he chose to be defiant and adamant. He duplicitously said, 'We three must retire.' I asked him why. Then, he said, 'Let us have give-and-take.' At first, I did not understand he wanted me to take action against the pastor who supported George Edward if I wanted to be out of it. Apparently he was bartering, but could not be trusted, for I felt he would make me punish the pastor and yet would sting me, as he seemed like a suave villain. Moreover, the pastor whom he wanted me to victimize did nothing deserving punishment and no way it was the matter of any offence.

In the meeting, I pleaded; the affidavits and the reports were prepared, and they were unwilling to lend me their ears. They managed some retired bishops to roar at me maliciously and one of them was living on the false promise of reactivation, as he was eager to take chance, however, he was disappointed. The Priests of Vengeance were desperate to suspend me and when their hopes brighten, mine blinked; Stanley Downes gibed and whispered, 'Thirteen is unlucky,' hinting at my birth date. I felt, he was a bit insensitive, and expecting him grow wise with age was useless. I wondered if he believed in numerology and occultism, incompatible to Christian faith, and yet it seemed to influence his thinking. He ridiculed me and did not show spiritual flavour and mature theological perception. The crux of the matter was craving to take revenge on concocted allegations. Unspoken words were louder, the furnace of hatred, jealousy, and revenge was far more intense than the warmth of love and forgiveness. Even in such situation in vain I believed the power of love would bury hatred; however, there was no such charisma. I was shocked at the sinking piety of the bishops who were inflamed by inflated ego, revenge, and timidity than the spirit of reconciliation, love, and forgiveness.

By 12:30 noon, they asked me to leave the meeting while they conspired. I sat out, waited for hours, hoping I would be called back. There was no word from them. Then, I beheld, one of the retired bishops was coming out of the meeting with a mischievous smile. I was aware of his dislike for me, nurturing apparent bitterness, as he could not be elected as bishop before I was. I asked him what was going on. He ascended his upper jaw (maxilla) to holdback a mouthful of stuff, which he was relishing, perhaps *pan parag* (the mixture of tobacco and beetle nuts). Like most church leaders, I was not surprised and did not know if he realized he was enslaved to it. What a pathetic spiritual condition of the bishops of the church! He gleefully said, 'It takes time to prepare for crucifixion,' the bad taste in his mouth. I sensed it was a prelude and I was stunned and deeply hurt by his barbaric expression; the message was short and simple that they would cheer revenge and not abandon the conspiracy. It was irony; they persisted in their wrongdoings and yet the same time sat on the judgment seat to punish me for my prophetic voice. The entire episode was spiteful, the bishops unjustly acted, which was unexpected of them. I was frustrated and returned home, sat in my office, and sank in my chair with gloom on my face; no one was around me and visitors eluded me. The Priests of Vengeance were in a majority among the voting members of the Council of Bishops, thus they were ready to solemnize the ritual of revenge. I knew they could easily suspend me in travesty of truth. After I left the meeting, I heard Sampath Kumar did arm-twisting, threatened to resign if I was not suspended. In the past, by such tricks he often achieved his goals. I was grieved; he settled for nothing less than my suspension for not supporting his deviant ways and presuming that I was eyeing his honeycomb. They marginalized, oppressed, and sordidly treated me. Until then I could never imagine that the Friends of Convenience would act like the immortal Brutus. I was shattered; how come they forgot my support in the time of their crisis.

In the late evening, Nimrod Christian, then president of the Council of Bishops, though deserved disciplinary action for being found implicated on serious charges, got along with him S. S. Singh, who was addicted to silences, to my house. I was sitting in my office; he motioned him to serve the letter of suspension on me, while he watched. I accepted it; I wish I did it under protest. I was dismayed to read, they suspended me for six months to inquire whether I had gone to court of law directly or indirectly in the light of prepared affidavits and premeditated inquiry reports, in utter disregard to the constitutional right. Devoid of justice and absolute absurdity, they assumed extra jurisdictional power. They choked the right to hold different opinion than their own and seeking justice before the Judiciary of the land, which is the constitutional right, and some could not bear to see speedy church development work in the conferences under my charge. Not being mindful of the episcopal office they held, they indulged in massive conspiracy and gloated to victimize me. In malice and revenge, the hate sword spilled more blood than the love spirit could gather. I was agonized, for it was seen that the bishops did not practice what they preached: be angry, but do not sin, let not the sun go down over your anger; do not make friendship with those who are given to anger. It seemed the eloquent preaches forgot their call and refused to tread the path they showed to others. The Priests of Vengeance used disgruntled ones to cut me to size, who felt the heat of my decisions although in the best interests of the church that shook their narrow personal ambition. In colossal violation of the constitution of the church, they put the mask of their own picture of things to justify the ill-conceived, ill-intended, and illegal action of my suspension.

The news of my suspension spread like a wildfire; words are insufficient to describe the agony I have undergone. I wrote in my diary on May 6, 2004, the night seemed longer like an evening shadow, and I was sleepless throughout the night and flapped like a wounded bird, depressed by revengeful and unjust suspension. I felt my strength was descending like sinking sand; however, I mustered enough toughness to survive. I asked myself why God did not hear our prayers. Those who nurtured grudges merrily made stories and diffused, and others had no idea of the conspiracy, they were like *tabula rasa* – they readily absorbed it; it was intended to dent my credibility. Regardless, at dawn, I gathered enough courage to inform my well-wishers; one of them who held a key position in his church said, 'I fear none, but clergy.'

Not long after, Nimrod Christian called on me. I could perceive dislike in his eyes and uneasiness on his face. Outwardly, he gave the impression as if he cared for me; however in the recess of his mind, he contemplated to inflict me more. I did not pay any heed to his words, as he tried to justify his innocence and wash his hands from the conspiracy. As he was still talking, I felt like innocent Edmond Dantes, Alexandre Dumas' main character in his celebrated novel, *The Count of Monte Cristo*[4]. I asked myself, 'Was it not true in my case as well?' Every situation turned hostile and everyone took chance to take revenge on me. They conspired, either to take revenge or to survive in power by keeping me out of the bishopric. In my brokenness, I realized, it was my folly to believe the Friends of Convenience and hoped in vain to get justice in the church.

Stage-Managed Inquiry

On June 17–20, 2004, John Wesley's Tercentenary Celebration was held in Bangalore; my supporters convinced me that I should attend it, so I went uninvited. Joshua Samuel welcomed me at the entrance of the Lincoln hall, I was amused at his magnanimous gesture and insisted I sit on the podium along with other bishops. I could not figure out the reason for such changed attitude. Not long after I learnt he was agitated; despite throwing weight behind the conspiracy and assurances of his father's second coming in the episcopal chair, nothing happened. I was appalled by Karriappa Samuel's burning ambition and did not appreciate the ways in which he wanted to make over his image. I observed Nimrod Christian was bitter and resentful for being ignored. Sampath Kumar, Taranath Sagar, and John Hanchinmani were at the helm of the affair; however, John Hanchinmani stole the show. As I walked out of the hall, someone in the crowd said to me, look there, pointing towards Ebenezer Shivapur, one of the men who signed the prepared affidavit. There was perception that he was there to ensure Sampath Kumar and Taranath Sagar would keep their promises. As follow-up to the celebration, on June 25, 2004, Nimrod Christian organized a similar programme for the Delhi Episcopal Area in Ghaziabad. I could not believe I was invited, not so much out of velvet feelings but to send a strong message: if they treated him like nobody, he would change his side. I attended the function. Sampath Kumar and Taranath Sagar could not bear to see me; however, not long after, they merged their ways.

Then I learnt that the Priests of Vengeance were trying to appoint one or two advocates to conduct inquiry. They called D. V. Sitharam Murthy, an advocate from Hyderabad to Bangalore. Pradeep Samuel, who attended the meeting, informed me that the advocate expressed his inability to conduct the inquiry on terms of a letter of suspension. Sampath Kumar persuaded him to conduct inquiry and assured they would pay him any amount of fee he would ask. I do not know what conspired, but he finally agreed. He misguided them to prepare a chargesheet against me by absolute lack of understanding of the procedure given in the Bluebook. I recognized such step taken in criminal matters, after FIR and inquiry. He claimed he knew the Discipline pretty well; however, his acts did not justify his claim and led them astray. I heard he was an advocate of repute; perhaps he was. However, he was not so much acquainted with the Discipline. The bishops were all out to victimize me; in anxiety they accepted his advice in subversion of the Discipline, it was another procedural lapse and a step closer to the topple line. Suspending me without a written and signed complaint and abandoning the reconciliation process were other violations of the rule of law of the church.

I thought by my suspension Sampath Kumar would be mollified. No, he was barely sanguine over the scanty harvest of his animated mindset. As he foretold, he would take over the Bombay Conference within a couple of months after the General Conference 2003, proven he was by no means less oracular; right on the prediction, wrong on the timing. He was unhappy over the delay and in a hurry to inflict his wrath on those who resisted his despotic attitude. He was triumphant over politically grabbing my Bombay Area responsibilities, as it was envisaged, Sampath Kumar to the Bombay Conference and Nimrod Christian to Gujarat Conference. No sooner did they seize the Bombay Area jurisdictional power than they indulged in inferior acts. They were furious, tormented those whose prophetic voice was conflicting with their self-interest and undone what I painstakingly did. Unbelievably, Taranath Sagar admired their nerve and kept them charged to do the inconceivable and undesirable.

Until then, three inquiries were held, but none was just and fair, and by conspiracy, inquiry after inquiry was conducted to target me and varnish their normlessness. There was no ground for suspension and conspiring to oust me from bishopric was a highly oppressive act. Having realized that in the long run the ground for suspension would not stand the judicial scrutiny, they then attempted to cook up some serious allegations. They imagined, I must have soiled my hands in some inappropriate property deals and extorted secret money. Sampath Kumar was gloating to fling on me some irrefutable charges to legitimatize my suspension and subsequently built the case to oust me from the bishopric. In forensic ingenuity, he relentlessly run hither and thither with Pradeep Ahaley, a pastor of the Bombay Conference who was a close associate of Taranath Sagar, to sniff the financial and property handlings; however, his malicious adventure did not find the joy of his hallucination, so he acted like a savage person. Recognizing that I handled the matters with integrity, then with growling vengeance he concocted trivial allegations and exaggerated them to accuse me. He coerced pastors, craftily held forced confirmations, denied my rights, and wilfully defied Bombay High Court's order of August 2, 2006, to frame me for failing to perform duty, and to substantiate it, he himself complained to the Council of Bishops, balked to my reply and falsely alleged that I did not conduct confirmations. A confirmation is the religious ritual, baptized children affirm their faith in Christ and his redeeming grace thereby enable them to participate in the Holy Communion or Holy Sacrament. In the Holy Sacrament, Christians participate in eating bread and drinking wine, in the perpetual memory of Christ's passion, death, and resurrection, and consecrated bread and wine are symbols of Christ's body and blood. In contrast, the Roman Catholic Church believes Transubstantiation and Consubstantiation is associated with Martin Luther; however, modern Lutherans reject the claim. Anyway, in the Methodist church tradition, after the confirmation ritual, confirmed candidates are received into full membership. It was interesting that a full member in the church may get voting rights at an earlier age than a society bestows on them without being ready to discharge responsibilities. However, I could not get to the roots of Sampath Kumar's psyche, and Nimrod Christian did unbelievable things to inflict me and Taranath Sagar eulogized their aggressiveness and kept their passion burning like volcanic fire for the sake of ruling supreme in the church.

Pastors and I during Holy Communion Service at Bowen
Memorial Methodist Church, Mumbai, September 2001

Not long after, they conspired to script the false
chargesheet in gross violation of the Discipline. The
work was assigned to a vibrating scribe, Taranath
Sagar, to which they were to be judges. He was full of
cheers that he got the chance to prepare the vengeful
weapon to dislodge me and script his own destiny.
There was barely any doubt that in collusion with the
man who aggressively opposed me and in consultation
with the Hyderabad advocate, he politically cooked up
a spurious and malicious chargesheet. The Aggressive
Opponent ran hither and thither with uncontrolled
fury as if a storm cannot be calmed, fully focused
to remove a bottleneck like me for their vainglory.
Taranath Sagar was prejudiced, unfair, and personal,
and had gone far beyond the scope of inquiry as
stated in the letter of suspension and in intense spite
inked concocted allegations. As far I know, until then

Council of Bishops never framed a chargesheet against any of their colleague bishops or inquiry was never conducted on such flimsy allegations. However, settled trivial issues were picked up and the frivolous matters, which were more than three years old, were revisited, and they made a mountain out of it and slapped on me and forced me to face inquiry in contravention to the rule of limitation. With ulterior motive and by over anxiety, they skipped to ascertain whether such so-called allegations actually constituted as charges in accordance with the provision of the Discipline, and by the full vigour of their vengeful attitude and extra sense, for the first time, the framing of a chargesheet procedure was adopted in the history of the church. He picked up the so-called allegation of parallel worship from the Aggressive Opponent's complaint, which the Council of Bishops did not maintain (long after, the Aggressive Opponent changed his position and said, wherever a bishop is present in a worship is not parallel worship). However, there was a strong sense that Sampath Kumar, Taranath Sagar, and John Hanchinmani swayed him, and he filed the nonmaintainable complaint to heal the wound of their hurt ego. By recourse to framing of chargesheet, the bickering of his political clique, time-barred and settled issues were included in it by the full vigor of their inferior desire, ferocity, and outpouring of hatred, like what the Romans did to a king – the weapon was prepared, and the noose was ready to destroy me[5]. The allegations were mere excuse as said, I was not averse to their inclusive political ambition, but the root cause was of my refusal to say amen to their collective defiance of the Discipline. The Aggressive Opponent was passionate and obtrusive and kept inflaming hostility against me. I recognized there was more than one reason for him to do so. He misconstrued my good intention of making things right and it seemed his relatives' assignments were not to their expectation. And, perhaps he felt humiliated due to his defeat in election and displeasure over of my efforts to stop the auction of the Robinson Church property in Mumbai by Municipal Corporation in the matter of the recovery of pending property taxes and repair cess. He was bitter over the disciplinary action against the pastor who alienated the church's institution and funds, as he was his blind supporter. I felt, although he had genuine concern for the church, however, there was a strong perception that he was coercing his views and norms on everything and everyone. In the Regional Conference session 2003, I felt he exceeded his limits, and on the spur of the moment, I chided him; he was deeply hurt and I realized I erred. I could have avoided it; it did not strike me at that moment, for the human nature is intricate. As for the Priests of Vengeance, he was a big boon; they infuriated his hurt-complex against me, and although internally they did not relish him, but purported to harness the full potentiality of his hate expedition against me. I perceived that John Hanchinmani, too, was eager to use his scourging energy; he stirred him against me, for my voice was in conflict with his ambition to remain unchallenged. Ironically, he tried to soften his wrath against himself by calling him 'brother', as he was his critic as well, the way in which he handled the church funds. Out of the deflated social holiness of life, the Council of Bishops maliciously entertained the ill-conceived and absurd chargesheet in the outright gross violation of the Discipline, the denial of the fundamental constitutional right.

The bishops derided at the church's interests, brushed aside my vows to uphold the Discipline and my obligation to honour the church Judiciary. Barely was there genuine concern or any scant respect for the Discipline; in a ding-dong manner, the General Conference 2003 was held to continue in bishopric and elect episcopal aspirants who were in their own likeness. As said, never before had the Council of Bishops framed a chargesheet against their colleague or adopted procedure contrary to the Discipline and circumvented a show-cause notice procedure; it was the demise of natural justice, and enlarging the scope of the paid inquiry was a vengeful act. The right to hold individual views and going to the court of law could not be shackled, and the outrageous act of pious men was anything but eclipse of holiness of life.

Taranath Sagar was vibrant like a live wire; in malice he signed the chargesheet dated September 17, 2004, containing fabricated and trivial charges and smilingly sent it to me without any supporting document. I protested against the process, as it was neither supported by the Discipline nor by any precedence. The inquiry episode was anything but conspiracy. I was perplexed at their vengeful attitude and audacity to indulge in such political despotism, and conducting inquiry on the chargesheet as advised by the Hyderabad advocate was conspiracy as it did not fit the facts. As said, there was no written and signed complaint; elucidating charges against me by a member or members of the church in good standing, addressed to a competent person as per rule, in case of a bishop, the president of the Council of Bishops. In my case, the Discipline and holiness of life were not their guiding star. They shirked the church's procedure and led me to appear before an outsider with vicious intention. Nimrod Christian praised him; I became curious and cautious. He said he studied in a Christian institution and was persuasive in convincing me to go before him. He said he knew him well and was a good man who knew the Discipline, as he represented the church in legal cases in Hyderabad. I said this was all the more reason why he would favour the bishops, as first he misled them to frame the chargesheet, which itself was the clear evidence that he was not conversant with the Discipline; however, Nimrod Christian could no longer hold back his scheming little mind. He said, 'If you spend money, everything will be fine.' He assured me that one of the college staff whose name he mentioned was B. Vasanth Rao would handle him. I was uneasy at his uncanny gesture, as he could not be trusted. I was not sure if he was trying to get the cue to my honesty like Delilah to Samson's strength or involve me in the serious charge of graft or trying to extort money or do both. I was conscious, suspicious, and depressed. I brooded over it, I said to myself, I was struggling for a fair inquiry and justice, however, I would not get it and they would eventually succeed in appointing their own person, the inquiry would be farcical, for they would go to any extent to manipulate it. I mustered enough strength; I said to myself, I must not fall in his trap though they would still win by the force of influence. I was firm, I ignored the notice sent by the advocate and did not attend the inquiry at the place called Central

Court Hotel, Hyderabad. As said, his claim of knowing the Discipline was unbelievable and especially after he led astray the bishops from the church' rules of disciplinary procedure and overlooked the fact that the church was his client. It raised doubt about his integrity and impartiality. I was not sure if he was one of those few persons who would stand for the truth at the cost of losing his client – it was doubtful. What was more disturbing in his letter he cited the name of the person whom Nimrod Christian mentioned and who seemed to be a confidant of John Hanchinmani, too, and it made me even more suspicious and restless. Eventually, he withdrew from conducting the inquiry on my protest and under the pretext of the court case.

I had to face another inquiry ordered by the Gujarat High Court, Ahmedabad[6]. I was not a contesting and active party to the court case. However, at the near end of the case, incomprehensible circumstances misled me and I reluctantly signed an authorization letter for an advocate whom I never knew, met, or gave briefing to. Anyway, as per compromised order, I was to choose one out of five persons; it was as good as they appointing an inquiry officer. The bishops decided five names in my absence, overruling my protest. Thus, I had no option but to pick one of their persons. I felt it was like a last wish of a condemned prisoner – making him choose the mode of annihilation. I was bewildered to read the names. R. K. Michael, the former director of Ingraham Institute, Ghaziabad. He was bitter, as I did not give him extension after he reached superannuation. Monohar David was under Sampath Kumar's appointment and was a stranger to me. Joseph Massey, the co-complainant with the

Aggressive Opponent, wrestled to coerce members of the inquiry committee on the Civil Line property at Nagpur to sign his self-prepared malicious inquiry report; however, they snubbed him. The other two were Pradeep Ahaley, an avowed opponent and a subordinate under my appointment, and Anjana Masih, an advocate, whose legal services were used by the Delhi Regional Conference under Nimrod Christian. It was a ploy, devoid of fairness and justice. I wanted to challenge the calculative, pick and choose names, but I was told I had to do so in the court of law. I avoided it as I was already blamed for going to court, directly or indirectly. I was left with no option than to fall in line and choose one of them. Long after, I realized it was like suicidal; I should have challenged it in the court of law in Mumbai, as the bishops were ceaselessly conspiring.

In good faith, I chose Anjana Masih and believed that at least she would be fair enough. In the beginning, she seemed neutral; however, as the time passed by, she acted like she was programmed. I was put on trial, as the court of law does, although inquiry was to be conducted within the scope of the letter of suspension and the meaning of the court order that did not suggest prosecuting me on the chargesheet. In fact, the court order was on the appeal against the order of the notice of motion of the City Civil Court, Ahmedabad, in which my suspension and conducting inquiry for going to court of law were challenged. The departure from it was illegal, but it seemed Taranath Sagar's chargesheet mesmerized her or she lacked legal acumen to decipher discernible difference between an inquiry and a trial like spotting sheep from goats, or perhaps, she was confused or deliberate. Instead of conducting the inquiry, they held a trial that begins after inquiry by court and played magisterial role and applied rules of the code of civil procedure, convenient to their intent. As I was not familiar with the process of trial and the provision of law, I could not soon figure out that I was actually on trial and I suffered endless miseries. In the air of importance, the inquiry turned trial was conducted with bias, lapses, anomalies, and inconsistencies. Crucial aspects were flouted, and it was a one-sided affair. Curiously, she took from me hundreds of pages of meaty evidence, documents pulling curtain from the conspiracy, only to treat them like trash, and in flagrant denial of justice, the questions of law raised by me were shelved. The moot questions of whether the frivolous allegations constituted as charges and whether bishops were competent to frame a chargesheet against their colleague in accordance with the Discipline were, in malice, brushed aside. A half-baked trial was a melodrama in the name of inquiry, and it was farcical and stage managed, vital issues were not dealt with, and it was merely recordings of evidences of the venal men of the Priests of Vengeance, there being no other evidence on record than the prepared ones. Curiously, the afterthoughts of their witnesses swayed her, and what my witnesses said did not matter to her. George Edward was made to depose; I saw him for the first time, he seemed in his mid-fifties, tall, stout, dark complexion, trimmed beard with some grey heirs, and wore bulky golden necklace, bracelet, and his fingers decorated with rings studded with auspicious stones. He spoke too fast some incomprehensible words, and his witness evidence was to be taken on record only after the production of his original affidavit; it was never produced and yet she unfairly relied on it. Stanley Downes deposed, explained the church's rules like a martinet. I remember, he scornfully abused his office and inducted a local elder into a non-Methodist church in blatant violation of the Discipline. There was petition against him before the Judicial Council on the matter; however, he tricked to counter the charge, so it was referred to the Council of Bishops to decide, which was until then pending[7]. And not long before, by abusing his position as the general secretary and in collusion with M. A. Daniel and select members of Oldham Methodist Church, Pune secretly facilitated to change the scheme of the Trust and bring the church property on its schedule. Then as residing and presiding bishop, I tried to set things right; however, they did not cease to fume. Anyway, at the end, he trembled and, in satire, said, 'I do not like to comment on my colleague bishop.' I thought she knew that sarcasm had no room in legal sanctity, but it pleased her to treat his babble utterances as evidence than the law of evidence could justify. In excess and abuse of power, venal and unbelievable witnesses were entertained. When I did not choose Pradeep Ahaley, he schemed to thrust himself into the inquiry, first he chose to depose, and then withdrew to assist the bishops' presenting officer. I objected, but she roared like a judge, 'The objection not sustained!' Then it was evident, she was won over. He became the co-inquirer and dominated the scene; the presenting officer felt relieved as she was soft and obliging. I was perplexed, every time she sought his nod before proceedings further, it conjured injustice and there was no need to have ingenuity like that of Solomon to understand it. I observed that she was in the ambit of the influence of the Priests of Vengeance and a mere tool in the conspiracy and the inquiry turned trial was mere farcical in the absence of just and fair handlings. Then I realized a priori findings to hold me guilty were in store. I contemplated to withdraw and challenge it in the court of law; however, again, I restrained, as then I did not think that it was wise to get entangled in a legal recourse, not realizing I was already being trapped in it and giving up to it to be swallowed by it.

As said, they buried the original issue of going to court of law, and in bitterness, the Priests of Vengeance's hired witnesses deposed to prove their amplified and wild allegations, and my protest voice was strangled. At her insistence, Taranath Sagar tried to support the chargesheet with photocopies of prepared affidavits, time-barred unreliable and unrelated letters and papers, and she embraced his concocted and frivolous stuff, ignoring rule for what is and is not admissible in fair inquiry turned trial. There was not even a single certified or true copy, and by injudicious imprudence, she did not ask them to produce original documents for inspection. I found Anjana Masih was not even conversant with the Discipline, precedence, practices, and was happily swayed by the wind of the conspiracy. Having held me no guilty on the count of giving money for court cases, it was absurd to hold me guilty on the count of instigating members of the church from Sampath Kumar's episcopal jurisdiction going to Judiciary of the land to make bishops abide by the Judicial Council Decisions. I was appalled by the travesty of justice; she dared to ignore the constitutional right, Calcutta High Court's order, and the action of the church's Executive body[8]. I struggled to make the Priest of Vengeance depose; however, no cognizance was given despite my repeated pleas. I felt, in all fairness, she could have called them to depose as they alleged, made complaint, and were deeply involved; the entire conspiracy could have been unveiled, segregating fact from fiction. However, it did not happen; the prejudicious report of the unfair trial was labelled as inquiry report and, in premeditated grandeur, held me guilty on several counts, as the court does and without deciding what rules of the Discipline I violated. Until then, I never heard of such shoddy way of handling an inquiry in the church. I understand that in an inquiry, investigation into charges is done, but not trial as court does. I was voicing that they would manage inquiry, and the same thing happened; it was like a self-fulfilling prophecy.

On December 20, 2005, the Council of Bishops' meeting was held in Mumbai. I expressed my concern over my being isolated and targeted while serious complaints against other bishops were kept dormant. Barely influenced by John Locke' philosophy of equality or Thomas Jefferson's advocacy for equality, in disguise they chronologically listed complaints against bishops, but in malice, prepared complaints against me were listed first to scorch me; it was like the last was first, and the first was last, whereas complaints against them lay buried. Curiously, Sampath Kumar and Nimrod Christian were absent. Taranath Sagar presided over the meeting. He found himself helpless in their absence. The reaction to the principal of parity was outrageous; they met in a secret conclave in Bangalore to decide their future course of action against me. Perhaps Taranath Sagar scared them with imminent peril and painted the grim picture of their hope and aspiration, while in his heart gloated to thrush on them the retire status and schemingly pushed them into the capsule of his hallow sympathy to get their support first, and then to oust me from bishopric. There was a rule in the church, if the 65th birthday of a bishop falls in between the General Conference Sessions, then a bishop continues as active until the end of quadrennium and retires in the next Regular Session of the General Conference. Sampath Kumar and Nimrod Christian were anxious to exploit the rule, especially the latter one by skipping retirement in the Regular General Conference 2007. Therefore, it was inevitable for them to stand by Taranath Sagar to achieve their goal, and vice versa, he, too, needed their support to rule supreme. They were craving for each other's support to sail smoothly in the political rocking boat, thus they were glued politically with each other to overcome the challenges of losing power. I observed Taranath Sagar was politically shrewd, playing tricks with them from the beginning; first he won the confidence of Sampath Kumar, and then together they induced the power-ambitious Nimrod Christian. He enticed them into his political trap; it was too tempting not to escape, so they thrived to collaborate and reciprocate in mutually inclusive interests and unrelentingly conspired to oust me. Then they were scheming to call a special session of General Conference to elect a bishop in my place and delay the Regular Session of the General Conference to escape retirement and continue in active status. Some bishops insensibly believed Taranath

Sagar and nourished his plan against me. He had the knack of politically influencing people, at least I knew two influential women in the church who ardently supported him in his episcopal election and one of them took active part in the conspiracy.

The Priests of Vengeance spearheaded to call requisition meeting of the Executive Council, signed the requisition letter on February 10, 2006, for considering the recommendation of the Council of Bishops and calling of the General Conference, but until then, neither such recommendation was passed, nor was there any urgency to fix dates for the General Conference. The signature drive was launched in early January 2006, immediately after their secret conclave and at the time, the inquiry report was neither signed nor circulated; it was signed on February 14, 2006. On March 10, 2006, S. S. Singh, the then president of the Council of Bishops, dispatched the copies of the inquiry-turned-trial report to the bishops after much pressure from the Priests of Vengeance. He vouched, the inquiry report was in his possession in the original sealed cover; however, it seemed they knew its content. Thus, if the bishop can be believed, then there was no way to know its content unless Anjana Masih herself disclosed or, in collusion with them, scripted it; the sequences of events are boldly unambiguous. It showed the finesses of the conspiracy, it was premeditated and an irrefutable evidence of their malicious adventure, so they were as sure as dawn after sunset.

On March 29, 2006, a special meeting of the Executive Council was called in Mumbai by cancelling the scheduled meeting of the management committee of the Executive Board. There was no doubt about

Anjana Masih's role in the conspiracy, the Performer was in contact with her and Nimrod Christian deputed pastors under his charge to influence and pressurize her to go against me. They even claimed themselves as church and abused authority; it was blasphemous! Then I could never imagine she would act in such poor integrity. I curiously watched her when she used to come to Mumbai, socializing freely with my opponents by falling short on neutrality and inquiry standard. I observed John Hanchinmani was tactfully influencing her and the witnesses and perhaps imagining my absence in the church's meetings. He was personally concerned about her comforts, air ticket, and incidental expenses; it was strange, incompatible with his nature. There was a perception that he was frugal to others, generous to himself. One of the members of the Executive body asked for the information on court expenses, but he never provided them. However, I could get some insight into the colossal legal expenses from the financial report for the year 2008–2009. In negative balance, ₹ 1,07,96,601/- was spent; it was recurring expenses. The church properties were sold to grease the church's administrative machinery and one-tenth of sale proceeds like tithe were exclusively set aside for legal expenses.

No sooner Anjana Masih held me guilty than she was held in sycophancy and effuse praise from obscurity in the church. On May 4, 2007, I was dazzled to see her with the Priest of Vengeance's men in the courtroom of C. K. Thakkar, a judge of the Supreme Court of India, it was like unwrapping the shroud of the myth of her neutrality, it left no room for a benefit of doubt. She looked at me and gave an artful smile, perhaps with a sense of guilt and my suspicion of her being in collusion with my conspirators surfaced, for the falsehood could not yoke the truth too long. It was startling, no further proof was needed and I was agonized over her pitiable integrity. In February 2010, during my conversation with Nimrod Christian, I asked him about her presence in the court, he spontaneously said, Taranath Sagar asked her to remain present in the court; it was inconceivable that he was not a party to it. What else to be said, collaborating to oust me in the farce inquiry turned trial was not enough, she came in open to oppose me. I could never think she would overtly lose her self-respect, not even in my wildest imagination, and taking sides, holding me guilty, and her unjustifiable acts and deeds exposed her pretension of neutrality. And I wondered if she cared a little for the value of honesty and integrity; however, I perceived, it was conspicuously untraceable. Actually, the inquiry turned trial was paid and stage managed with her support. I learnt that even their presenting officer said to one of my well-wishers, it was a bogus and there was nothing against Bishop Agarwal; it endorsed my stand that truth and justice were shackled by the power-obsessive ones. I was aware that no justice would be done to me in the manner in which things were unfairly handled, and I perceived she chose to betray truth than to lose her pious client, inasmuch a generous paymaster. Truth and justice were of no concern as they premeditated massive conspiracy with concerted efforts.

As said, the Friends of Convenience schemed to continue as active bishops; however, in the nick of the time, they were ruthlessly ditched and I was not surprised for making them face the situation like Columbus' experience. It came to light that John Hanchinmani and his political close-knit were resolute to retire them, sickle their ambition to continuing as active bishops, and assured delegates at the seat of the General Conference Session 2007 in Kolkata that he would stripe them off their active status at first available opportunity, so he stirred delegates and once again proved, what he said, he meant it. It was a pity; never had they realized their cherished power ambition was like an unsustainable human pyramid. Then, Sampath Kumar ran in utter bewilderment and, perhaps with a feeling of homelessness, looked out for the spokesman, and when he spotted him, he confronted and reminded him of their covenant; however, he whisked away. Taranath Sagar, John Hanchinmani, and the spokesman were in the secret covenant with Sampath Kumar and swore by his reactivation; what went wrong was his insistence on his never-let-go obsession with the Bangalore Area, which they stoutly balked, so he yelled at them. People were not agog, for they knew that they would meet their destiny in that way; however, they never imagined or dreamt that they would be treated like this after they ousted me. It was catastrophic; they could not survive in the power! I felt it was the reward for their treachery and unshakable faith in the unreliable loyalty and unchecked credibility of Taranath Sagar. Not long after, they were penitent for their historical blunder and excessive reliance on his episcopal elevation; it was anything but overvaluing their political alliance, not realizing the magnitude and force of his political shrewdness. They reclined in retired status and were living in the perpetual fear of the reopening of their pending charges and inquiry reports if they crossed their limit.

Judiciary's Remiss

When I received a copy of the inquiry report from Anjana Masih, as it was titled, in solitude, I sat in my office. In anxiety, I browsed through the pages and then carefully read it. I was stunned and shocked by the lavish findings of my guilt, and randomly turned pages over and again. I had no words to express and no one to turn to, I said to myself, what I heard came true; it was not just the grapevine. The Priests of Vengeance succeeded, they were sanguine in what they did thus far and confident henceforth. I could think nothing better than to challenge it before the church's Judiciary. On March 10, 2006, the petition challenging the inquiry report was sent to the Judicial Council. I hoped, in fairness and in the interest of justice, the church Judiciary would stay the report; however, it did not happen as the church Judiciary seemed reluctant to act on it, the wounds of the clash between the church Judiciary and the Executive body were still raw. The Judiciary, in routine manner, asked the Council of Bishops to reply, which they overlooked, and contrary to my expectation, the Judiciary was remiss in dealing with my petition and shown indifference to adjudicate the serious issue that affected the church. There was barely doubt that the Collusive Clique influenced the juries employed in the church and warned those who lived in the church-owned houses with vacating if they did not oppose my petition. The church Judiciary knew the conspiracy; however, they lacked courage to speak out like in the past. I felt the juries acted like defeated justice warriors; they were demoralized, functionally crippled, and keen to avoid yet another fiasco.

I challenged the inquiry report before the church Judiciary, as insiders had in-depth understanding of the Discipline, convention, and precedence and would get speedy justice. Then I did not know that the wait would be unending and justice would be elusive. In the interest of natural justice, I expected swift decision, but it was my wishful thinking and wasteful wait, just to receive the evasive reply after long under the pretext of sub-judice. The bishops were impervious to the truth and rose to destroy me. By looking at the Judiciary's laxness, I realized it was barely independent and free from pressures and interferences to deliver flawless justice. However, if at all, it did, the Collusive Clique would make it noncognizable and ineffectual by some lame excuse if their Decision would not suit their political scheme as they did to Decisions 575 and 576. I was shocked, on September 28, 2006, they repeated their past performance in the excess of their power and Decisions 584 and 587 were made ineffectual in their endeavour to deprive me and conceal the constitutional right of every Indian citizen to knock the doors of the court of law. In disgrace, they consigned the Decisions to dustbin; however, perhaps being short on memory, they published the Decision No. 558, nullifying their own impious intention in God's eternal sovereignty[9]. In anxiety to hide the conspiracy to oust me, bishops submitted a copy of the inquiry report along with their response to prejudice the court and show to the church Judiciary that my petition before it was sub-judice. They prevailed on their men in the church Judiciary, not to adjudicate my petition under the pretext of sub-judice matter, although the court order of June 30, 2006, clearly said that the church Judiciary would deal with the inquiry report. The bishops defied the church's laws when it hurt their political ambition, and on contrary, expected others to obey rules. They played divisive politics through their men in the church Judiciary to obstruct justice, stirred some unjust juries to declare my petition sub-judice by the use of rules. They maneuvered all things to deny justice when it was not convenient to them, and when it was, in malice, they chose to enforce rules. I perceived no impediment to deciding my petition and in fact, the Judiciary of land prefers the settlement of disputes in one's organizational arbitrary body. Had not the bishops became obstacles to justice, the church's precious time and money as well as mine could have been saved. It was melancholic; the 'sub-judice' trick was unjustly used to deny justice and some matters were deliberately said to be sub-judice. I recognize that the purpose of sub-judice rule is to avoid dealing with any proceeding, which might be prejudicial to a case awaiting or undergoing a trial[10]. In my case, it was not the case; the inquiry report was not challenged before the Judiciary of land and it was not even part of the trial proceedings, but the Priests of Vengeance instigated their men in the church Judiciary to declare it sub-judice to deny me justice. Pradeep Samuel, the then general secretary of the church, was called out of the procedure and under pressure to give information on court cases during its meeting held on December 14,

2006, in Mumbai. The secretary of the church Judiciary absconded until the information was placed on the table. I was shocked by his insipid move, for I knew him as a person of integrity. He seemed yielded to pressure, threats, and perhaps a warning message of losing the covetous position that he held. Only after the information was received, he descended in the meeting, and I was denied opportunity to present my side. The Priests of Vengeance's supporters in the Judiciary did not budge until my petition was declared sub-judice.

I observed the juries under the bishop's appointment, and most of them tended to lose freedom and there was perception that some were lured by money in the guise of the travel claim, and the rest wrestled to deliver justice. One of the juries informed me that he noticed hefty envelops on juries' bedside tables. I could believe him, for such practices were common in the church and this was how members of various church bodies were influenced; it was anything but a decent means of graft. At the end, those who were committed to adjudicate my petition gave up in frustration after strenuous struggle. It was an irony that the bishops expected people not to go to the court of law to seek justice and at the same time interfered and obstructed justice in the church as well. The bishops whose stakes were high indulged in such kind of inferior activities and barred some members of various bodies of the church, the rest were either under their influence or pressure or prone to graft or acted as spokesperson. The poor conduct of the bishops seldom inspired or gave any hope to the church members to approach the church Judiciary for justice. Of course, it is a good system of arbitration; however, it was made a lame duck by constant interference and infringement, and influential church leaders and some corrupt juries tarnished the image of the institution of justice.

There was barely doubt that the Priests of Vengeance stirred some members of the church Judiciary to render my petition sub-judice to cover up the conspiracy and deny me justice. They glorified their voting power, and as said, they were in majority among voting members of the Council of Bishops, resolute and aggressive in achieving their end goal to oust me. They did not care whether they had such power nor was there any valid ground, but for imagined fear, they felt if I was left unhooked, then Taranath Sagar would face an unsecured future and their buried complaints, serious charges, and inquiry reports would resurrect. In 2004, not long after my suspension, I spoke to Taranath Sagar on telephone; I ventured to sponge his psychophobia, but he said, 'How can I believe you?' He sounded like a cynic; I abandoned my efforts. They sprang in the fullness of vengeful attitude, made concerted efforts to oust me, and lay to rest their future uncertainty by putting the unjustified seal of the Council of Bishops and the Executive Council on it. They thought, if it was not done by March 30, 2006, then the Gujarat High Court's restrictions on me would hold no good and they would find it tough to achieve their inclusive narrow ambition. Thus, under the guise of keeping the deadline, they misled and pressurized the Executive Council members, as if the deadline to take disciplinary action was set by the court.

Judges to Own Cause

On March 25, 2006, an emergency meeting of the Council of Bishops was called in Mumbai to act on the inquiry-turned-trial report. I protested the participation of the bishops, who were the complainant, inquirers and witnesses in discussion and decision on the report, but M. Elia Peter in silent conspiracy turned down my concern for natural justice by saying, 'We will decide it.' Then I placed in writing the need to examine Anjana Masih's the biased inquiry- turned- trial- report and picked up holes in it; however, by conspiracy and seared conscience, they throttled my voice and damned me by saying, 'I was speaking against Anjana Masih,' the messiah of the conspiring souls, trying the left hand not knowing what the right hand did. They were stirred, closed their mind to truth and justice, and by conspiracy, everything was concocted from start to finish. I failed to arouse their seared conscience. I said the report was challenged before the church Judiciary, S. R. Thomas confirmed it from the secretary of the Judiciary by calling him; however, in strife and fury, they denied justice and proceeded to destroy me. The scornful wave swamped their conscience; their hearts were hardened and persistently pretended to be pious men of God, as if they were infallible.

There was no hope for justice, revenge was the norm, and the process was awfully violated. There was no sign of conversion, but yoked under the velocity of hatred, as said, the bishops framed me even on flimsy issues without power and named five persons of their choice and one of them was even the co-complainant, and the rest were prejudiced. Some scornful pastors and venal laypersons were deposed. Stanley Downes deposed callously and participated in the deliberation on the report and endorsed the recommendation of my termination. Taranath Sagar, paired with Karriappa Samuel, maliciously conducted inquiry. The Priests of Vengeance paralyzed truth and justice. In the gross violation of natural justice, they were complainant and inquirer or witness, like judges to their own cause, and adopted arbitrary procedure, used inferior means, suppressed truth, and buried justice. I felt the Council of Bishops was like a treasure chest of white ants, feasting on cherished values of the church, which became a potential threat to civil liberty guaranteed by the Indian Constitution. Retired bishops having no voting right stirred to rattle and be raucous. I thought if the fire of charity purified their hearts, they could have held on to the truth; but no, they were thrilled to be part of the celebration of treachery and conspiracy. Some bishops felt sanguine to take a chance to settle their embalmed grudges, and others acted out of selfishness in utter disregard to justice. Nimrod Christian was tricky; he said, although I was not found guilty on all counts, on majority of counts I was. He was desperate to get extra years to his active tenure, so he was somehow trying to fix me by quantifying logic. The rest of the bishops were uncannily deathly still and silent like the brooding Pyramid of Giza. I perceived the bishops in pulpit acted, as if baptized by the fire; nay, they were anything but the inferno of negative energy and their despotic side of persona shone like epiphanic dazzle. They humiliated, mentally tormented, and asked me to leave the meeting, usual tactics while they celebrated conspiracy, sacrificing saintliness and sanity. I struggled to make my voice heard before I left, but it was a useless venture like chasing wind or conquering gravitational force. Not long after I left, I learnt that Taranath Sagar vibrated and mimicked Sampath Kumar's resignation trick, unsupported by any syllogism or rationalism or metaphysics.

Out of conspiracy, the bishops treated the inquiry-turned-trial report like the gospel truth, and without issuing show-cause notice and by the loss of savoir-faire, eulogized the Priests of Vengeance. Out of retaliation and malice, behind my back, Sampath Kumar moved and Nimrod Christian seconded the resolution recommending my termination, an episcopal colleague of their equal rank and one of the six active bishops in the excess of their power and not commensurate to so-called proven charges. By tyranny, they charged me for exaggerated trivial and spurious allegations, while varnishing their own mountain-size serious charges and unlawful deeds. I was shattered, sank in the thought of the church's junk justice balance and power politics. They oppressed and victimized me for doing what the church expected me to do. Obviously, it was an unfair and absurd justice system, in which three bishops could conspire and decide the destiny of their episcopal colleague of their own rank, elected to the bishopric by two-thirds of the votes of the General Conference delegates present and voting.

Victor Raja and S. S. Singh came to call me, asked me to come over to the Methodist Centre. I went and sat down with them. I was puzzled; they were persuading me to take voluntary retirement. One of them was a newly elected bishop, an introvert and reclusive personality, who until then posed as my loyalist, if not whole-heartedly, at least pretended to be so, and the other one was the one whom I tried to rescue from the political paws of the Friends of Convenience. I asked them why they were playing in the hands of the Priests of Vengeance. Then, they called me back to the meeting. Nimrod Christian was rhetoric; he said, on humanitarian ground, voluntary retirement could be considered. I was stunned at his malicious move, aspiring to be like Francesco Petrarca. They intimidated and used pressure tactics to force me to opt for voluntary retirement, so that he could continue as active bishop beyond his term and put the lid on the conspiracy. I said it was a crucial decision, I need time and I asked them to give in writing, but they refused. Then I wrote myself what they said about voluntary retirement and vainly waited for reply. The letter was intended to show that they intimidated me to take voluntary retirement, it was no way my reply to show cause as to why disciplinary action should not be taken on the inquiry-turned-trial report; however, they used it against me to mislead the Judiciary of the land. I thought I was clever, only to realize I did a stupid thing by unnecessarily writing and miserably failed to imagine that it could be used against me like a weapon, and for long time, I did hell of explaining to bring heat out of it. At no point of time, either before the disciplinary action or after the inquiry-turned-trial report, the show-cause notice was served on me. In malice, they used the letter against me to cover the serious procedural lapse and denied me natural justice. There was strong perception that misleading the court of law, an unrighteous disorder was the life style of some bishops; however, I was firm and refused to yield to their iniquitous desire despite mounting pressure. I stood firm, for I was on the right side, and pressurizing me to take voluntary retirement was making it involuntary, while I struggled for justice. I believed if anyone had to take voluntary retirement the then bishops who infringed the Discipline and found guilty on serious charges were the ones who should do so, for they profaned the holiness of life. I recognize that in the world, the righteous suffer and struggle and evil ones thrive; however, I was perplexed to experience that the church was barely an exclusive stock. They stirred their own kind to oust me from bishopric to hang on to power, and those who fought the court cases were, in one way or another, rewarded, while they victimized me for their glory that sponged the social holiness. Sampath Kumar's obstinate attitude and recklessly flouting the Discipline forced people to go to the court of law, for which he was applauded in great honour and praise, while the truth was crucified and barbaric justice was becoming the norm.

To propitiate the power avarice of bishops, their political kith supported them to victimize me. None of them had prophetic courage to warn them of the danger of effacing the idea of truth and justice in the church. Until then, I never heard of such unbelievable injustice in the church. I suffered and struggled, for they believed my prophetic voice was hindrance to achieving their inclusive narrow ambition. There was awareness in the church that most bishops were found guilty in one way or another on some serious charges of either finance or property matters but they were covered, escaped disciplinary action by political compromises. Seemingly, the leaven of the bishops was briskier than those of the Pharisees and the scribes, whom the Lord Jesus Christ asked to, throw the first stone if they were sinless. They, being alive to the voice of their conscience, threw no stone against the woman caught in adultery and left one by one. In contrast, the bishops of the church threw vengeful stones on me, all they could pick, while they carried a load of their inferior deeds and inquiry reports in their baggage that found them guilty. Not perplexed by it, they obsessed to find the speck of sawdust in my eye, not the plank in their own eye, as though they suffered with Lowell's syndrome. I could have stepped down from the bishopric if I was on the wrong side, but I was not. As the victim of conspiracy, I struggled against the fountain of lies, oppression, and collective offensive of the bishops of the church until God gave me strength.

On March 27, 2006, Nimrod Christian agreed to meet me in Delhi. I knew he was enigmatic; however, I still wanted to meet him, so I could convince him to abandon his chosen path. He came to receive me at the airport, did not come by his chauffeur driven car, and no happiness radiated from his face. I felt he was trying to keep our meeting out of public eye like the one Nicodemus did. I raised the issue of show-cause notice with him, he conceded the procedural lapses. He said, he suggested to the bishops to seek first my response on the inquiry report and if the response was unsatisfactory, and then serve 'show-cause notice'; however, he said Sampath Kumar and Taranath Sagar were unmoved. As we were on our way to the Vansant Continental Hotel, Vasant Vihar, he was frequently calling the Performer. He even asked me to contact the Aggressive Opponent to mend differences with him and said I could even mention his name that gave me the idea that they used him like a weapon against me, and now in turn, he was forcing them to oust me. I could imagine to some extent the depth and width of their conspiracy. I spent the day with him and I felt he was skilfully displaying his contrast persona like Jekyll and Hyde. I figured out from his talk that he was one with Sampath Kumar and Taranath Sagar, predetermined to oust me, as they assured him of his continuation as active bishop for another four years. I also got the impression that had he a chance, even he would go after Sampath Kumar, for he was voicing bitterness and sporadically expressed his desire to do so throughout the time I spent with him. The more I came to know the finesse of the conspiracy, I became breathless, completely exhausted, and frustrated in my struggle for truth and justice in the church, and melancholy returned to Mumbai by evening flight.

After the Delhi trip, I was strained and despondent, and the doctor advised hospitalization for observation. On March 28, 2006, I was admitted in Saifee Hospital, Charni Road, Mumbai. The next day, the Executive Council meeting was held in Mumbai under the chairmanship of active bishops. I could not attend and no notice was served on me to remain present to face subsequent disciplinary action. In routine manner, I sent Rayhal and Virtu with leave application and a doctor's certificate to S. S. Singh, the then president of the Council of Bishops, but Taranath Sagar dissuaded him not to acknowledge and sign. Then I realized, regardless if I was present or not, it would hardly matter; they would ask me to leave the meeting, as usual tactics under the pretext of free discussion and intimidate subordinates to go against me. However, when my leave application came up, the spokesman contended, it was not before the Executive Council, and the Council of Bishops was the one to decide on leave of bishop. Active bishops with right to vote were the co-chairmen of the Executive Council, and in malice, they chaired in rotation. Unbelievably, they were unfair, unjust, and anxious to celebrate their conspiracy. They neither placed the inquiry-turned-trial report on table nor allowed any discussion, and in my absence, they coerced members to approve their own draconian recommendation of my termination, presided and voted by them to strife me off from bishopric like blood law and without any force of authority and after I served the church sacrificially for decades. They were aware of the provision in the Discipline that the Executive Council, a subordinate body of the General Conference, devoid of power to either elect, appoint, or take disciplinary action as competent authority against a bishop. Such power were vested with the General Conference, in conformity with the law of the land that the appointing authority can only take action against an employee, but in strife, the Collusive Clique acted like brutal tyrants and did even what the General Conference could not do. I recognized the Executive Council was less democratic and more oligarchic. As per rule, even the General Conference had no power to remove a bishop; at the most, it could give him a premature retirement, if it was deem it necessary[11]. The Discipline restricted, not to revoke articles of religion, privileges of ministers, episcopal administration, trial and appeal and general rules. Concisely, they treated me as an obstacle to relishing temporal power; however,

I could not betray my conscience to join the Collusive Clique, defying the Bluebook, so I balked with their unacceptable ways, which they chalked out to achieve their cherished ambition. Having realized the gross violation of the Discipline and natural justice, and to camouflage it, as after-thought, they prepared their men to move amendment petitions, and long after, the Executive Council itself did so to incorporate provision in the Discipline to terminate a bishop – General Conference to terminate a bishop and, in between its session, the Executive Council. They could not succeed in fulfilling the requirements necessary to carry out amendment, so it was lost and until then the status quo was maintained.

Nimrod Christian, in the guise of a well-wisher, during the meeting, made last-minute frantic efforts to break the deadlock on my voluntary retirement and pretended to rescue me from the termination furnace. He was neither sympathetic nor sincere, but hilarious, swayed by the wind of his insatiable passion to survive in power. Vasant Raiborde, a common person between Nimrod Christian and me, said Nimrod Christian pressurized him to come to the hospital. I learnt he stood at the reception counter with a great hope of meeting me; however, access was denied and he returned with despair. Then, in desperateness, he telephoned to Sharon and chanted voluntary retirement; after hearing him patiently, she said, 'You three were together and Dinesh helped you both in the time of your crises, now what is going on?' On hearing her, he was shattered, became furious, and recharged his vengeful sting to act in the bitterness of his heart. Then he strived to call a special session of the General Conference to fill the vacancy in my place and evade his retirement, but he was unsuccessful. Sampath Kumar and Taranath Sagar deciphered his sensitive ambitious nerve and enthused him to harness the full potential of his fertile destructive intent for their own game plan.

On April 3, 2006, I received a letter from general secretary informing me that my services as bishop were terminated. No sooner had I received the letter than I protested and then he wrote a letter to the Executive Council members seeking their advice. Some of them replied to his letter and confirmed what I have narrated. It was interesting that the members who approved the recommendation forgot that the illegal delegates of the General Conference 2003 elected them as well and the malicious bishops raised hands to approve their own recommendation in the meeting presided by them against the interest of natural justice. I learnt that Sampath Kumar was bullying members who were under his appointments and Taranath Sagar was poisoning minds with spurious tales to stir them. S. R. Thomas acted like an idealistic, voiced his concern in private conversation with me that punishment should be proportionate; however, in public, he acted just the opposite, seemingly neither he had conviction nor commitment, as in his mind, he still could not digest his defeat in the episcopal assignment race against me. He was overwhelmed that the Friends of Convenience were against me, inasmuch as it was a self-satisfying scenario for him. In fact, the prepared flimsy charges did not call for disciplinary action by any standard, much less termination from the bishopric.

The Priests of Vengeance, assisted by other high priests, solemnized massive conspiracy, and the inferno of revenge engulfed all those whose voice differed. The Collusive Clique overflowed with joy; it was anything but Christlessness and the antithesis of truth and justice values cherished by the church throughout its history, and I believe the future will judge the heinous history they made. My protest against their unlawful action ignored and chanted my genuine outcry as rubbish. I hoped in vain for the seventy-times-seven attitude; however, the wait was fatal. As I mulled over the events, the words of Alexandre Dumas, 'incomprehensible details assumed their real significance', became alive, which until then lay dormant. Prepared evidences, induced and venal witnesses, unlawful chargesheet, persistent jurisdictional violation and tyranny, a priori findings of my guilt in the paid inquiry, and abduct abomination acts and deeds were incompatible to the holiness of life and ministry of the church. I could not imagine the finesse, extent, and tenacity of the massive conspiracy, I lamented over my lack of comprehension of the bishops' narrow inclusive personal ambition, for it seemed they were not like consecrated spiritual material. Then all doors to justice in the church closed, the Judiciary of the land was the only inescapable way, though not a smooth and sure way to justice. The wheels of time and the tide did not favour me, so without loss of time, I challenged my illegal termination before the Judiciary of the land to fight against injustice of the bishops. I got into the legal mire from where it was not easy to escape, and in vain, I waited for the church Judiciary to decide the legality of the unfair inquiry-turned-trial report.

WILDERNESS DAYS

Walking a narrow way and having prophetic voice were like living in the political furnace. Truth, justice, and equity were applauded, but few stood by me in my wilderness days, an experience of being cut off from familiar people and places in the church. Nevertheless, inspired by the life-stirring stories of God's people around the world, I kept on going. I remember when the prophets of the old spoke against evil deeds of kings; they faced their wrath and reclined to solitude places to escape acrimony and annihilation. And the people who caused the rise and fall of great and mighty powers and caused political upheavals were often under the tyrannical yoke and disappeared from the public scene, seized and locked in cages and dungeons, ate meager morsel, stripped of natural freedom, tortured and killed for the sake of crown and kingdom. I read hardback *Nelson Mandela in His Own Words*. I am astonished, not long before; the champion of apartheid was in solitary confinement for his struggle for apartheid. I felt it was perhaps one of the examples of awful life in seclusion in our recent human memory. As his life story goes, he was in the cell, perpetually lit by one bulb, and for weeks utterly isolated, nothing to read, write on, and no one to talk to, and every hour seemed like a year. He wrote, 'I found myself on the verge of initiating a conversation with a cockroach'[1]. I did not suffer like him or Richard Wurmbrand, Romanian pastor of Jewish descent; however, I did have the woeful experience of loneliness and betrayal after I lived a vibrant and active life in the church, as the bishops venerated their inclusive narrow personal ambition as Israelites did to the golden calf. I suffered and struggled like passionate crusaders of truth and justice. The vengeful and malicious acts of the bishops rattled my life, ruined my ministry, deprived and isolated me, and I was agonized even more.

The trauma of vengeance kept hurting me. Then, I did not know God's purpose for such sudden turn of events in my life. The words are not sufficient to describe it; however, the Bible promises were like balm to my hurt and humiliation, all things work good to those who are called according to God's purpose. I felt relieved, drew strength to face the unknown future, and God alone was my anchor, as the Priests of Vengeance thrust me into the wilderness. It was one thing to hear about it, and it was altogether different to experience it. Indeed, it did not speak for the piety of the bishops; once, I considered them as spiritual giants; however, I was despondent to find that they were anything but power-crazy lots who were swayed by the wind of power and became intolerant to the prophetic voice when it clashed their political ambition. It was pathetic and a cultural shock, for without even a second thought, they were ready to destroy those who adored the universal values of truth and justice, as they perceived them as obstacles to their self-fulfilment. I was looking for the tolerance to the voice of dissent in the church, I seldom found it. I remember my conversation with an influential pastor who was a delegate to the General Conference. He said his colleague pastor who was ready to compromise anything for his political prosperity asked him do things, as he did, so he, too, could enjoy all the good things in the church like him, but he said he was not convinced, so he declined. Obeying ones' conscience is a great challenge and struggle and it seemed it is seldom liked by the church leaders of narrow selfish vision. I was firm in my vision for the church and the rule of law, never to betray it for the sake of temporary gains. Some people often asked me, 'What did you gain?' As for them, of course, I gained nothing for my being ideal, except illegal termination and unending struggle; however, in that, too, I felt a sense of fulfilment. In vain, I expected the bishops to walk the way of holiness of life, but they preferred their way of life, as they loved to occupy their chair by any means, so they were as adventurous as they could. There were some among the church leaders who rose to defend the Discipline; however, they were often whipped politically by the iniquitous church leaders and the principle of 'no individual is above law' was conspicuously absent in the church. I was glad that at least a handful came out to protest such injustice, though they could not sustain for long because of intimidation, as inclusive narrow interests of the Collusive Clique were camouflaged and adored, as the pro-church to mislead the masses in the church. They said and did things as they pleased and perceived right-thinking leaders as their adversaries when they did not support their narrow selfish ambition and iniquitous means, and by inferior politics, they destined them to doom. In their opium of power, they bent the rule of law of the church, bruised reason and logic to remain or ascend in the church hierarchy, and I witnessed the painful moments. I vainly thought, at least in some remote corner of the church hierarchy, reasonability existed; however, it was my utopian thinking and it made no difference inside than the outside the church. Unreliably, the Priests of Vengeance and their coterie seized truth and justice and thrust me in the wilderness for my prophetic voice.

Doing Right

From time immemorial, just and innocent people suffered and the wicked prospered. Theologians, both evangelical and liberal, burnt the midnight lamp to know its mystery like biologists tried to know how the leopard got spots but found no satisfying answer. The commonly held belief is that our sins and wrongdoings bring suffering, but I think it is a too simplistic explanation of the intriguing problem of suffering. In all ages, evildoers escaped unhurt and prospered, as God's judgment is slow but sure. In contrast, those who adored benevolent values, principles, and ideology miserably suffered. In my situation, most church leaders were anything but incurable power avarice, an inherited trait evolving human nature in his short sojourn on the earth, which will perpetuate until the end of the age. However, there seems to be no satisfactory answer to the dilemma of suffering of the righteous and the prosperity of the wicked; it baffled all, sometime or another. In my theology class, I recognized, there was general belief that the prosperity of the wicked is short-lived, inasmuch as the suffering of righteous ones could be part of God's plan. It was tangible in the lives of the Bible characters. Moses, the suffering man of God, fled into wilderness after clumsy failure to deliver Israelites from the Pharaoh's slavery, exploitation, and indignity. Joseph, youngest son of Israel, was sold as a slave who saved people from starvation and death. Daniel was thrown into lions' den, as he was monotheistic and did not bow down to any other god than he believed, defying the inescapable ordinance of Darius, the king of Persia. Elijah stood against the king for killing of righteous, fled to wilderness out of fear and the ravens fed him. John the Baptist was beheaded in prison for his prophetic voice against unlawful marriage. A host of missionaries and men of God suffered and lived in isolation for the sake of their faith and ministry. The Bible words, blessed are those who suffer for righteousness, meaning doing right things influenced my thinking profoundly and sustained me in all my humiliating experiences; it was just opposite to yesterday, when people held me in honour and respect, and now all changed. I was isolated, tales of spurious allegations diffused, and people said all sort of things when I was deprived of my episcopal chair.

I could not comprehend my sufferings, for it was like catching falling leaves of a tree, and several thoughts came; however, none was satisfying and comforting. A person dear to me said, you are suffering, perhaps your decisions might have hurt people and their cry might have reached God and so now, you are undergoing suffering than no other bishop in the church. The voice persisted, I should have not chosen, the less travelled path unlike others, however I could not reckon to such stereotyped thinking. I searched my heart in the search light of my inner voice, I was convinced and my conscience was clear that I never intended to harm anyone for my own sake and had no ill feeling towards anyone for personal gain. I felt, perhaps I was too zealous and high on expectation on the work delivery, which was often misconstrued and resented. My desire to make things right and do things right came on the way of the power-obsessed and inward-looking church leaders who dissipated the vigour of those who were otherwise. I remember, and then there was serious thinking to find ways and means to overcome galloping financial shortfall in the church. I was surprised; Sampath Kumar emphatically said, 'I do not want to be saviour.' I perceived, he sounded like the rich fool – unmindful of the church needs, while some toiled to find ways, and still others sat on the fence to wait and watch. It seemed, in years to come, the church finances would be an impediment to the ministry of the church and may discourage new initiatives. A great deal of time and energy was spent on the maintenance of the church structure, nothing significant done for evangelism and the church growth. I was sad; most church leaders wavered on the vision for the church that did not facilitate the mission of the church. I was convinced that I should not do a stereotype work and I do not regret over my decisions except a few, although I was sincere and clear in what I did. Advancing the church's mission was my priority; and my call and duty perhaps paralyzed the self-serving political ambition of some leaders who dominated the affairs of the church. No way was I discouraged, for the zeal of the Lord was my strength and in doing right things and making things right, it was my humble endeavours. I recognized that sometimes my decisions were not liked by all and those who felt the heat of them reacted in one or another, but I did not waver.

I stood by those who suffered injustice and my heart always went after the poor and politically feeble ones. I am convinced beyond doubt that my suffering was not the wages of my wrongdoings, as some might be tempted to think, but it was the cause of the fusion of negative energy and the cocktail of inferior interests, as my prophetic voice was paralyzing the conspirators' inclusive narrow personal goals.

The church history is the witness to great charismatic personalities who stood against the tides of moral and spiritual decay of their times, as compared to them, my role was small, feeble, and humble, and limited to the context. However, I often remember, the golden rule, suffering makes man perfect. In my wilderness days, I learnt meaningful lessons in more than one way and the life of great crusaders of truth, justice, and equity consoled and inspired me, and my hurts, pains, and misery were my challenge as I struggled against the venom of the Collusive Clique.

Defamed and Deprived

The Priests of Vengeance defamed and disgraced me before the church to varnish their inferior report cards. Out of hatred, they tried to tarnish my image with the active support of their followings. Unbelievably, Nimrod Christian was influenced by the knack of calumny and maliciously distorted facts before media in Delhi, of my suspension. The reason for the suspension, he said, was anti-church activities and mal-administration. It was an irony; he himself was not above reproach, but he raised an accusing finger at me. What I heard was true, how short human memory is, and it was all the more so, in his case. No sooner had he wriggled out of the furnace of the inquiry report than forgot how miserable he was, craving for my support. He gave filtered briefing to show that he was a better man than I am. I was deeply hurt by his deliberate concealing of facts. The *Light of Life* magazine lifted the reporting from the *New Leader* magazine and published it without verifying from me. When I read it, I questioned Nimrod Christian on his reporting. He assured he would write to the editor of the magazine to clarify the ground of suspension, and since he did not do it, I wrote several reminders; however, he was unmoved, making it clear that he was not as good as his words. I felt dismayed; Google, too, lifted his inflationary reporting, perhaps from the World Wide Religious News and without verifying from me, posted it. His aim was to humiliate and tarnish my image before the church and the world forum. Regardless, I felt good when people called me to assure their support and some of them satirically reminded me about the

Friends of Convenience, expressing disapproval of my supporting them. All knew, had I not stood by him, he should not have been there to defame me. However, I failed to measure the size of the man who did not return in gratitude what I have done for him. It was an irony, the man who barely cared little for the church's interests more than one-way then clamouring concern for the church and others soaked with the pride of their power, attributed themselves as church, profaning Christ's words on St. Peter's great confession. The wind of their ego swayed them and they never realized that one day, such attitude would lead them to misery. They furiously run after me, as I was invoking the Discipline and supporting the church Judiciary that impinged their personal ambition, so out of fury and anxiety they chose to project me as anti-church. Nimrod Christian's scornful words were piercing – they belittled my sacrificial service to the church.

Undoubtedly, over-stepping the church Judiciary to survive in the episcopal chair and conducting the General Conference 2003 with illegally elected delegates in contravention to the Discipline was surely anti-church persuasion. The Priests of Vengeance acted like lords and contrary called those who raised voice against defying the Discipline as foes and maligned them.

It seemed that the Aggressive Opponent contacted a news reporter of the *Mid Day News*paper, Mumbai, with the help of his friends and published the twisted news of my suspension with intention to show me in poor state. He made copies of the news cutting and the Bombay High Court order of February 26, 2007, printed in a booklet and distributed in Bombay, and the Gujarat Conferences and the Priests of Vengeance rejoiced at his hostile mill. I was in cultural shock, as a few were won by the truth, many by canards. They rejoiced; however, in their heart, they knew it was no Christian way, inasmuch as it was the follow-up to their conspiracy, so they exaggerated it. Never had they realized its velocity would vanish in graft and corruption practices in the church. I recognize rumours are short lived, inasmuch as they are like a storm; however, I felt the time would come when their untamed motive would become known and haunt them like a ghost.

As said, the news of my suspension spread, and many could not believe what they heard while others quickly criticized and humiliated me, old stories were revisited, they picked up the concocted tales of the property matters, and still others were happy to settle their personal grudges. I could not explain to everyone; it was hard to do so as most people were led astray by the tides of the concocted stories and I did not think it was worth to justify myself under such hostile storm. I believed the time would come when they would be ready to lend their ears to the truth; only time would unfold the truth. Then, the situation favoured calumny. However, I worried; by the time the truth would shine like light, it would rupture my reputation. The entire experience was tragic and the warmth of the love of my sympathizers and my cool rationale could not remove the creases of my hurt and humiliation. None was around me whom I could speak to, and those who used to flock around me were in hiding for days and all communication was paralyzed. I did not know what was going on. After days, in the midst of gloom and despair, the assurances of support and consolation poured. I felt relieved to know that there were people who believed me and my family comforted me. Encouraged by them, I was prepared to fight for justice, while they tried to tarnish my image; however, they could not succeed, for it was my priceless treasure. They won the battle, not the war against the truth, for people did not appreciate their iniquitous adventures; however, they did prolong and intensify my suffering, but no way could they quell my endurance.

There was no end in sight to my sufferings, so I felt, I should seek the help of James K. Matthew, a United Methodist Church Bishop, and knowing him as a good friend and supporter of the church, I wrote a letter to him, requesting to advise the bishops to stop in-fights. There was no word from him; perhaps they advised him to keep himself away from it. In such deprivation, my agony and despair were like my shadow; however, I did not lose heart. I could not imagine the things they did to crush my hope for the early end of my sufferings and the Bible words, 'If you do not stand firm in faith, you shall not stand at all,' kept me going[2]. Then one of my disguised faithful ones told me, what the Performer said to him that they would drive me to the brow of a hill, but not push down the cliff. It seemed it was their initial strategy; nevertheless, they threw me in the valley of suffering from where no one could easily escape. They deprived me of my ministry and privileges, and my financial support was withdrawn to make me suffer and surrender to their growling desires; it was common sense logic to cut the source of my livelihood. For in the situation like this, I needed money for my living and legal expenses, and if it was impaired, then the survival would be harder and surrender would be easier. They hit the nail, however, at the wrong point and failed to recognize that man does not live by bread alone, and there is always the divine providence in the life of those who walk in the integrity of their heart. Nimrod Christian with his unquenchable thirst for power harboured to infringe my support. He gloated to cut my salary increment and to hit me hard for attending the Billy Graham Conference in Bangkok from October 11 to 14, 2004; during the suspension period while others travelled and did globetrotting without adoring the holiness of life and witness of the church, they forced me to live in seclusion and suffering. I spent my precious time preparing reply to the letter of suspension, and then I never realized that no one would care to read it. I perceived Nimrod Christian in the guise of a friend used to visit me to measure my agony, spy on me to know my moves, and to plan counter stoke. During one of his visits, I said to him, I spent a lot of time on preparing the reply; he looked at me, as if it would be treated like a worthless piece of paper, for they were of one mind to demean me and derive pleasure from it. He said that he too did the same and I felt he was not genuine in all he said and did. Once, I observed the way in which he closed the main gate of the Bishop's House when he left. He hopped, his face flashed with mischief, giving him the sense of satisfaction that he succeeded in making me believe his words. Whenever I think about it, I feel hurt, it dents my inner feelings like a meteor does and it leaves me with the deep sense of relative deprivation. I searched my heart to know what I lacked that my colleague bishops have that put them on higher spiritual level. I did it, not out of spiritual arrogance, but of spiritual necessity. Most people in the church knew they left behind them indelible footprints of their inappreciable deeds; however, by the sudden turn of events, they gave the impression as if they cared for the holiness of life. I could not imagine the extent of sufferings that I have undergone and as a human being I felt relatively deprived. I could not decide if I should agitate like Mahatma Gandhi did, for it would be merely a futile struggle, as it seemed there were not many lovers of truth and justice in the church, and those who were, they were reluctant. I could never imagine that the Collusive Clique would be so stiff and tuff for others and conceal their own inferior acts. It seemed the call of their conscience fell on their deaf ears, as their ways were anything but antithesis of the constitutional rights. In my wilderness days, the sovereign God led me and I felt he has a purpose for me, so I did not lose my temper or hope. As said, after clouds come sunshine, but clouds and sunshine had come and gone, and yet there was no lasting sunshine.

I recognized my predecessors and colleagues had professional jealousy, when the spiritual and temporal work of the church gathered momentum in my episcopal area, they could not bear to see that I did more in less time. People made difference; however, some disgruntled persons whose political aspiration did not find fulfilment were resentful and some bishops were spreading hostility, instigating and supporting their followers for mutually inclusive political benefits. Sampath Kumar and Nimrod Christian by collusion and conspiracy took over my episcopal area, deprived my right, and afflicted me. They oppressed pastors and the church workers who disapproved their vindictive politics and sinking administration, but fed their supporters with temporary bones to keep them in great humour. They imagined my supporters as threat to their covetous political ambition and seldom cared for their holy calling or realized, as perhaps said by Stan Lee, with great power comes great responsibilities. It was a painful situation, the good work of the church suffered. It gave the message that yielding to the wishes of those who held bitterness against me was far more important than truth and justice. The holiness of life was barely adored, how to torment others and me was their incurable ambition. They oppressed me, caused unimagined hardships, and feasted on the conferences' precious scare resources with malicious intent, which I raised painstakingly at a great risk; their aim was to keep my opponents and those who were potential political vexation to them in cheerful mood, as frivolous allegations were a part of my being faithful.

Deprived of preaching and fellowship, I could not keep myself away too long from it, after I had until then more than thirty-one years of active life in the church. In solitude, I used to think about worship service, pastors' fellowship, leadership seminars, and prayer breakfast meetings; inasmuch as being cut off from all those activities was agonizing, however, their pleasant memories kept me going in my painful struggle. The Priests of Vengeance coerced pastors to keep me out of the ministry of the Word of God. I used to get up at 4 o'clock in the morning, as often I could to pray; however, due to the sadness of my heart, my prayer life was shattered and there were long breaks.

I felt sad that I neglected to pray and immersed in the thought as to why God was allowing my conspirators to triumph over me. While I was despondent and worried, the testimony of a devote Christian inspired me that made me return to early Morning Prayer.

Sundays reminded me of the joy of sharing the Word of God; however, it also gave me pain. My family members could go to church as much as they could. I, too, attended the church services like other churchgoers or watched God or Daystar channels on a cable network or heard messages on YouTube. When church members saw me, they urged me to occupy a seat at the altar side; however, I humbly declined to keep the pastor out of disciplinary action. Then I felt it was good to avoid attending Methodist churches, as my presence embarrassed pastors who were under surveillance and virtual threat from the Friends of Convenience. Most of them were scared of calling me to pray or preach, but I could not ignore my inner call of attending church too long. I thought, if not Methodist church, why not another church. I, therefore, like a common worshiper, attended other churches' services. I wrote in my diary, on 2004 and 2007 Christmas, I attended St. Ignatius Catholic Church at Jacob Circle, Mumbai. St. Ignatius was the patriarch of Constantinople who refused Bardas, uncle of the emperor in Constantinople, Michael III, sacraments for his unsavoury reputation. In retaliation, the emperor unlawfully removed him. My attending the church, dedicated to his memory, was in somewhat identical circumstances and a shear coincident. Anyway, I felt it was a great ecumenical experience and I learnt the lesson of humility and simplicity. As a bishop, I sat in a high back chair, next to the alter and preached sermons from high-rise pulpits; however, now it was altogether a different experience to sit in the last pew, identifying myself with the universal church, common worshippers, and the priesthood of believers.

Although the Judiciary of the land allowed me to do my day-to-day spiritual work, the Friends of Convenience by the force of their office did not allow me to do my duty, for their contemptuous indulgences were their way of life. Some pastors took risk, invited me to preach, only to face their wrath and the pastors who were under their influence eschewed me. They called them for rituals, ceremonies, and special events with the aim to humiliate me. From the very beginning, preaching is my passion, people liked my preaching and after the church service, some came to tell me how they were blessed, recalling the words that touched them and urged me to write down my sermons. Then I felt I would never be able to do so due to my busy schedule. However, in the wise working of providence in my wilderness days, I penned them in a book, and not long after, its Hindi and Marathi versions were published; I felt it should touch many lives. They prevented me to preach in the church, but the preacher in me could not. I could have sued them for the contempt of court; however, I realized it was unwise to open another front in my struggle, as it would change the direction of my focus, and they being habitual in defying the law of the church and court orders, barely could have made any difference.

Then, there arose differences in the Collusive Clique. Nimrod Christian and Pradeep Samuel insisted that I attend the function organized on 150 years of

Methodism in India and Silver Jubilee Celebration in Lucknow. I reluctantly agreed. I informed the host, S. R. Thomas and the then bishop of the Lucknow Episcopal Area of my attending. In the beginning, he was cooperative, agreed to book a room for me in a hotel with other bishops. Encouraged by their good will gestures, I reached Lucknow on October 19, 2006, past midnight and checked in the hotel. In the morning, I joined the bishops at breakfast. Their spouses accompanied them; some were happy to meet me, others were dismayed. By seeing me, Sampath Kumar was restless and fuming, without losing a fraction of a second, he asked the spokesman to take up the issue with S. R. Thomas, who in turn asked me not to participate in the celebration and occupy the hotel room at my own expense. The spokesman even said, 'It is prudent to leave the place.' I was grieved over the double speak of the bishops and diminishing sensitivity to the holiness of life and imagining Methodism without Wesleyan holiness of life was like Christianity without love and forgiveness. However, I felt, having come so far; I had better attend the opening function. I asked S. R. Thomas if I could do that, he said anyone could attend, however, for the rest of the function, only those who were invited. The invitees were men and women, assembled from all over India, well dressed as usual happen on such occasions. They were busy exchanging greetings. Anjana Masih was there, looked sublime and getting preferences over others like a luminary. Mulayam Singh, the then chief minister of the Uttar Pradesh, was the chief guest and bishops and others were finding their way closer to him and squeezing to appear with him in photographs and videos. I felt, for the sake of solemnity, the celebration could have started with the praise and thanksgiving service and if necessary, the programme could have so adjusted to his convenience.

On the occasion, they decided to write the history of the church, following John N. Hollister's writing, an American Missionary[3]. It was a good move; the bishops held several meetings and assigned portions of the proposed book. It seemed that their minds were puffed up with encyclopaedic historical information and fertile by power ambition than spiritual experiences, and impoverish minutes and bulky documents that pulped out of their untidy bookshelves boosted their aspiration. The suggestion to ask a professional within the church to write the book did not go well with them. Perhaps, they thought it was their life's rare opportunity to go into annals of Methodism. They wrestled with it, and in lack of coordination and clarity, they set to write the history of the church. I watched how desperate souls they were to appear in a new role, as men of letters. Some of them were serious; however, everyone was eager to play a bigger role; thank God, they kept me out of it. Synergy was missing and the whole was no greater than the parts. Sadly, it ended as chaotic endeavour, the occasion came and gone; the book had seen no light of the day and the prodigious expenditure drained out of the church's money and time.

In the celebration, the people who worked under my episcopal supervision ignored me and behaved as if they did not know me, and others conveniently avoided meeting me in open, out of fear. I observed the celebration turned less contemplative and heart searching, it looked like a political gathering; inferior power politics was the epithet rather than the holiness of life. They were determined to chase me out; however, they never realized that the holiness of life was not a sterile spirituality, but it is like the Damascus experience. I asked Nimrod Christian, 'Why have you insisted on me to come to Lucknow, if you intended not to support me?' He said, Sampath Kumar and Taranath Sagar threatened to walk out of the celebration if I participated. Such was the spiritual decay; their hearts were full of hatred, while they claimed spiritual leadership. The political differences between them quickly settled when they heard about the negotiation between the Performer, a close associate of Nimrod Christian, and my supporters. Having sensed the danger of losing Nimrod Christian, Sampath Kumar and Taranath Sagar cunningly agreed to call the General Conference's Session early to evade his retirement and to go against me. They cast me out, as if I was the only sinner among the infallible bishops. I grieved over the paradoxical situation, they were celebrating Methodism while paralyzing the holiness of life, and the emphasis on John Wesley's spiritual experience of strangely warm heart was missing. As there was no one who could speak for me, the next day morning, I returned to Mumbai in great agony, treating my visit as a bad dream. They deprived, tormented, and treated me like untouchables. I ran from pillar to post and the Priests of Vengeance forced me to live in solitude and misery.

Tyranny

I was under vengeful fire; pastors and others, who once surround me, were living in fear and grief as well. They were worried if the Collusive Clique would come to know they were meeting me, they could be victimized, transferred or their families could be tormented or they could even face frivolous charges and suspension, for it was the order of the day. Pastors and church workers were worried, for Friends of Convenience were victimizing those who did not fall in line with them. Unbelievably, Sampath Kumar seemed acrimonious and did not hold above dispute his episcopal position.

In my early days of wilderness, I confined myself to my office room; windows were kept shut to stop people guessing what was going inside and the Methodist Home workers spied on us. At times for a little while, the north side of the office door was open for fresh air and natural light. Rarely, there was a visitor for months; it was like living in a prison without prison walls. When the oppression of pastors and others became acute, they gathered courage to meet me. There was strong opinion that Sampath Kumar was actualizing the vindictive advices of Taranath Sagar, who hailed from the Bombay conference. Sampath Kumar was resolute to ruin those who did not appreciate his leadership style which appeared like fascist policies and alter ego. Personal contacts with me became rare and risky, so they avoided. These were painful moments; telephone was the only means of contact, although expensive; however, I began to contact people on telephone and at times had anxious moments when I was unable to get them on mobiles or landline in emergency due to the service provider's poor quality, especially during the court hearings in Ahmedabad and Godhra. As the time passed by, people came to know about the great injustice done to me and showed sympathy and visited some time to encourage me.

The thought of my suspension used to pop up in my mind; however, I was helpless, it was like spilled water on the ground that cannot be gathered. I was agonized by the anxiety of an unknown future. I asked myself why God allowed bishops to crush me with injustice, and then I remembered the smoothing words: no matter what your future is going to be, you know who holds your future. That comforted and encouraged me to move forward with hope and faith. I recognized more than before, when people are committed to doing right things in the church, they face hard times, as if doing right things no more merited, but how good you are in collaborating with majoritarianism did. Some appreciated good work; others blew negativism. In fact, those who did good work faced opposition more than those who barely worked and were considered as threat to their flourishing self-image. I spent sleepless nights, thinking, what I was struggling. Sometimes, tears rolled on my cheeks; never had I faced such torturous experience. I read my diary, on October 21, 2004, 'At about 6:00 in the morning, I felt, I was sitting in the corner of my office with tears in my eyes, thinking about the conspiracy.' I shared it with my family in tears the intensity of my agony and painful moment, which I was going through at the hands of those whom I rescued from crises. The very thought gave me pain and dried up my strength. It was not my nature; I had gone through sufferings and faced hard times; however, it was all changed! Sometimes, I was in tears, talking to myself, God you know I am innocent, and yet my adversaries are oppressing me, then my inner voice said, 'You are not the only innocent person suffering in this unfair world and living in the bottom of a dry well,' that brightened my face and strengthened me to move on. I consoled myself, I said, I was still in better condition than many who were tortured and persecuted in concentration camps around the world. In monologue, I debated, however, the church should not be like the world and the inner voice said, 'It is no exception and there are many vices in the church, which did not reflect the holiness of life or the baptism of fire. It seemed the situation was barely different from the days of Christ, the church turned into the den of political trades and church leaders preferred people like Barabbas. Some self-righteous think that the devil is active only outside the courtyard of the church, I feel it is the spiritual arrogance; the ideal typical situation does not exist in the church, for the wicked grew and prospered more than devote servants of God. I recognized the lack of spirituality was fading the golden era of Methodism in India; elections, unfruitful meetings, church politics, and property development issues occupied the church elites and led them to cutthroat political competition and election winning crafts. The outward show was maintained; however, substance lost its fervour; it was change with continuity of merely faith in the holiness of life. A great heritage of John Wesley's holiness of life, also called social holiness, was reduced to mere symbolism that lies imprisoned in history books.

People barely appreciated my inclination to be a disciplinarian and perfectionist, inasmuch as it troubled my family. In my anxiety for 'need achievement', I changed the assignments of those who did not do well to my expectation. Some thought I was hard and those whose assignments were changed turned bitter; in the midst of such poignant feelings, I felt sanguine to learn; those who experienced me said that although I was tough on 'need achievement', I was soft and compassionate and my experience made me appreciate that everyone is not equally endowed with the same gift. As I said, I emotionally used to get stirred by people's suffering; this instinct motivated me to help bishops, pastors, and church workers who faced hard times in their ministry. I stood to defend them when I was convinced they unjustly treated them for opposing those who habitually defied the Discipline for self-fulfilling political ambition. I had tough times; however, I did not lose heart. I spent 230 days in great pain and agony, which were like years, every moment was intense, soaked with despair and hope, waiting for some miracle to happen, and it kept me praying and going.

It was a scary situation; my supporters were oppressed, crushed, and intimidated. I entered in my diary, on December 3, 2004, a pastor advised a layman not to enter my house from the main gate when visiting. He said, 'After all we need to see our own future.' It gave me an idea of the extent of the threat perception, inasmuch as I was grieved. I did not expect the pastor to think like that, for I supported him for many years, even prior to my becoming bishop. There were occasions when I confronted my bishop for his sake. Sadly, I came across mostly such kind of people in the church who lacked courage and were obsessed with self-welfare and seldom stood by people in the time of their distress, who meant so much to them. From May 6, 2004, onwards, such tendency was tangible, words are insufficient to describe the misery of the pastors, church workers, and laypersons who supported and sympathized with me. They lived under the perpetual threat of victimization and despotism. As the Friends of Convenience showed ferocity, pastors and some lay members were cautious to avoid their displeasure, least get shackled by their impious wrath; however, others chose to confront them from the beginning. There was huge reaction to Sampath Kumar's one-sided way of handling things; pastors and lay members strongly protested; however, it was perceived that he did not cease to act like Goliath. One from the Collusive Clique informed me that on hearing my name, Sampath Kumar used to get the fit of anger and with a distorted face used to spit on the ground, and stamp on it with all his vigour like a ruthless ruler, scourging truth and justice. Such was the velocity of his hatred towards me, while Nimrod Christian was secretly finding crafty ways and means to drag me into spurious criminal cases, it was inconceivable aggressiveness.

Disguised Faithful

Some disguised as faithful to gain favour. In the episcopal administrative system, the bishop has to pick up his team from an existing stock of pastors and laypersons to carry on his responsibilities. There were political coteries and I chose the persons on my team whom I considered of a great help to smooth running of programmes and projects. My criteria were a reasonable competence, commitment and cooperation, and confidentiality. I had no personal preferences to choosing certain persons over others, then thinking they were the best picks, and although competence desirable qualities to make a success story, I realized that faithfulness and transparency are crucial. I agree I failed to feel people like the earth's motion and especially whom I choose. Then I did not realize, perhaps it was important to involve troublemakers in the decision-making process as well, if not in the core areas of the church's ministry. I think, I could have avoided political jujitsu, nipped in bud self-serving tendency of those who were on the team and achieved even greater things if the voice of dissent was politically not blown up out of proportion. It is very well said, to err is human, and man learns from his mistakes. Long after, I realized most of those who surrounded me had deflected honesty, as I felt. They had hidden agenda, which they believed, best achieved by disguising like loyalists. It is the same story everywhere and perhaps use until useful attitude was dominant in the church. They liked to be on winning side and in the good book of bishops. I was not an exclusive victim of it, other bishops too had such bitter experiences; in my case, it was bit excess. Then I never knew, one day they would drive me into troubled water and strain my relations with my colleagues and others. Some boasted their proximity to me and said and did things of personal interest by keeping me in the dark. There were misgivings that what they said and did were with my blessings. It caused animosity and hurled fear in the opponents' camp – defeat in election, failure in expectation to get creamy appointments, and corrective measures to make things rights were misconstrued. Its cumulative effect was the sustainable bubble of political hostility, blown up to their advantage. I was amazed when the storm of conspiracy paralyzed my bishopric; the faithful flock, without having a second thought, deserted me at a time when I needed them most and disguised like faithful as long as I held the chair and they reaped benefits.

One of them claimed he was a good chess player. I have a very little idea of the game; all I know is that contesting players make cleaver moves to capture each other's king. However, on the chessboard of the church politics, he never ceased to make swift and sharp political killer moves, intuitively like chess grandmasters. I was amazed that for the sake of political ambition, he embraced the ruling side than principles and values. In my wilderness days, at times, I waited for him, but he never turned up or called me. Surprisingly, no sooner had he perceived I was gaining the lost ground than he appeared, made some lame excuses for his long absence. He loved to be thrilled to imagine himself as a big and busy church official; it seemed he was in ambit of megalomaniac. He had political knack to please people in power who could help him protect his interests. He could go to any extent; giving dinner, gifts, bowing down at feet, were his adored political tools, and he even advised me dinner diplomacy, as its practitioner and unsuccessfully tried to shape me in his mould; however, it was incompatible to my nature and purpose. I wrote in my diary, on December 24,

2004, after two days of extensive verification on court order, he came to see me. Again, on January 10, 2005, I wrote in my journal, I advised him to keep himself out of the conference work for the sake of good relations. He was apologetic and persuasive in getting things done; some projects or works which he cherished were pressed for curious reason. He never relished anyone getting close to me. I wrote in my diary on January 21, 2005, that he was often critical of the pastor who, he felt, was closer to me than him. I asked him to keep out of conference politics, he was resentful and could not swallow the idea of vanishing from the political scene of the conference; it mirrored his inner craving to remain in the limelight in the church politics. Again, I wrote an entry in my diary, on March 21, 2005, he came in the evening to meet me, stood in front of me, swore he did not change sides. He pleaded to trust him, asked to forgive, folded his hands and touched my feet and I could not believe my eyes I dissuaded him doing it. I was stunned by his drama. I realized he could go to any extent to win a person. It seemed that it was his political art; never had he realized that it would work no more on me. I discouraged him, but he was not wary of gaining excess and favour from bishops and other church leaders who could satisfy his political thirst. He moved strategically close to bishops, prevented others coming closer to them like a chess player. He failed to restore his deflected credibility in my sight and my relationship with him oscillated until the time of the Adjourned Session of the General Conference Session 2007. After a month of the conference, he called me to tell that everything went on well, as if I was eager to hear him say so. He expressed no regret that my rights were denied. I did not react; I simply heard him. Until then I never realized the kind of the person he was, who loved to be on winning side. This was long before I spoke to him. By then, it seemed he was mixing up with the Collusive Clique and perhaps hibernated to my struggle. After seven years, he occasionally contacted me; I forgave him as God forgave me and he somewhat paid the bill of my favours.

Although he was sometimes helpful, I was dismayed; his personal and political interests came before all other things. I faced a lot of hard times and unexplainable misery because of his slothful and careless attitude. I had a few unforgettable experiences. From July 25 to 31, 2001, I attended the World Methodist Conference in Brighton, England. He too, came as a visitor. I was to go to the United States from Brighton on the invitation of the India-Reconnect Project of North Illinois Conference of the United Methodist Church. In Brighton, I met the person responsible for the itinerary. He informed me that there was change in the programme and would prepare a fresh itinerary. I could not figure out the reason for such abrupt postponing of the programme. Not long after, I learnt that C. Joseph Sprague, resident bishop of Northern Illinois Conference, was supportive of the project; however, it seemed other members held different views. Regardless, I went to London to cancel my air tickets along with others and he accompanied us. After the work was over, we had the city tour, waited at Victoria bus coach station to go to railway station to catch train back to Brighton. I had to go to the restroom, so I left my shoulder bag with him. After I returned, I asked for the bag, he looked for it; it was not on him. In bewilderment, he gawked without blinking and kept munching snack as fast as he could. I was shocked that he was insensitive. There was not even the slightest stress of anxiety or remorsefulness on his face. I was stunned to know, it was stolen. In the bag, there were my passport, air tickets, and money; I lost them all! I lodged FIR with the Belgravia police station; the police asked me to watch the CD (CCTV footage), I did so; however to my great agony, and the camera did not cover the seating area from where the bag was lifted. I was surprised to learn that old women were involved in the stealing enterprise. The next day, I rushed to the Indian High Commission to obtain an emergency certificate and air ticket to return to India. I had gone through hard times, for he was not being careful in the handling of office matters too. The Collusive Clique amplified it, made it acute, and inspired the Aggressive Opponent to target me for his work inefficiency, as I was then his Board's chairman. I was amazed he masterly managed to remain in the helm of the church politics, and his proven tricks of appeasement and submission perhaps helped him pursue his political ambition, no matter who the bishop was.

The second one was unlike him; the first one described him as a man who loved to live in conflicts of one kind or another. He said, 'It thrills him.' He was then reluctant to reconciliation and conflict resolution, except through legal remedies. He used to file court cases and, without taking it to its logical end, would pick up another. I could not quite understand why he did it. I felt that perhaps it was his way of life. There was perception that he acted like a social activist;

however, people did not appreciate his overwhelming appetite for money. The chess player brought him close to me that breathed paradoxical interests. He was in the opponent political camp, never close to me. In the past, he was an enthusiastic supporter of Taranath Sagar and it was said that, in early stages, he contributed a lot to his political success. I overlooked these facts, believing people do change and could be useful in the church's work. There was political change, Sampath Kumar was bubbling to victimize him and to propitiate his hurt ego and political interests, for the second one was vocal against his despotic attitude and faced the political fire of the Collusive Clique, as he stood to defend the Discipline and the Judiciary. It seems, he believed, when no efforts yielded any result; legal remedy was the only way, so he stood by those who were fighting court cases and the chess player took part in it. He untiredly toiled on political arithmetic, on rules, paper work, and deliberation. They were not transparent with me, but my colleague bishops misconstrued, as if I yoked them to litigation, so they began to inflict me. In my wilderness days, he seldom met me, as he, too, was vociferously fighting his own torment and perhaps gloated over his secret plans. Sometime after June 15, 2006, I expressed my concern on dubious working of the principal of a newly started English school. He appalled me by his despising attitude and said that the principal alone could not be targeted. Thereafter, our relationship was not warm enough as before; during and after his bad days, he came to seek my help; I was willing to help worthy cause; however, I perceived he was bitter, realizing I would not nourish his tendency to alienate the church property and institutions by exploiting loopholes in the church's structures and laws, then he did not show up. I was puzzled to know his disapproval of my stewardship concern. He was loud and clear with some pastors and laymen that I was not a good bishop and not a cut for the church politics but for intellectual pursuits. I think, to some extent, he was right, but expecting him to have compatible thinking was my delusion like medieval alchemists trying to turn base metals into gold.

The third one was quite different from the first two. He was spiritual, more devoted to prayer than I was, lifted me in prayers for many years, and we liked him. I was for him from the time I heard his life story and painful experiences and suffering at the hands of his senior pastor who was from his own linguistic stock. He bore all kinds of humiliation for years, for the sake of his ministry. He was anxious to build his image as an influential pastor in his community by showing his proximity to me and the power to influence pastors' appointments. Some from his linguistic group were his staunch antagonists, so in intolerance, they raised voice against his activities. I advised him not to talk about their in-fights, however, share only his problems, if I could be of any help to him. By being short on understanding, they targeted me for his alleged activities. I was amazed; he said he usually took rounds of Bishop's House even when I was out of the city. Then I was intrigued, all of a sudden, he went in hiding, broke contact, except on July 24, 2008, the day I had surgery for hernia; along with his wife, in the evening, he came to see me in the Bombay Hospital and asked if I needed money. I realized, he was keeping away from me because of his son, a pastor, for he worried his son could be oppressed. His son had some kind of dysgraphia. When I was in the Delhi Episcopal Area, I arranged to show him to D. W. Thomas, cardio-thoracic surgeon and the director of Methodist Hospital, Agra Regional Conference, who recommended to see a specialist in Mumbai, after which, his life changed. On March 27, 2010, at 9:35 in the morning, I heard the sad news that he slept with saints in Jesus Christ. I was grieved; without wasting time, I visited his family, consoled and prayed for them. Then I rushed to John Pinto's mortuary to pay homage, where his body lay; however, I was unable to see him, for it could have been difficult to maintain -7° degree temperature, if his body was taken out. My family members and I joined in his last journey at the Christian Cemetery, Sewri, Mumbai. I felt sad, for he was with me in my good and bad days.

In my wilderness days, I realized, most people in the church behaved the same or in a similar way, so long as I was useful to them, they flocked around me like bees to a honeycomb, and when I was not, they acted like migrating birds to live in a comfort zone. However, I did not expect such sudden turn of events in my life.

Tormented

The Priests of Vengeance fully charged to politically chop me like a coconut; however, I struggled against injustice and the affliction hurled on me, and having stood firm against their powerful stokes, sometimes I gained the lost ground, and other times, I was gloomy and helpless. When I was the winner, the Priests of Vengeance became more aggressive; they evolved new strategies to crush me and in more than one way made concerted efforts to implicate me in criminal cases, for they knew that exaggerated, concocted, and trivial allegations would not go a long way, so vengefully they pursued me, somehow tried to scourge me with criminal cases. Imagined fear, not stoic idealism, was the driving force. They thrived on negative energy and tried to block all avenues, for it seemed they thought that if I occupy the episcopal chair, I would take revenge on them; such thinking reflected their own mindset and could not think better than the tit-for-tat attitude. It was sterile to make them think sensibly, for then it was the norm in the church, and expecting them to think otherwise was like moving a mountain. I perceived that Taranath Sagar and his faithful political flock were impediment to justice. The bishops did not aspire to become role models or strive for the Christ-like spirit and saintliness. They said and did things that suited their political ambition, flimsy allegations were conceived, as unpardonable sins and despotism quelled the truth and justice and tormented me. The disciplinary process was a measured move, in the absence of grace, malicious roles were played and they adored inferior means to stay at the pinnacle of power: the desire for holiness of life was lacking. The prophetic voice was shackled and labelled as anti-church. In the name of inquiry, they axed my rights and privileges and throttled my voice to reign in my place. There was no hope for a fair and just deal, as the custodians of law were acting like its reckless breakers. They were passionate adventurers like Everest climbers to either secure or gain position in the church's hierarchy, and advancing the church's mission to the world was their least concern. In deflected fairness, everything and everyone was maneuvered either by the influence of office or by some reward. They denied me natural justice and in travesty glorified their deeds and I was even more agonized by their duplicity. There was a perception that the bishops blew the trumpet of truth and justice in public; but in contrast, they were engrossed in doing just the opposite, and the talk of truth, justice, and equity was a mere pulpit rhetoric.

I was helpless. A number of pastors and laypersons who rallied behind me slowly dwindled as time passed by, and at the end, there were some who prayed and supported me; everyone was worried about their election and position and did not feel wise to take the risk at the cost of their political ambition. My voice against unfair means stirred and disturbed them; I stood against the storm of injustice and flourishing falsehood; however, they succeeded in their conspiracy, pushed me into the valley of suffering, and threw sackcloth on me.

There was no end to my agony; they plotted to thrust on me criminal cases and to frustrate my struggle for truth and justice. The Teachers Girls' Training College, Godhra, Gujarat, was in crises. The college admitted more students than the Education Department of Gujarat Government allowed. Then, the department filed an FIR for alleged violation and donation for admission; some members of the Admission Committee were arrested. After much struggle, they were released on bail, but it displeased those who opposed them. It seemed Nimrod Christian was the force behind it; his close associates worked overtime to drag me in it, then being chairman. He instigated a Christian man to implicate me in it and poisoned the mind of Methodist Lay Association members against me. There was a strong perception that a huge secret sum was spent on it and that, perhaps, the source of funding was south. As the time passed by, his followers came to know the truth of his ulterior motive. I was amazed; they turned against him and became my staunch supporters that hit him hard. One of the pastors, whose name appeared in the FIR, said he prompted and pressurized him to take my name in the donation for admission mess; however, he never yielded to his tempting promises and threats. In the integrity of his heart, he refused to involve me falsely that thwarts his malicious game. The Gujarat police called me for recording a statement and I did go. When he came to know that there was nothing adverse against me, greatly disturbed, he revived his efforts, instigated again the same man to file a special criminal application in the Gujarat High Court, Ahmedabad, to include my name in the FIR and for CBI or CID inquiry, and in that, too, he could not succeed, for the truth was on my side. I was regularly receiving information on the vengeful activities of the Priests of Vengeance that became my nightmare and gave sleepless nights and anxiety. I thank God that I did not suffer stroke or heart attack.

Nimrod Christian was working against me like a demon when he was at the helm of the affair in the Gujarat Conference, by the force of revenge, greed, and lust for power, fiercely driving his unedifying schemes against me. Then the Education Department issued a show-cause notice as to why the recognition of the college should not be withdrawn. He took away the notice and related office files from the manager of the college in disguise of taking up the matter with the Central Government, New Delhi. Having assured the manager he would take up the matter at highest government level, he kept silent in a calculative move to blame me that the college was closed because of my administrative negligence. Had he been concerned about it, perhaps a lot of hardship and heart palpitation of many could have avoided; however, for him, casting aspersion on me was more important than saving the institution from chaos and closure. It became a very sensitive and inferno issue of every Methodist Gujarati household in Gujarat and aboard. He turned the heat on me for some time, flexing his political muscles to keep the issue burning to condemn and scorch me; however, soon people came to know the truth. Then, the rumour was spread that a member of the Admission Committee said that the donation for admission was authorized by me and the part of it was passed on to me. The member vehemently denied having said it and gave the written statement to the Pastorate Committee (Executive body) of the Sharon Methodist Church, Vododara. He and his coterie made me go through immense mental agony and face unforgettable ordeal. The Aggressive Opponent was spreading rumours of my imminent arrest; he told everyone that the Gujarat police would reach Mumbai anytime to arrest me, for I realized that it was their heart's desire to see me behind bars, at least for some time. They devised schemes, mobilized people, spent huge sum of church money to torment me.

There was another incident in the Methodist Technical Institute, Vadodara. A young woman, who worked as secretary in the director's office, fell in love with a non-Christian man. Long before, the family of the woman knew it, however then they did not make any fuss about it. Not long after she stopped attending the office, as she eloped with him and I learnt, it was out of fear and safety. Then, she conceived and gave birth to a child, although personal issue, it was twisted and blown out of proportion. Nimrod Christian kept his vengeful attitude replenishing against the director, who was also the president of the church Judiciary, for his refusal to tilt justice balance as per his wishes. He was a PhD and prior to his joining the Church's service worked as an officer on special duty (Research), Uttar Pradesh State Assembly. There was strong prevailing awareness that Nimrod Christian instigated the young woman's brother to file FIR against him, for alleged sexual misconduct, however the young women refuted her brother's allegations. Not succeeded in it, then her brother moved the Gujarat High Court with Habeas Corpus writ, alleging both the director and the police, then she appeared before the court and the writ was dismissed. Then he filed the criminal application in district court, asking for the custody of the young woman and her child and their DNA test, as well as of the director. I learnt the woman's family was not well to do; it was unbelievable her brother could file cases without external financial support. Anyway, the woman, in her statements before the court said neither the director nor anyone else had any role in her private matter, and it was her own choice. Failed to trap the director and link me to abetting him, and then indulged in unimaginable acts. The Priests of Vengeance were eager to damn me by hurling criminal cases on me. There was strong thinking that Sampath Kumar was envenomous church leader, power penetrated into his head and by stirring impulses asked to those who wanted to see him on the church matters to file criminal cases against me first and then come to him. Whereas, Nimrod Christian vowed and repeatedly said to the Catholic priest, who was one of the Board members of the Holistic Child Development India, a NGO and then working in Nagpur, that he would never let me resume my episcopal work.

He vowed to remove the director, so chased him after having failed in his attempts to frame him in the alleged sexual misconduct and then made the emotional issue of his non-Gujarati origin. The parochial language issue kept politically burning and then out of desperateness, the students of the institute instigated and indoctrinated. On December 13, 2004, they ran in rage like a horde to the director's office and tried to thrust into the office. The director said, he hid himself under the office table to escape murderous attempt on his life. Failing to seize the director, ran like a herd of wild beasts to his bungalow, spattered windowpanes and burnt his private car to ashes. On hearing it, I was shocked for the loss of ordinary human feelings and the way in which the students were demonized. There was no word of remorse or condemnation from Nimrod Christian, the then in-charge Bishop. It seemed, cozily sat in his Delhi episcopal residence, pretended, as if unaware of what was happening, I could not believe it, perhaps on hotline, directing the scene, for there was no evidence of one's best efforts and condemnation.

I was melancholic about infallible bishops; as they posed, did not even order an inquiry on the serious incident, nor did any church leader condemned it; odious act was a blot on the church. The Director at the most could file a police complaint and named him in it, however the investigation could not reach to its logical end in his absence and it seemed Nimrod Christian managed to choke the process. On March 1, 2005, he resigned, I apologized on the behalf of the church for the shameful act, he left the institution and we settled his compensation; however, money could not weigh humiliation and the murderous attempt.

The Priests of Vengeance were spiteful, did not abandon their desire to involve me in criminal cases. In 2004, Taranath Sagar's former political mentor filed a mandamus writ petition in the Aurangabad bench of Bombay High Court. I was not aware about the case for a long time however; it was for a worthy cause. He prayed that the election of bishops conducted in the General Conference 2003 be declared illegal and unconstitutional, and restrain Sampath Kumar from acting as in-charge Bishop of the Bombay Regional Conference. Sampath Kumar and Taranath Sagar were shattered and there was perception that they visited secretly to manage the case. The Chess player too, was serious about it, as he was worried about his losing job. The case filed with a big bang, pursued with vigor for some time, however eventually lost its luster and tenacity and left it to natural death. Taranath Sagar like Sampath Kumar was reacting, waiting for an occasion to take revenge. Then, it so happened, Taranath Sagar's man and his former political mentor's wife fought over the handing and taking over the charge of hostel managership, it turned intense and led to a police case. I made genuine efforts to reconcile the matter within the church, however sadly, they were defying. In 2002, an English Medium School was started in Udgir, Maharashtra. There was a good response from the locals, as the school did well and upgraded to first standard. However, by overlook the mandatory permission from the Government Education Department for the first standard was not obtained. Seemingly Sampath Kumar schemed to take advantage of the situation to inflict me and Taranath Sagar supported him, and perhaps prompted his man to file a criminal case against his ex-political mentor, and to implicate me as chairman. Sampath Kumar was all along venomous and fuming and perhaps financed the case. Long after, Block education officer filed the FIR for admitting children to first standard without statutory permission and collecting school fee. My name was in the FIR, the arrest warrant was issued and on June 15, 2006, police were at my doorsteps. I did not know about it, as I was in the court. The Aggressive Opponent, who ritually attended the court proceedings said to one of my supporters in the courtroom that the police would reach at any time in the court. I thought he wanted me to skip the crucial court's proceedings, but indeed the police were actually waiting for me. Providentially, I escaped a well-planned dragnet. Within days, I filed an application for transit bail in the Bombay High Court, it was granted. Then I got the regular bail from the Aurangabad Bench of Bombay High Court and filed an application to quash my name from the FIR; the

Honorable court granted my prayer, as then I was not acting as chairman. These were tormenting moments, I was in agony and tears for days and help came from unknown sources that gave me courage; unknown people came to support and stand by me. The Priests of Vengeance picked up even microscopic issues to mentally agonize and demoralize me to secure their position and frustrate my struggle for truth and justice.

In 2008, there arose a man in Mumbai who was like a separatist. He tried to entangle me in another criminal case. Sampath Kumar appointed him, as the manager of the Bombay Conference Centre (formerly known as Friendship Centre), Mumbai by defying the appointment procedure. He found very tough to take the charge, so agitated. He filed a police complaint that I was exerting my influence and interfering in his administrative work through the person, then the Executive Secretary of the Bombay Conference's Regional Board who was occupying an office in the Centre. His office secretary filed a non-cognizable FIR against him, which gives details about the incident. Actually, he trespassed into his office in his absence, stole office files, papers and indecent photographs. Given the seriousness of offence, tried to come out it by filing a false criminal writ petition against the church and me in the Bombay High Court. I was amazed, he lost the balance of his mind, made defamatory averments and exhibited indecent photographs of Taranth Sagar's former political mentor with his secretary, showing him as me to mislead the court, tarnish my image and obtain an order to register the crime against me; however the criminal writ petition dismissed. Then, he rushed and filed a criminal complaint in magistrate's court, Mumbai. In the course of court hearings, he spoke to me, asked me, whether I would succeed in my lawsuit, I did not comment. Then he said, he had close contacts with the bishops and would negotiate to settle my issue, if I withdraw my lawsuit. He said, 'I studied your case and found nothing deserving such action, you are merely the victim of circumstances. Then he said, "I went against you because you dissolved Rasayani Pastorate", a place close to Mumbai. I said, as per rule whenever a local church's full membership slips below thirty, it loses administrative and representative privileges, however worship and pastoral care continues as usual and the status restored when it regains the requisite number of full members. He was not satisfied with my explanation, for he appeared like a language fanatic. The case went on for more than a year before it was dismissed.

The Priests of Vengeance had hostile attitude; I was mentally agonized, and they put me in a great financial hardship and deprived me of my rights and privileges. The charisma of fictitious issues and the use of free flow of church money could not help them seize me. By divine providence, I stood firm against their massive malicious stokes.

Spiritual Strength

I was longing to have the spiritual strength to face the ordeal I was going through. I was comforted and encouraged by the life and witness of men of God who were unshaken in their testing times, never were they despondent even at the risk of losing life, reclined in wilderness, revived spiritual strength and sharpened their understanding of God's purpose for their life. These thoughts were like balm to my pains, kept me focused and steady, and energized me in my wilderness days to live the life of faith and hope.

I turned to God in anguish and tears. In monologue, I asked why God allowed my antagonists to crush me. I searched my heart in my loneliness, pondered over my failings and waited for answers. I said, God, you know the conspiracy; nothing is hidden from you and do I deserve such sufferings disproportionate to my shortcomings? The answers to my juvenile inquisitiveness came from the Bible; it enlightened, strengthened, and stabilized me in my struggle against falsehood and injustice that shook the roots of the church's spiritual and moral values. I perceived power seekers among religious leaders were not alive to spirituality and people were indifferent to it. In my loneliness, my faith shook, I could not think like Job, the Biblical figure. At times, I was tempted to think if God really cared for me, as he watched me like an automatic watchmaker while I suffered pain and agony. I heard my inner voice say, wait for God's hour, and would you accept good from God and not troubles, the voice became clear and loud and rebuked my insane thinking, mellowed and inspired me to trust him and his divine justice in the times of sunshine and shadows. I felt satisfied, revived, and spiritually strengthened that kept me going in my faith, even if it meant to lose the joy of life and live in a valley of darkness, for I believe that God does not test his chosen ones beyond their endurance; it was my ultimate source of strength and comfort.

The Priests of Vengeance misled, stirred emotion, and coerced people to gather yes votes to destroy me. I felt sad; the democratic process was often abused in the church. Generally, leading persons did not oppose bishops in the open, as most of them were either under their appointment or some obligation or pressure. I observed that the church democracy was sinking; it became like ochlocracy and the prophetic voice was not taken in good spirit when it impinged the interest of those who mattered. In such circumstances, I needed spiritual strength to face the Collusive Clique. Once, a good Methodist elaborated the pitfalls of such farcical democratic practices in the church. He said that it ruined the good work of the church. He drew my attention to the success story of the Roman Catholic Church and said that there are no unnecessary interferences in administration of institutions. I understood his view point; however I recognize, there exists no absolute authoritarian or democratic forms of church governance either in Roman Catholic or Protestant churches, and such exclusive dichotomous patterns of the church governance do not exist. However, it seemed that the Roman Catholic Church leaned towards authoritarian order, whereas Protestant churches tended to be ochlocratic or oligarchic. Regardless, I think dedication to calling is critical to a success story, irrespective of the forms of church governance, Episcopalian or otherwise. A democratic form of the church governance without dedication was futile, and democracy and dedication are mutually inclusive. I found that crucial decisions are often irresponsibly taken by unfair play of democratic practices and pressure tactics and voters were swayed to raise hands like a horde in ayes or nays, not knowing what they were doing; it was common sight in the church. Persons with oblique motives misled horde to interfere in the institutional functioning, bishops tended to abuse their prerogative to appoint pastors and church workers either to get support or oppose colleague bishops. I perceived democratic practices were increasingly bruised, honest and sincere church leaders woefully suffered. It was pathetic; the church's democracy reduced to oligarchy or ochlocracy to achieve personal ambition that tended to mould others in their own likeness. I was embroiled in the massive conspiracy and needed spiritual strength to overcome it. In February 2009, I happened to speak to John Hanchinmani on some matter; I asked him, why injustice melted to me. He discreetly said the problem percolated from the bishops; however, he secretly toiled to make them porous like an earthen vessel and to strangulate my prophetic voice. He was simply shifting blame on others and I did not react; however, his words echoed in my ears that gave me more pain than relief.

The wilderness days were awful; every day was like a year, pregnant with challenges; however, I survived with the prayers of people. Sometimes I felt if it was not for prayers, then what could have happened to me? I could have been without spiritual strength to endure affliction and agony; truth and justice could have perpetually shed tears in a remote corner of the church sanctuary. I hoped the church would adore truth and justice, but in vain, I was dismayed. A number of pastors, church workers, and laypersons said they prayed for me. I believed God would lead me to justice through the prayers of saints, for prayer is power. I felt moved when I heard some people were in tears before God and others prayed for me every day before dawn. I felt small, said to myself, how much more I should do so. The prayers of God's people rejuvenated me to rejoice in my painful suffering. I never knew how I got strength to face challenges and some were agog at my endeavour. I thanked God; at last, my unwavering struggle against falsehood and injustice was recognized; it was the answer to people's prayers, for its power was mightier than wickedness.

Those who came to know that the gross injustice was done to me because of my prophetic voice were dismayed. They hit me hard by negative energy, so I stopped resisting and surrender to their naïve ambition; however, more they pressed, more I persisted. The words of the Bible encouraged me: 'Better to surrender to God than men', for at least, he would have mercy on us. I was aware, I was under severe financial strain, as all my financial support was withdrawn and we were not living the kind of life we were used to. While, they lived in affluence, they tried hilariously to make me live in misery; it was like antithetical of the Bible parable of the rich man and the beggar. We endured pain and agony like the struggle and simple living of my early ministerial days. The divine providence did not make us bow down to the ungodly desires. We curtailed our expenses, spent on bare necessities, encashed our savings, and liquidated property assets. God kept us alive like lilies of the field in our affliction and gave us our daily bread. I did my best and left the rest in God's hand and it did work, it was a longest agonizing struggle for the truth and justice ever fought in the living memory of the church. Nearly all deserted; I was lonely; however, I always felt God's presence, as I was tossed from pillar to post. If it was not for God's providence, I should have confined to ashes.

The pathetic spiritual condition of the bishops dismayed me; however my faith in the institution of priesthood was not shaken. There was perception that most consecrated religious leaders were short on their calling and acted on unaccepted standard than professionals did. In disguise of the divine call, they pursued hatred and revenge that was defiling the holiness of life and the bishopric in the church. By remarkable political flexibility and speed, they collaborated and competed with each other, either to retain position or ascend to a higher position or destroy others who were seen as obstacle for their vain glory by inappropriate means, unchristian principles and practices; it was the norm of the day. The church leaders by their narrow political mentality acted like proverbial Indian crabs in a basket, obstructing honest persons to taking up leadership in the church. The ministry to the world was neglected and the spirit of love and forgiveness was missing. They preached the message which they did not believe and did not realize that there were better and bigger things to do than to conspire like Pharisees and Herodians.

In my loneliness and suffering, I learnt life's valuable lessons. I concede I did mistakes in judging people by their face value and my senses of seeing and hearing misled me. I recognized that to know a person, one needs to experience him, and my simple understanding of intriguing church leadership caused me irreparable loss. Then I felt men in religious robes should mislead none. In my suffering, wise words, suffering makes a man perfect, and it energized me and enabled me to be cautious. I also learnt the need to treat all in political equality, for you never know what future holds for you, as most church leaders are like wondering stars and live in conflict of interest, ready to abandon a sinking ship without caring for those on board, so was my experience in the wilderness days.

The church expected me to do good work; when I did, I barely received support. I conceived my success was part of allegations and envy to those who failed to do so when they had chance to do it, for they preferred to swim in a swimming pool than in troubled waters. Some bishops were critical of my work, unwilling to appreciate its speed and diligence. I recognized that doing good work in the church causes bitterness and kills initiatives, for ideal was far from real, and the satisfactory answer to the antipathy was intriguing. However, I felt it does not mean one should do only the stereotype, oscillating like a pendulum until death do us depart mode. I did not keep on hold new initiatives for the fear of criticism and latent political ambition of a few who tried to strangle it; however, my zeal for 'need achievement' never diminished.

Everyone recognized that the charisma of John Wesley and the early missionaries was missing in the church. The church needed a prophetic voice and revival, as the spiritual legacy of the men of God in the church was seldom invoked and internalized; authoritarian attitude was ruining spirituality and pushing the holiness of life in the backyard of the church. It was melancholic situation, the religious leaders were inward looking, self-absorbed, and self-adoring. The church's spending was disproportionate to the church work and income, and unchecked prodigious spending and greater reliance on property sale proceeds had bearing on the ongoing church work and spirituality. Overall, the church's growth was more or less static, and in most parts even dwindled. The political ways of doing things and the laissez-fair episcopal administration was of a serious concern. It seemed as if the situation was heading towards the point of no return. I mulled over these intricacies during my wilderness days, which otherwise could have escaped my attention.

No Way to Justice

The Bible parable of the widow is thought provoking, for her perseverance to get justice from an unjust judge was unbelievable as he neither feared God nor had any regard for anyone. It was an amazing struggle that symbolized untold miseries of millions around the world, especially in Indian context, who are anxious to get speedy justice. No sooner had she approached the judge than she was shown door; however, she had unwavering passion, never lost her head and hope, for she believed that one day she would succeed, and repeated refusal did not dampen her spirit to struggle for justice. In the end, the unjust judge felt that if he did not do her justice, she would wear him out, so he granted her request, but in the church, it was so different. I was struggling against the despotic and oppressive action, anxiously hoping to triumph over the conspiracy, however languished. Contrary to my expectation, delaying tactics was a norm to deny justice. I had seen many gave up the struggle for justice in the church out of frustration and with the hope to get it in the other world, and those who resorted to crooked or violent means; interestingly their voice was heard, as though Darwin's law was a sure means of quick justice in the church. I observed that most church leaders did injustice in pursuit of self-interest and did not learn to turn another cheek or walk a second mile, as if it defied human logic. Such spiritual fervour was elusive and perhaps was conceived as a sign of weakness, although it was indeed a sign of greatness! It was a pity; the way in which the bishops frustrated justice did not edify the church.

It was shameful, one had to struggle and survive political tricks and falsehood to get justice or fair deal in the church. Honest and committed church leaders were languishing in the inferno of hostility. In vain I pondered, how come such things do happen, have we not taken a long step forward from survival of the fittest or muscle or brain power to love power, and yet we were lost in a never-ending debate over the supremacy of muscle versus brain power. I was pacified by my inner voice, which said, after all, we are not living in Christ's kingdom of God or Plato's ideal state; it was utopian thinking in the prevailing scenario, the ideal typical situation did not exist, all the more so inside the church than outside. The justice scale tilted, a deep-rooted sycophancy of parochial tendency overshadowed democratic values and social pressures, and vote bank politics thrived. The church's think-tank spoke loudly on justice issues, seldom delivered justice. They were indifferent to what went on, made lame excuses when the interests of political clique was at stake, and scrupulous democratic practices flourished in the church, which gave rise to an anomic situation, defiled social holiness and tarnished the image of the church.

The struggle was between order and disorder, spiritual and material; it was egocentric, driven by craving for temporal power. I recognize, ambition is a powerful force and I bore the brunt for not following those who cherished disorder. The bishops whom I rescued from the political furnace of their opponent bishops conspired and betrayed me. People reminded me for my folly of helping the Friends of Convenience. I realized it was too late to do anything about it. I was reluctant to go before the Judiciary of the land and I found the church Judiciary was lukewarm, remiss and reluctant; barely was there any hope of decision on my petition challenging the inquiry-turned-trial report as, under one pretext or another, it was differed. As said, while the inquiry-turned-trial report was before the church Judiciary, the Collusive Clique spearheaded the massive conspiracy to oust me. No reason, logic, and law could dissuade the conspiring bishops; 'do what you like' was their loud and clear chanting. in such vengeful political mindset; there was barely any hope to get justice. The hostility against me was spreading like a wild fire, driven by the political wind and the bishops spearheaded their own spiritual annihilation and bent on obstructing the free flow of justice. They knew they were acting in partisan spirit like judges to their own cause; anxious to deliver barbarian justice, boasted shamelessly about it, and drew immense pleasure from it. The crisis of conscience loomed large;

religious leaders were absorbed in sordid acts, which even a common worshipper would not dare to do it; it was a sort of spiritual watershed and compromise with unchristian principles and the craze for power gave rise to the tendency of subjectism. The bishops were malevolent, rarely tolerant to prophetic voice, a typical syndrome found from grass roots to highest levels. The spiritual and temporal leaders thrived on manipulating the rule of law and actuated it for the sake of survival in power.

As said, the vengeful bishops did not wait for the decision of the church Judiciary, but in undue haste and wild rage proceeded, passed, and approved the resolution to oust me under their own chairing and, of course, for their own cause. The principle of natural justice, love, and forgiveness barely found any room in their scheme of justice. I thought I should struggle like a *satyagrahi* does (*Satyagraha* broadly means struggle or persistent nonviolent agitation for truth); however, I realized I would not stir the imagination of the horde in the church, as most of them were docile and it was not a property issue. As I mulled over it, I remembered the wooden cross in the Delhi Bishop's House on 12, Boulevard Road lay abandoned in the office's store. It was until then in a good shape about 1.4-inch-thick and 3.4-inch-broad wooden plank, and about five feet in height and its ends pointed, and painted with black colour; however, by the lapse of time, its colour faded. Out of curiosity, I probed the reason for it being laid abandoned and the amazing story emerged. In high drama, it was fixed in the Battery Lane property, not so far away from Bishop's House, and not long after, it was removed secretly to stir the religious and emotional sentiments of the community to achieve an oblique motive, as most are sentimental to mission property than spiritual inheritance. Moreover, to give a big boost to it, at India Gate, near Boat club, New Delhi, on April 10, 1991, the agitation was staged, not as precept but as method to restore the sanctity of the desecrated holy cross. Under impulsion, some bishops and the church leaders reached the place, and the horde from the neighbouring areas that was agog arrived at the scene by Lorries with emotion and passion. After three days, it vanished and the bishop who spearheaded it curiously withdrew; in bewilderment and despair, the horde left and the cross that was fixed was removed and laid abandoned in the office store for infinity. I felt I would not be able to arouse such horde for the cause of truth and justice. I would hardly pull them out of the comfort zone of their living room in my support and sustain it, so I abandoned the thought. I had no other way than to go with a heavy heart before the Judiciary of the land, a nonviolent means to justice, although a costly affair, not an easy and torturous one; however, my only strength was my innocence. I hoped in vain to get speedy justice, and then I never knew the wait would be much longer than I expected and never realized it would be like Armageddon.

Judicial Journey

People cautioned me that the judicial journey could be long, expensive, and risky. I was in ambivalence whether I should go before the Judiciary of the land. After analyzing pros and cons, I felt at least it would not be like the church Judiciary, which was under intimidation of the Collusive Clique who believed my ouster was the solution to all their woes and worries, like the philosopher's stone. They were rejoicing that they would hear no prophetic voice chastening their cherished political ambition and would achieve it at remarkable ease. Faced by the compelling and inevitable situation, I decided to go before the Judiciary of the land, not knowing what I would face on the way. All I knew was that it would not be an easy way and there would be legal bumps and jumps with uncertain outcome. The truth was only a galvanizing force for me to struggle against the conspiring bishops. Thus, I was ready to struggle for justice, freedom of expression, and sanctity of the Discipline, which the Collusive Clique devoured. Challenging the Collusive Clique who was at the helm of the church's affairs was not easy and simple. I recognized I would be struggling against all odds. I was aware of abundant institutional money at their disposal, which would tempt them to circumvent justice, as in the past, and the personnel at their command were unbelievable. I wondered how I would withstand against the bishops who acted like ancient warriors. I could do nothing more than to rely on prayers, meager financial resources, and expected God to work a miracle; however, some people helped me when they came to know about the massive conspiracy, and it kept me going. I got warning messages from their men to sensitize me, who said that the Collusive Clique would spend the church's money; I would have to spend my money, and if need be, they would not hesitate to sell the church properties to raise funds to fight the legal battle till the end to frustrate my struggle for justice. Truly, it was a scary scenario, for they were competent to envisage any means, for the Priests of Vengeance made it their prestige issue of their inferior deeds under the cover of the church. They tried to demoralize and dissuade me to break my judicial journey; however, I was determined to continue as long I could endure, for it was not my struggle for survival in bishopric any more, it was for truth and justice, and I felt that I was a least means to it.

A layman from the Gujarat State whose name was Gideonbhai Christian, '*bhai*' (brother), a curious suffix added to a person's name in Gujarat, challenged my suspension in the court of law. I did not know him or heard of him; however, it seemed his kinsman whom I knew inspired him. Right-thinking people were shocked by the unfair and contemptuous suspension. The bishops infringed the Discipline and ignored their own vows, justified vile indulgences, twisted the issue and context, and in profuse self-admiration, profaned the constitutional right of an Indian citizen. I was amazed, he unwaveringly fought the legal battle, and justice-loving pastors and lay members supported him. However, I was skeptical of its wise handlings and yet I was indifferent to it. Regardless, challenging the vengeful and powerful bishops was the rare show of courage and conviction. I remember his kinsman once shared with me about his contemplation, I entreated him, not to push me into it; however, one day, I was taken aback to know that the action of suspension was challenged before the City Civil Court, Ahmedabad. I was not the party to the decision of going to court and I neither consented nor was aware of the reason for such a great haste. I felt if the court doors were not knocked, I could have escaped the long unfruitful and torturous struggle for truth and justice and perhaps the Priests of Vengeance could have made no lame excuse in the name of the church to achieve their inclusive narrow self-ambition. When the bishops received the court notice, they asked me to sign the advocate's authorization; I signed it without any hesitation. I was defendant no. 5. The Priests of Vengeance were panicky and furious, for they spearheaded the conspiracy. The matter lingered on for a long time, and at the end, the court observed, 'In this case, there is a prima-facie case, still, however, this court cannot help the defendant no. 5 since he has not filed the suit.' Then he challenged the order of October 20, 2004, on the notice of motion in the Gujarat High Court, the court stayed the suspension and granted the interim relief like aspirin for a cold. Not long after, I realized it was the colossal mistake that led to a spiralling litigation. Neither I could escape from it, nor did I have any control over it. The Priests of Vengeance vowed to fight, infuriated by the negative energy, what it may come. Taranath Sagar shaken awfully and desired intensely to challenge it, Sampath Kumar stood by him, and Nimrod Christian gave him unfailing strategies like Chanakya. They moved as if the speed of light, approached the Supreme Court of India, poor Gideonbhai Christian could not imagine their formidable speed. The order was not set aside, and the court asked the Gujarat High Court to dispose the matter on or before March 31, 2005.

Pradeep Samuel, Kariappa Samuel's elder son and the then general secretary of the church, represented in the court's proceedings in trial court and Gujarat High Court, Ahmedabad, who is known by the nickname

Sunny, and seemed politically shallower than his father was. I remember the nefarious act; by malice, my bio data given for episcopal election purpose was wriggled and printed under another episcopal candidate's name in the General Conference's journal. Out of it, an unsuccessful and absurd attempt of criminal intent was made against me. I probed into the plot, as all leads seemed to suggest, and it was Karriappa Samuel who was brooding to harm me in the secret chamber of his mind. Then, Pradeep Samuel was an episcopal aspirant, keen to prove his legal acumen and coordinating efficiency to gain the confidence of the bishops. He vowed to fight it out by any means and believed in managing court orders that intrigued me. Perhaps, he thought, it was a rare opportunity to expiate his father's wrath also than just doing his official duty. They naively believed that I was one of the causes of his father's political downfall because of my stand on CORAR's matters. Nimrod Christian mentored Ajay Christian, his political follower, who locally monitored the legal case and the Aggressive Opponent was his irresistible companion and tool. They travelled by air, checked in star hotels, spent prodigiously large sum of the church, and played all kinds of mischief. They were hostile. Pradeep Samuel suppressed the truth and raised fabricated and irrelevant issues before the court by exhibiting the names of pastors who either resigned or left on their own. On the instigation and without knowing the facts he alleged, I drove them out. In utter disrespect and the dignity of office he held, he prompted the local horde to fill the courtroom to influence the court. As said, I never attended any proceedings; however, by lack of comprehension, I signed for an advocate whom I never met or had given any briefings or he ever contacted me. The appeal was decided by the compromise order to face inquiry and the court allowed me to do my episcopal duties with certain restriction.

It was a clumsy legal affair; those who pursued the lawsuit did not get committed legal help and had no working knowledge of the Discipline, or else they could have put to an end successfully the stretchable legal battle. It did not happen; however, Nimrod Christian's ego was hurt. There was perception that he assumed himself as a supreme leader of the Gujarat Conference, played foul politics, crossed all norms, and hugged all kinds of questionable stuff; it was phenomenal! Then Sampath Kumar's words echoed in my ears, 'He is not a cut for bishop.' I was amazed; despite it, Sampath Kumar was flexible to him when he sensed perils to his ambition. I was grieved over Nimrod Christian's unbelievable moves, and his scathing reaction to Gideonbhai Christian's humble efforts was nothing but an arrogance of power. I conceived he misled and maneuvered pastors and lay members to prove he was a better episcopal leader than I was. Unbelievably, he harnessed every small and trivial issue and amplified them and gave to it his own meaning. However, the truth was on my side. I came out of it after I suffered pain and agony. Not long after, people realized his self-serving leadership style and every action he took had hidden agenda; it was flavoured with favouritism and driven by punitive tendency. It is known to all that eventually people rejected his leadership style and sank his credibility and respect even among his own linguistic affinity and in the sight of those who then held him in honour.

No way could I know how the legal case was pursued. There was perception that the role of secret money was at play, as at the nick of the time, Gideonbhai Christian's advocate curiously remained absent in the court without any convincing reason, and I felt that it was like a picture, worth a thousand words, giving clues of apocalyptic legal misadventure. I felt Mumbai could have been better if the legal remedy was to be sought. My authorization for an advocate was abused in my absence; the compromise order pulled me like a powerful magnet into a legal death trap, and the fertile political ambition of the Collusive Clique was ultimately crushing me. It appeared that the lawsuit was like a jackpot for those who pursued it. As said, the massive conspiracy enlarged the scope of inquiry, added prepared evidences and venal witnesses, and named their own persons to conduct the inquiry. Pressure tactics, the reward of position, and free flow of money helped. The Priests of Vengeance anyhow wanted to show that I stood on the wrong side.

As said, the bishops were barely concerned for their holy calling, relied on managing the trial turned inquiry, hastily acted and did not bother to give any cognizance to my petition before the church Judiciary. The Priests of Vengeance were unwavered to oust me without any force of authority, and before the church Judiciary could give its decision, the rest of the uncanny bishops burst into atrocious doxology. It was treachery; they hardened their hearts, closed their minds, and proudly walked away from the truth and did not show courage to face the truth, while I hoped in vain for the miracle of reconciliation. I recognize in serious matters, punitive action may be necessary, or when corrective or reformative efforts yield no desired results; there existed no such situation. The bishops, ignited by negative energy, choked justice, gnashed teeth, and oppressed those who raised prophetic voice against their action of vandalizing the Discipline, as it was a stumbling block to their political ambition; they consciously and consistency bent and broke the rule of the law of the church to remain and gain the positions of power. In mathematical certainty, they thrived to ruin my ministry and life and frustrated my efforts of seeking justice in the church. The situation was pitiable, self-preserving, and perpetuating. In my simplicity, I expected fairness and justice in the church; but being driven by the passion of power led them to conspiracy, loitering logs in their eyes, no way did they dissipate their zeal to act as judges to their own cause; obviously, it was mitigating justice, and imagining swift and flawless justice was inconceivable.

I recognized that in such vengeful tendency seeking justice was like moving the Himalaya Mountains. While my petition challenging the inquiry report was still pending before the church Judiciary, the Collusive Clique hastened to terminate me from bishopric and thus the urgency led me to challenge my illegal termination before the Judiciary of the land. In the Gujarat High Court, the lawsuit was pursued with legal imprudence ended. On April 10, 2006, I filed the lawsuit in the City Civil Court (trial court) in Mumbai against the illegal recommendation of the Council of Bishops of my termination and its approval by the Executive Council. I felt, if such power was bestowed on bishops, then they would be perpetually occupied settling egoistic issues against each other. I could not imagine and appreciate their political mindset; they assumed extra constitutional authority to which they were not entitled, and instead of spreading love and forgiveness, they rose to destroy those whose voice conflicted with their self-ambition, which was least adorable. It suggested that the bishops of the church lived a parallel life and in the crises of conscience, and their calling was barely their guide. The political life style of church leaders was not conforming to the Christian character. In-fights and disputes accelerated, which were antipathetic to the holiness of life.

The court gave the ad hoc interim injunction against the resolution of the Executive Council within days of knocking at the court's doors, on the ground that the 'show-cause' notice was not served prior to taking the action. Then I received notice to attend the Council of Bishops' meeting. By seeing me, Stanley Downes became restless and bitter, as I tore down the smokescreen of his pretention that he held in honour the Discipline. They ignored him and I chose not to react for the sake of collegiality. Then the lawsuit shuttled from City Civil Court to Bombay High Court and back to the trial court, Pradeep Samuel represented the bishops. He even duplicitously advised me to go on a long leave until the General Conference 2007 and then take voluntary retirement. I perceived some sinister plan in it and dissuaded my supporters from visiting me and slanderously called me an enemy of the church, as if I was. I felt it was unwise to react to his political rhetoric; one day, they would see themselves through the mirror of their inferior deeds and know who they were. On

June 30, 2006, the City Civil Court passed the order on notice of motion, making it absolute in my favour. The court held that the Executive Council did not have power to terminate the services of a bishop. In fact, there was no provision to terminate a bishop. It was also observed that the inquiry-turned-trial report was challenged before the church Judiciary, and the court expected it to decide. However, it was a short-lived success of my humble struggle for justice. The Priests of Vengeance felt small and the Collusive Clique was nervous. They were anomie and ambitionist, seeking to ruin my life and ministry for the sake of propitiating their hurt ego in the guise of the church, which was antithesis of Christ's command to love and forgiveness. Then they appealed against the order in the Bombay High Court. After some hearings, on August 2, 2006, an interim order on the appeal was partially in my favour, the court observed that on prima facie, there was no express provision in the Discipline, giving power to the Executive Council, a subordinate body of the general conference to terminate a bishop. The court allowed me to do day-to-day spiritual work; despite, as usual, they frustrated my every effort to do my spiritual duties; office budget was withheld, and pastors and heads of institutions were intimidated, not to cooperate with me, which was the contempt of the court. I wrote a letter to the treasurer to release the episcopal office budget; however, by political manoeuvring, he replied that he would seek the direction from the bishops. Not long after, the committee was appointed to deal with the payment of my salary, and the then treasurer deprived me of my support by playing the card of S. R. Thomas's absence in the committee and then decided to release the money on legal advice, which was skilfully managed. Sampath Kumar in the Bombay Conference and Nimrod Christian in the Gujarat Conference vociferously acted. They obstructed me to do my spiritual duties and committed the contempt of court. I avoided filing contempt petition to stop multiple litigations and deepening bitterness. They kept watch on pastors and heads of institutions who supported me. Some of them received 'show-cause' notice, others were hastily and unlawfully terminated from the church's ministry; it was an unprecedented phenomenon.

In December 2006, there was a perception of play of secret money. It seemed the bearer cheque of ₹ 5,00,000/– was issued in the favour of the Aggressive Opponent, jointly signed by John Hanchinmani and Pradeep Samuel. I was at loss to know its purpose, as he neither was the church worker nor did he hold any executive position, and yet in a rare devotion he pursued the lawsuit; the desperate soul never remained absent in the courtroom, even when no one showed up. My advocate informed me that he approached him; however, he warned him if he dared again, he would hand him over to the police. Around same time, the counsel whom I engaged for advocacy shocked me. He was present in the High Court, but despite my urging him, he refused to attend the hearing by giving the lame excuse that he had to attend the Supreme Court directed matter. However, my experience tells that the court had barely taken up such cases on warfooting unless they were timebound; his evasive reply utterly dismayed me. He chose to sit idly in the courtroom, raising doubt about his professional handlings. Then

I thought it was unwise to stick to him any longer and felt relieved after I substituted him. On December 22, 2009, although late, I wrote a letter to the treasurer, to ascertain about the cheque after he said, in our telephone conversation, he would reply; however, I received none. Not long after, in a personal meeting, he said that he did not reply to avoid correspondence. His lame excuse did not convince me. I felt it was mere excuse to conceal some inappropriate deeds. There was a perception that a good sum of secret money pumped from the South to win the lawsuit; however, I was not discouraged by it. I thought I might even lose the case although the facts and the law were on my side. Once, the judge who heard the case hinted at my advocate by saying, 'I know you have the trump card,' in obvious reference to the potential power of the Calcutta High Court order. Then I was baffled and grieved over the court's handling; the judge argued like defendants' advocate. On February 26, 2007, the order was passed, and the trial court's order of June 30, 2006, on the notice of motion was set aside. Prior to the order, the court gave me three days to consider taking voluntary retirement; I declined as I felt it was an attempt to muzzle the justice. I informed the court; I intend to challenge the order in the Supreme Court, so there were a total of six weeks' time from the date of the oral order, and the written one was not ready for some curious reason. They were thrilled for their success; misery and suffering engulfed me. I could not believe that when I read the order, it was unreasoned, as it exceeded the brief and defendants' argument. The judge said, just the opposite in the final order after having said that there was no express provision to terminate a bishop, unsupported by any explicit rule of the Discipline or by any law.

On April 10, 2007, I filed the Special Leave Petition in the Supreme Court of India. My counsel argued that the Bombay High Court overlooked the fact that the Executive Council was not an appointing body; neither had they the power to terminate a bishop nor was there any provision in the Discipline to terminate a bishop. The General Conference was scheduled to meet in the month of May 2007. On May 4, 2007, the court asked me if I would like to go before the General Conference; I requested for time to think it over, so the court adjourned the hearing until May 7, 2007. On the next date, I said to the court, I was willing to appear, provided the Executive Council rescinds its resolution. The bishops turned it down and the court adjourned the hearing.

Thereafter, one of my supporters helped me engage Salman Khurshid, Oxford-educated eminent senior advocate, and long after my case, he became the Union Minister of Law and Justice. He conscientiously applied his legal mind to my case and concluded that the Bombay High Court did a major mistake. In July 2007, the court issued the notice to the bishops to file their reply. One of their contentions was that the General Conference declared vacancy in my place but could not elect any bishop. On November 16, 2007, it was brought to the notice of the court that the Adjourned Session of the General Conference 2007 was scheduled to meet at Paramankeni village, near Chennai, and likely to elect a bishop in my place to frustrate the end of justice. The Supreme Court took the cognizance of it and passed the interim order: 'In the meanwhile, if any election of bishop is made, it will be subject to the final as well as further orders of this court.' Then, the case was listed on February 29, 2008, and again on March 28, 2008, for final disposal. My senior advocate could not attend the hearings, as he had to attend the Indian Congress Working Committee meeting in the Northeast, so the case listed after summer vacation. On July 11, 2008, the bishops' senior advocate argued that they had already elected bishops and, thus, the Special Leave Petition was infructous. On observing facts and circumstances of the case, the court remanded back the case to the trial court with direction, not to be influenced by either the observations made by the trial court or the High Court and to decide the lawsuit preferably on or before December 31, 2008. It seemed, drawing attention of the court to the order of November 16, 2007, slipped from my counsel's mind and on the spur of the moment, he said to the court that in view of refusal of interim relief, the bishop might have to vacate episcopal residence. However, the court allowed me to occupy it subject to giving undertaking of vacating if I lose the suit. Although it was borne out of anxiety and concern for me, I felt it was unwise and unnecessary to raise the issue, as neither the house issue was the part of the brief nor defendants pressed for it that pushed me into needless legal fire fighting. The bishops did not cooperate to conclude the trial proceedings soon. They were inhibited by delay tactics, until I was frustrated and reached the retirement age, so the aim was to obstruct me resuming my episcopal duties, deprive justice, and muzzle my prophetic voice.

On July 17, 2007, the trial began in the right earnest and recording of my cross was crawling to close. Then

I lay my hand on important piece of evidence, so I filed the Chamber Summon (Application) to add the subsequent events of deceptively declaring episcopal vacancy in my place and conspired to bring rule for termination of bishop to legalize their illegal action. The trial court allowed it and made it absolute. Then the bishops filed Chamber Summon to amend their written statement; however, they were not allowed. By sensing that they would not succeed in the lawsuit, they stalled the trial proceedings by challenging it in the Bombay High Court and intentionally waited the appeal period to lapse. Then, on January 19, 2009, they filed Civil Revision Application, a wrong move with intention to delay endlessly. On February 5, 2009, the appeal came for hearing, and on technical ground, it was rejected; however, the court allowed them to turn it into writ petition. Then sadly, the case once again came before the same judge who set aside the order of the notice of motion. I was apprehensive of his fair handlings. I asked my advocate if the matter could be transferred to another judge or he be requested to rescue himself; however, none of those things happened. I could not engage the counsel, I wanted for advocacy, knowing his bias attitude towards him. On February 17, 2009, he stayed the proceedings of the trial court until February 20, 2009, but on that date, mysteriously, the case was not listed. Then, I requested the trial court to proceed with the trial since the defendants failed to bring stay on the proceedings. On March 12, 2009, the defendants' advocate by giving a short notice mentioned the matter before the same judge despite my advocate's prior notice, informing him that he would be out of the city on March 12 and

13. My advocate's office informed me about it, so I appeared before the court and requested to adjourn the hearing until my advocate was present. I struggled to get the judge's attention and when I grabbed, I handed over the copy of the notice and pleaded him to list the case on March 16, Monday. To my utter dismay, I could not paralyze his prejudice; he passed the order in the absence of my advocate, not to precipitate before the trial court and adjourned the hearing until June 19, 2009. Then I said, according to the Supreme Court's order of July 11, 2007, the suit was to be decided on or before December 31, 2008. I was amazed at his preposterous logic; he said there was no order of the Supreme Court after February 11, 2009. I was shocked and amazed, as if approaching the Supreme Court was like going to the cafeteria, that too, for deliberate intricacies. Anyway, after realizing his overriding, he tried to correct himself and asked me to file a civil application to resume the trial, yet another procedural delay. My worse fear came true. I was perplexed and dismayed at the court's handling that expected me to overcome legal hurdles by another lengthy legal process, augmenting delay and cost, which could have been avoided by fair handling. I could not comprehend, why it could not be made simple than to complicate, delay, and deny justice. In contrast, some judges were aware of courts failings causing injustice. Justices R. V. Raveendran and P. Sathasivam of the Supreme Court said, 'We have been coming across several instances, where in their anxiety to do justice, courts have gone overboard, which results in injustice rather than justice'[1]. I was bewildered at the court's curious soft corner for the defendants' advocate. I wondered if the

judge was overreacting to the Supreme Court picking up holes in his marathon judgment, setting aside the order of the notice of motion, calling it as preliminary observations and directing the trial court to decide the lawsuit, uninfluenced or inhibited by it. I was puzzled as to why the judge was in a great hurry to report his unreasoned order, which was rendered ineffectual like fused dynamite and yet it was found posted on the court's website. After strenuous struggle, the case was preponed to April 4, 2009, then the bishops' advocate played yet another legal hat trick; he said he was authorized to appear only for the church, not for the bishops. It was merely a legal trick; the general secretary of the church represents on the behalf all officials of the church in all legal cases. However, I had no other option than to comply with the court's direction, so notices were sent to the defendant bishops, such was the vagary of law. As we walked on the corridor on the court, after strenuous struggle in the courtroom, my counsel could not hold back his feelings and remarked, 'Bad luck is pursuing you.' I was stunned to hear that; however, I said to myself, it was not bad luck and after a while I said to him, 'It is devil's tricks to harass me.' He asked me to pray, I said, 'I do pray.' Then he said, 'There could be some deficiency in your prayer.' I replied, could be, but actually, the egoistic bishops were chasing me like my shadow; he nodded his head in concurrence. The civil application did not appear on the court's board despite best efforts. Then the case was listed before another judge, and before he could hear, he went on leave and never returned. By seeing the delay, I gathered enough courage to file a Special Leave Petition in the Supreme

Court. I reached New Delhi on March 27, 2009, and the next day I went to the court to sign papers. I spent the day in my advocate's office. In the evening, I rushed to the airport with my well-wisher to take the flight back to Mumbai. I asked him for my baggage, which was kept in his car's boot, he searched in vain, it was not found and obviously was stolen! I was awfully shaken, it could not be measured like a Richter scale; court papers, personal clothing, money, identity, and credit cards and air ticket, all were lost. I immediately called Imitiaz Ahmed, an associate advocate of Salman Khurshid; I narrated the happening, he asked me to file FIR immediately, as my credit and identity cards could be used in a crime. I could not do it myself, as I had to take flight, so I asked my well-wisher to do it, which he did. The flight to Mumbai was ready to take off and I could get boarding pass after much persuasion. I had nothing on me except the boarding pass when I travelled back to Mumbai in utter disgust, pain, and agony. Awfully shocked by the theft, I mulled over it throughout my journey. I could not get relief, as I hoped, the Supreme Court merely requested the Bombay High Court to expedite and dispose of the matter. Then, no regular judge was sitting to hear such matters; however, there was one who did bench hoping like a professor going one classroom to another. Shortage of judges was impediment; however, justice delayed was justice denied. At last, regular judge was sitting to hear writ petitions. On the strength of the Supreme Court order, the case was listed and finally seen the light of the day on August 5, 2009. The court allowed the defendants to carry out the amendment in the written statement within four weeks on production of authenticated copy of the order before the trial court. The court also allowed me to file additional evidence affidavit. However, I could not come to term with such time given to amend written statement. There was yet another legal hurdle, my trial court's counsel said, 'As per rule, filing of evidences without written statement is not as per law.' Then again, to overcome it, a Chamber Summons Application was filed to amend my written statement as well. The trial court permitted to do so, which was challenged by the writ petition before the High Court on the ground that they too be allowed to file counter to it. After few hearings, my counsel agreed, they amended their written statement, which they could have done otherwise without rushing to the High Court.

The defendants' advocate cross-examined me like drilling a dry hole. He asked sarcastically, why I wore purple (episcopal) shirt like a sacred Brahminical thread and he ridiculously told the judge that they call themselves 'minister', perhaps keeping in his mind Indian politician and unaware of its Biblical roots *diakoneo*, the Greek word meaning 'care or service' and the words deacon and minister derived from it. Then under the instruction, asked me if I would take voluntary retirement with all monetary benefits and compensation. While in the box, I said, 'I am seeking justice.' Not long after, my trial court's counsel said, he called me obstinate. Then I recalled, what he said to my previous High Court counsel who uncannily chose to sit idle, 'We will drive him out with bags, baggage and barrel.' Anyway, by the time my cross-examination closed, I was exhausted and my precious time, money, and energy were lost.

I could perceive premeditated move to delay the court proceedings to frustrate justice. However, the recording of defendants' cross began after marking some documents earlier not admitted. Subodh Mondal was the then general secretary of the church who was generally perceived, as having a brusque personality. He deposed against me; however, his cross-examination could not continue, as they skirted to submit the original requisition letter of February 10, 2006. The document was critical to unwrap their conspiracy, and by delay tactics, adjournment after adjournment was taken, but the document was not produced. Then came the summer vacation knocking at the court's doors, the case was listed after the vacation, as the judge, too, was not very keen to take up cases, as he was due for retirement. They deliberately delayed to produce the document even after the vacation and then the summer vacation was not good enough; then again, adjournment taken to produce it. Then the court was a bit stern on them, asked them to give undertaking that they would produce it within ten days. I realized, with such delay tactics, there would be no end. I was perplexed, expected my trial court's counsel to protest premeditated adjournments; however, he seemed soft with the defendants' advocate. The delay wasted the court's time, drained out my money, and denied justice. On seeing his indifference to their delay tactics, I asked him if I could tell the court, and he consented. I entered the witness box, the court allowed me to speak and I said to the judge that the Supreme Court asked to decide the suit by December 31, 2008, however the defendants made hair-splitting distinctions between expedited and time-bound matters although the Supreme Court had given the time frame. By seeing the order, the court agreed for short listing; however, they could not tame their delay instinct and the trial stretched under one pretext or another. Then I requested my Supreme Court's advocate to press the Special Leave Petition, which was filed but pending and he did it after seeing the suit progress. The notice was issued to the defendants on May 12, 2010, the court did not pass any order, it said already order was passed and as such, there was no need for further order; however, the court gave liberty to come before it, if there was any need.

On the next listing, there was another obstacle; by mistake, the case was listed for the afternoon than usual morning time. By taking the advantage of the error, the defendants' advocate mentioned the case and wanted to move for adjournment, which was protested and the court kept back the matter 1:30 afternoon. When the matter was called, again they pressed for adjournment on the ground that the case was listed for 2:30 afternoon, but the court refused the adjournment and decided to take up the matter 2:30 in the afternoon. However, the case was not called as 2:30 afternoon's listed cases were taken up first, which went on till 4:00 in the afternoon and then no other remedy was available than adjournment. After mammoth persuasion and delay, at last the evidence document was submitted, and the cross-examination resumed. I was amazed, the Aggressive Opponent sat in an advocate's seat, in the first row, next to his advocate and tried to tutor Subodh Mondal what to reply. By looking at his daring and lack of respect for the court norms, my trial court's counsel pointed out to the court. The court rebuked him and asked him to leave the courtroom at once. After loitering for a while in the court's corridor, he pushed off; however, Subodh Mondal did not show sensitivity to the 9th commandment.

After much pressing, his cross-examination crawled to close. Then the defendants filed the application to close the cross-examination, and then after some time, in a dramatic move, strategically withdrew it, the court imposed fine on them; it was the second time during the proceedings that they paid fine. Then they said they have more witnesses to be examined; however, on the next date, they mischievously retreated by saying those who were to be examined refused to come. In the meantime, the judge retired, and after that, the one who came in his place was transferred and the opponents' tricky advocate was not punctual as usual and often absent, appeared in the courtroom like a lord, and waiting for him to resume proceedings was awful torture.

Then, there was debate as to who should start argument first, both side advocates said, the one who cross-examines first; however, the court was not sure, and it wanted to know the written law. After much wait and search in the library, the judgment was produced that satisfied the court. The defendants' counsel started the argument. He said he wanted to argue only on law, uncaring about the facts of the case, critical in deciding the suit on merit as the Supreme Court asked the trial court to do so. Anyway, finally he closed his argument after prolonging. Then he wanted the court to include the matter of vacating house, but the court turned it down. Then my counsel advocate passionately and diligently argued that lessened my pain and agony to some extent I suffered. When the court was giving the date for order, the defendants again came up with the application to file the charge of perjury against me, saying that I gave false statement on oath, as I was not present in the court in Ahmedabad; the court asked them to go before competent court. It was a blatant lie; they knew I never attended any court proceeding. After, nearly sixty four dates, huge expenditure and unbearable torture, the trial court throttled justice, dismissed the suit, and passed the decree on March 16, 2011. The judge seemed on my side; however, he changed side curiously. On reading the judgment, my advocate and I were shocked, speechless, and mortified, for the judge ignored sparkling facts and took limited cognizance of law. I felt that it was not like what Mahatma Gandhi said in his autobiography while he practiced as a barrister in South Africa, that facts mean the truth, and once we adhere to the truth, the law comes to our aid, but it did not happen and I was thrust into the millions of weeping justice seekers. Surprisingly, there was lack of usual excitement or firework in the opponents' camp. The judgment suffered with factual inaccuracies and surmises, and absurdities reified, it was anything but the bending of justice. The church juries had better comprehension of the church's laws, inasmuch as they were under intimidation and the lure of rewards of bishopric, so I chose the Judiciary of the land, only to discover it could not fully grasp the church's functioning and its rule of law. The justice balance tilted in their favour due to lack of comprehension of the Discipline, limited observations, and absurd conclusion. It seemed that the time and tide were unfavourable for the truth to triumph. I realized it would take time for the truth to shine; however, by then the legal suit would be infructous, the frightening legal casualty. I could find, no easy way to justice! I reconciled that it was time to move on, doing some worthwhile to advancing the gospel and serving humanity. Hence, I was not keen to file an appeal against the order. I was despondent and apprehensive of the fair handling by the court of law, as it is widely believed that there are black sheep among judges and there was a perception that the Collusive Clique thrived to buy justice, so I thought it would be a mere futile exercise. Nevertheless, my family members and friends did not think like the way I felt, and they prevailed on me to go in appeal; reluctantly I acceded, I filed an appeal against the order, and to my great disbelief, it was admitted. The active ones of the Collusive Clique became furious; in retaliation, they filed the contempt petition against me in the Supreme Court, for my failing to vacate the episcopal residence. I was disturbed and anxious over its outcome and did not know where we would go since we had already sold our apartment. Compelled by the situation, I opposed it, the court balked with them and found no case of contempt, as it is a settled rule that appeal is the continuation of the suit. However, the court asked the Bombay High Court to dispose the matter in three months. I felt relieved. Taranath Sagar and John Hanchinmani could not succeed in their desire to throw us out of the house; however, they felt as if I threw cob out of web. We continued to live in the house although it was in bad shape and not maintained for years.

As usual, the matter drifted, and again, I came across the new vital piece of documentary evidence, the Executive Council trying to bring new law for the termination of a bishop. In 2007, the two members of the Executive Council, who were close to the Priests of Vengeance and voted in the favour of the recommendation, made similar attempts, although those evidence documents were already admitted in the court, but the trial court failed to take cognizance of it. I decided to file application for bringing on record the recent document, for the proposal was by none other than the Executive Council itself, which approved the illegal recommendation of the Council of Bishops of my termination. The bishops' advocate objected, the court allowed the document to be admitted, but without further cross-examination, it was a big success!

I was anxious to have early hearings and disposal of the appeal; however, as usual, judges changed and the final argument eluded to take place, it was marred by uncertainty in spite of the Supreme Court asking the court to decide within three months.

The appeal was listed for November 17, 2012, but there was barely hope for the final argument. Then one day, it so happened, the board collapsed, and it came up, my counsel was ready to argue and even the opponents' advocate was present; however, the judge, after shuffling the appeal, said, 'Not before me.' Regardless, I hoped another judge would take up the appeal after the Christmas break, so my counsel tried to place it before another judge, but without lending his ears to our plea, refused to take up although the Supreme Court asked the Bombay High Court to dispose it off within three months. Whatever bounded rationality was, final argument matters lingered for decades, even in cases when appeals were admitted without any relief; it seemed like system failure. Then opponents' advocate, although aged, unexpectedly died, and his son, advocate by profession, took over; however, he seemed not so serious about it. Then they engaged another advocate who tried desperately to conclude the final argument as I did before. In the end of 2013, the date for the final argument was twice fixed, but nothing happened. By then eleven judges changed, I was melancholic and often felt to abandon my struggle for justice, everyone in the family was sick of it, I felt enslaved by it, not free to leave the city and serve the Lord; perhaps it gave sanguine feelings to my conspirators.

In the beginning of 2014, my hope brightened, however, of little avail. Then came summer break and the court opened on June 9, 2014, and unexpectedly, final argument started and finished on June 18, 2014. It was extended summer, the weather was hot and humid, I was exhausted and dehydrated; several notes were written and rewritten to the satisfaction of my counsel. Sometimes, during my broken sleep, I remembered some points and got up to write them down before I forget. I perceived the opponents' advocate was ill briefed, slipped into the realm of pre-inquiry and out of the scope of the appeal; picked up far too insignificant stuff, magnified to show me in poor state – I gulped it down and justified illegality of disciplinary action. After arguments, my counsel said, 'You have very strong conviction'; I felt good. However, out of nervousness and by any means, the bishops side thrust injustice, distorted the case facts, and settled law of the church i.e. the Judicial Council Decision 387, and the judge being not familiar with the Discipline and an outsider, happily swallowed distortion and factual inaccuracies and demolished the contention of nonissuing show-cause notice by espousing conjectures, surmises, and absurdities. Moreover, he seemed swayed and inhibited by the February 26, 2007, interim order of his colleague, forsaking objectivity. Curiously, in the open court read the order despite bringing to his notice Supreme Court order of July 11, 2007; however, discounted and continued. He never understood the disciplinary provisions as insiders do and gone overboard, flawed in comprehending it, balked with my side and dismissed the appeal; actually I won it in the sight of the church leaders and others who understood the Discipline. Although I had good case to challenge the order before the Supreme Court, but wary of injustice, I restrained, for the sake of rescuing my family from further sufferings. However, I refused to drink the cup of injustice of bishops and hoped the Judicial Council would take up my pending petition challenging the inquiry report, as it was no longer sub-judice, only to know that not long before, the Executive Council without any force of authority thrust the Judicial Council into the state of suspension animation. I was barely consoled, not even by the thought-provoking words of Philip Jenkins, an American renowned religion scholar, who said, 'God permits his chosen people to suffer defeat and dispersal, for reasons no mortal can discern at the time'[2].

Justice Administration

The lengthy judicial process was a nightmare. As said, one should skip, for it comes heavy on your purse, time, and health. Then I never knew, one day I would have to undergo the trauma of litigation. I found that it was truly awesome mystery mongering process for me, being the first-time litigant. I thought why not it made easy, less painful and inexpensive; however, I never got any satisfactory answer. I recognize it is essential to follow the procedure within legal framework, eliminate an element of bias or unfair practices, and minimize mounting delay; it did not happen. I felt, it was my idealistic picture of the legal system, and the twists and turns of procedural misconduct render litigants helpless, and trying to get speedy justice was like skipping rope on floating logs. Everyone agrees that legal remedy should be affordable and speedy; however, it seems that it would remain an unfulfilled wish of millions unless challenging legal reforms enacted to emancipate litigants from immeasurable and untold hardships. I believe the age old cumbersome process of administration of justice needs change and the scope of vagaries of law needs to be minimized if not eliminated and legal fraternity to internalize the integrity of their professional ethics. If it is not so, then in legal procedural abyss, litigants would be perpetually trapped and find it hard to escape. Legislators, intellectuals, and legal fraternity are aware of the need to cut on cost and time taken to deliver justice, and yet millions are lost in the jigsaw puzzle of the legal process. It was not so easy even for literate litigants to cope up with it, and thinking of litigants who were least literate was very scary. One has to lean on his advocate's advice, sometimes, even it may not be worth its salt. However, at times I was a bit fortunate to have advocates who heard me patiently, briefed me before and after hearing. Nevertheless, there were unexpected delays caused by abuse of legal procedural loopholes that frustrated me. At times, I felt, legal remedy was worse than carrying the yoke of the bishops' injustice.

I felt guilty for spending my time and money, and running from one court to another, and I wished I spent the same time on preaching the gospel message. Often, I thought of quitting the vicious circle of litigation; I was struck in the legal mire; it was hard to come out of it, though I wished in vain to escape. It was frightening to enter court buildings, and one needed enough toughness; however, out of my architectural inquisitiveness, I was delighted to gaze at gorgeous court buildings built during the British era. The City Civil Court building, Mumbai, formerly Secretariat, was built with brown and cream sand stones, whereas Bombay High Court is a masterpiece of Gothic architectural style, built with black stones with stretches of cream and brown sand stones and its walls are more or less two feet thick, even a heavy-duty drilling machine will not break it, so it was with getting justice. The carving on Burma teak and tracery in light and brown sand stones are simply superb, unlike the Supreme Court, New Delhi, round pillars and onion domes, built with cream sand and red stones, in a fine combination of Mughal and Rajputana architects. The height of each floor is high, like an entrance lobby of our modern high-rise towers. There are elevators, but not so easily accessible for litigants and climbing higher levels was a breath-taking experience and locating an advocate who might be attending some other matter, somewhere on higher levels, was too exhausting and frustrating and anxious litigants like me felt relieved when seeing their advocates entering in courtroom. However, defendant advocates could still spoil chances of going ahead with proceedings. Or, case would not be called before court the adjourns for the day or the judge may be on a leave or the court would dismiss the board for the day because of pre-occupation of the judge, or even the matter might have not been listed due to bugling in the registrar' office. Concisely, I faced numerous such risks and uncertainties; however, I dared to face them. I was scared and thought, if it was delayed, it would dash my hope of getting justice, my calculations would go wary and lawsuit would render infructous, a frightening legal casualty in procedural tangles. I had no other way, than to come to terms with it, the way justice administered or better say quit. There were inordinate delays when the defendants challenged the trial court's interim order in November 2009, every time the case came for hearing, something or the other unexpectedly happened. My advocate on observing it said, 'You are like a crane among crows. I can understand it could happen in politics or business; it is shameful it is so in the church.' I felt small and no way could I defend the church, for it was ceasing to be the witness to the world. As we know, the history of the world is full of stories of good men, who did bad things; however, I felt terrible that the bishops did no different and ceased to be the role model of holiness of life. The bishops were lowering the image of the church by rotten and stinking power politics that led to spiritual decay and insensitiveness to the holiness of life and becoming the prisoners of their own narrow inclusive power ambition.

I recognize, human and social factors, too, cause delays in delivery of justice, which of course were out of anyone's control. A judge or an advocate, as a human being, could fall sick or could go on leave for some urgent family or social matter. In the legal scenario of piling of cases, getting speedy justice was all the more difficult unless one was able to show its urgency, which of course was purely relative – what was urgent for me may not be necessarily urgent for the court. The crush of the matter was it gave me unimagined pain. I felt that the legal system was rather weak and cases were pending for years for one reason or another. There is a proposal to reduce time taken for final disposal of cases, only the future will tell; if at all, it will happen. However, the disposal scenario was grim, everyday new lawsuits added and the matters of public interests got priority over other cases. It is inconceivable; judges could dispose of so many cases at one go, give reasoned order, conquer the perennial problem of shortage of judges, and steadily reduce already piled-up cases. I was caught in such a scenario; it was, however, a great struggle and a long walk to speedy justice: the harder I tried, the further I got entangled in it. People often asked me about the progress of the lawsuit and assured me their support and prayers. It was the challenge that met by the prayers of people who were looking forward to my resuming episcopal work, for the good of the church; however, people seldom came in open, for the fear of victimization at the hands of the active of the Collusive Clique.

As I used to sit in courtroom for hearings, I eagerly watched all that was happening. I was amazed at the court's colonial customs, value-loaded words like 'my lord', 'your honour', 'learned judge', and 'my friend' echoed courtrooms. Advocates rushed from one courtroom to another, while entering and existing courtrooms, customarily bowed to respect a sitting judge who was too busy to pay attention. One could see advocates rushing to courtrooms, followed by their associates and assistants with the load of case papers, law books, and citations, and others walking on the court's corridor in their court attire of contrast colours that of a penguin. The litigants of all age group and gender were sometimes accompanied by little children, and even physically challenged ones squeeze their way into packed courtrooms. After hearing, I followed my advocates to confirm what I understood was right and to find out what would be the next step. As I reflect on it, I confess, I do not know how I withstood, as my entire experience was like culture shock. It was an unusual experience and I was in the whirlwind of unexpected litigation. The prayer of people kept me going in my struggle for truth and justice; however, I was determined to fight against the massive conspiracy and malicious desires of the bishops like resisting evil.

I understand, in the adjudication process, a judge observes juridical facts in a given dispute and within the framework of legal parameter and try to analyze them objectively to give his reasoned judgment, but it requires courage and conviction to remain unaffected by subjective factors while adjudicating intricacies of legal issues. I recognize at the most it could be minimized; however, it could not be wholly eliminated for a judge is human being and a social animal. In the process of adjudication, subjective influences may lead to error in judgment and social affinities, peer groups, the state of health, the state of mind, and media influence reasoning. When observing juridical facts, superfluous facts may validate as critical, or rely on the limited observations or considered absurd or not as concrete as critical like the fallacy of reification. The wind of designated senior advocate, former colleague advocates, and an interim order of their colleague tend to pull judges to their side. There are undesignated senior advocates who are equally competent, and some of them were acclaimed for their credibility and integrity. Some people advised me to engage a designated senior advocate and, at times, the advocate who had a face value before a particular judge. It seemed good to have such advocates appear for you; however, I felt that the trend was becoming exploitive, subjective, and as decisive as law. I could not always afford to have such kind of advocates, as their fee was exorbitant than other advocates were and my case was not so legally knotty. However, I could pay advocates' fee, sometimes, it was less or no fee; it was a miracle! And at times, it was like an extortion and betrayal experience. I observed good advocates do their homework well, churn legal materials, crystallize it, place it before the judge, and then support it by evidence and systematic and convincing argument. It was a tense moment to observe judge's response. I was asked to observe the judge's body language to guess fairly, as to which side the judge was tilting and what could be the possible outcome; however, often, it was deceptive. I found that some judges were known for fair handlings than others. People often asked me who was the judge hearing my case, when I mentioned the name, I received both positive and negative comments. I used to think on the nature of human nature while I sat in courtroom. I understand a judge is first a human being, then judge; it gives him an ample scope for free play of subjective influences in the adjudication process. One of my well-wishers nearly scared me; he said that a judge by a twist of his pen could put you in a legal mess that would be an awful task to overcome. Of course, law is technical, inasmuch as, it is a social force to maintain social equilibrium; however, the lack of in-depth understanding of law acts as spoiler or the scope to twist interpretation or meaning of a legal text leads to dismissal, appeals, and counters. In my extended exposure, I observed judges and advocates of lower court tended to take a narrow view of the legal process for inclusion of evidence materials unlike judges and advocates of higher courts; it was like studying a specific course at undergraduate level in narrow perspective and at the graduate level broad, in-depth, and for inclusive understanding. Sometimes, it was not so easy to convince my advocates for submission of some relevant materials to strengthen my lawsuit, as there were settled procedures and rules and any deviation could cause delay or defeat justice. Over and above the tormenting legal process, litigants whispered and top judges talked about corruption in the Judiciary, which kept haunting me. In the midst of it, there was good tiding to check such tendency; the government seemed to be concerned about it. However, it is the moot question, whether the Judicial Standards and Accountability Bill, 2010[3], and National Judicial Appointments Commission Bill passed by the Indian Parliament will become law or any other measure will help change the justice delivery scenario and rid of corruption. Regardless, I feel judges and advocates should be the persons of impeccable integrity and the legal process should be simple, short, and transparent to deliver speedy and flawless justice. There are increasing numbers of voices calling to deliver justice speedily, make affordable for common man and rid of corruption. I wish the spark of hope turns into a cleansing fire, dissipating the idea of tilting justice balance and removing flaws in the legal system.

Although I have not heard of any foolproof system anywhere in the world, let alone legal and doubt if half-hearted measures will eliminate or even reduce shortcomings. Despite the trauma of delay and the uncertainty of justice, in helplessness, people still go to the Judiciary of the land. Their hopes are still alive to get flawless justice, contrary to the scenario in the church, where the very idea of justice evaporated. I recognized, there was no way to justice and my hope to get quick justice was trimming, inasmuch as bishops were extinguishing it. I was melancholic; the religious leaders who were supposed to practice the holiness of life dissipated it. In my brokenness, I watched the justice tottered, injustice flourished in the church. I found the bishops did not care to respect the law of the land or work within it, as if they were like a State within the State. The bishops acted like lords, unmindful of their holy calling and lured others by the influence of bishopric; it was an unrighteous affair. The abrasion of justice was not enough, they seemed to be perjuries, threw people out of the church on frivolous ground to varnish their inferior acts and deeds, and lacked religious flavour, holding the outward form of godliness, however denying its power.

It seems politics does not very much infringe the Judiciary of the land unlike the church's Judiciary, inasmuch as it was shameful, the bishops choked justice in the church and used the institutional funds and means to frustrate justice seekers. The words of the people echoed in my ears that I would never win the legal Armageddon, any amount of money would roll out to buy justice, it was a real-life situation and no way to justice. Some believe everything has a limit, even money, and beyond point, it would miserably fail to bend justice; however I was yet to experience it and the lack of comprehension of the Discipline on the part of the judges thrust injustice on me.

CONFESSION AND CONSOLATION

As said, on November 16, 2007, I was in the Supreme Court, New Delhi for the court hearing. The interim order was passed; I wished it was the final order. Next day, morning, I went to my advocate's office to collect the order copy. While his office was working to get the copy, I was strolling outside the Supreme Court lawyers' chamber, named after M. C. Setalvad, the first longest working attorney general of India, along with my acquaintances who stood by me, prayed, encouraged, and supported. For a moment, I could not believe a call on my mobile, it was Saturday, 11:35 in the morning. The person who was calling was none other than Sampath Kumar, sounding like a contrite soul and asked me apology for the harm he did to me and wished I could come out of it soon. Another call after three minutes, I accepted it and on other side, the voice said, 'I am Nimrod'. I said, 'I recognize your voice!' He was trying to justify himself, how he strived; but, he could not succeed in rescuing me from the conspiracy and blamed Sampath Kumar; it was unbelievable that he had no part in it. However, I felt triumph, as they showed some remorsefulness for what they did to me, which purported my innocence. I did not fume at them and neither was occasion nor was I curious to know the reason for the change of mind, if not heart. On hearing, I said, I do not wish to live in the past, though the past shall live. I pondered over the conspiracy and their curious political conversion. I was amazed, I asked myself if not the triumph of the truth, then what else. It seemed, no sooner, they came out of the influence of power intoxication than realized their folly like Michael Henchard, the character in Thomas Hardy's novel, *The Mayor of Casterbridge*, who sold his wife and daughter in the drunken state. When he came to his senses, he realized his wrongdoing, unsuccessfully looked out for them, mourned, repented, and vowed not touch liquor for twenty one years. Much water flowed under the bridge than they realized what great harm they did to me. I recognize that time is important, for time and tide wait for none; it could either make or break a man and change his life. Like self-absorbed revengers, they were bitter and could not think good in the inferno of negative energy of hatred, revenge, fear, and egotism. I wished they restrained themselves from rendering me miserable and messing up my ministry and life. I consoled myself, as everyone will agree; it takes time for good things to happen!

As the time passed by, we conversed. Sampath Kumar was bitter against Taranath Sagar's nicotine politics who nourished his mind on imagined fear and canard. He seemed to be sorry for listening to him and without mincing words, in agony and shock said, he was at loss, Taranath Sagar could betray him. I felt, he was revealing some part of the conspiracy; however, I was keen to know, what he could do. I asked him about it, he instantly said, 'I will go to any extent to help you.' Fiery as before, however like a falling star ceased to shine. Whereas, Nimrod Christian lacked courage to confess the inconceivable harm he did to me. He babbled stereotype words as usual and blamed Sampath Kumar by saying, 'I told him not to go too fast and hard, but did not listen.' He said he was under the threat of reopening his pending inquiry report if he supported me; it could be so, for blackmailing and manoeuvring politics were used in the church, but he seemed barely fair and impeccable. However, it was believable, what he often said that it was the hidden political agenda of Taranath Sagar, John Hanchinmani, and the spokesman to divide us. Having realized their folly of relying on Taranath Sagar for continuing in the episcopal office, establishing him in bishopric, and destroying me, could do nothing to him, for by then they were devoid of power. No way can anyone go back to the past and redo things, except to move in the future or restitute, as the Bible says, 'In everything do to others, as you would have them do to you.'

Sampath Kumar was very upset and expressed displeasure at the episcopal election trend in the Adjourned Session of the General Conference 2007. He left long before it was adjourned sine die, as episcopal elections were sure to take place and there was no chance for reactivation or assignment to vacant episcopal area though now he was ready to accept any other episcopal area. Nimrod Christian said, he tried to convince Pradeep Samuel and John Hanchinmani to place the Supreme Court's order of November 16, 2007, before the house, but they refused. Then, he said, he advised them, at least, not to fill one episcopal vacancy in the light of the order, but they were in no mood to listen to him, as they thought he was paving the way for himself. John Hanchinmani, a political hard nut, perhaps worried that if it so happened, then his position would wreck and Taranath Sagar might politically rattle. Nimrod Christian said, in the situation, he was helpless, moreover retired and did not have a say. Not after long, in one of our conversations, he said, 'You are a strong man!' I felt, it was his honest admission of the power of truth than the wind of words. Actually, I was neither strong nor stern; I am simply frail as ever before the Almighty. Their agony and bitterness against Taranath Sagar did not dazzle me, for people knew, one day he would ditch them after untying our friendship knot and drive them to the brink of ruins of their ambition and to remain in the helm of the church's affairs. As said, he schemed in political shrewdness, first to destroy me with their support and then he won their confidence, convinced them I would go strong against their ambition if I was not thwart and swore anything, but their continuation, as active bishops in the same episcopal areas, at least in the case of Sampath Kumar. How tempting the plan it was, they yielded to his wishes with the political blind curb that hindered them to foresee political risks, for revenge and ambition are powerful force to involve anyone in vile politics. Taranath Sagar exhorted them by his uncanny political skill, made them act as he wished, and no sooner had he achieved his elusive political ambition than did to them like Aurangzeb. Taranath Sagar and John Hanchinmani attained political supremacy and decision-wise seized the church and acted like veto power. Tarnath Sagar knowing their inner craving for revenge and continuation in bishopric used them and not long after made them lick the political wounds of their great fall. Then, they realized, the blunder of trusting him, confessed mistakes and lamented over his elevation to Episcopacy. Sampath Kumar said, 'It was not you, but Taranath Sagar was the problem, suggesting that he played divisive politics to ascend to power and reign supreme.

I perceived, they lamented for failing to achieve their power ambition, whereas Taranath Sagar was hilarious and lived by power alone and proved he knew the political art of possible than they knew, and of course, I was no way near to any one of them. Then I was surprised Sampath Kumar said to me, 'Taranath Sagar, John Hanchinmani and the spokesman, the unholy trinity is spoiling the church.' I felt, it was his outburst against their failure to abide by their secret covenant and the truth was sparkling like a diamond and unravelling mystery of the conspiracy. Once, when Subodh Mondal came face to face during the court hearings in the Bombay High Court, he said he was not against me but was under compulsion. Perhaps he was, but in no way was he innocent of the conspiracy, as he, too, was one of the signatories to calling the requisition meeting and an aspirant to Episcopacy the goal impossible to achieve without their backing. Eventually, he was soaked in the line of their thinking. Taranath Sagar and John Hanchinmani were subtle and strong to block me by doing unbelievable things and citing the Executive Council's resolution, especially the former one, while the latter one pulled the strings of the lawsuit spitefully and strategically, imagining prophetic condemnation. In political convenience, they did not cease to shackle the truth and justice under the pretext of the lawsuit, persecuted me and justified what they have done, while worried if I succeed, they would lose their earthly paradise.

I grieved over the irreparable loss of my ministry and the family money. I sought God's purpose; it was not easy to know, perhaps the time would tell why God allowed the affliction to take on me. Sometimes, I wondered whether it was to bring change or transform an old person in me into a new one, for sufferings make man perfect, if God intends. However, unexpected confessions of the Friends of Convenience comforted me. I recognize that relative truth is perceived in different degrees at different times; however, pure truth is always the same, and cannot be camouflage or varnish for long, it surfaces more than one way. I pondered over their unexpected confessions and starling disclosures, inasmuch as about their changed position. The Collusive Clique played insensitive and decisive roles of one kind or another; Sampath Kumar had sown its seed, Nimrod Christian bountifully reaped, and Taranath Sagar and John Hanchinmani relished it by thrusting their hegemony and having a final say in the church and dominated the docile church machinery for their vainglory in the absence of creditable leadership. Their stony hearts and hardened postures were anything but personal desire to keep me out in the name of the church to secure their position and power, while it seemed now that the rest of the Collusive Clique had not much ado with me.

While the hearings on the appeal were slow, in August 2011, my family and well-wishers persuaded me to find a way by talking to my antagonists, as even the appeal was disposed off, in either of us favour, the matter would go on and I would get no justice I deserved. Besides, my struggle for truth and justice made me appreciate the value of reconciliation like Mahatma Gandhi appreciating compromise. I felt that nothing was like talking to them. Then I could think of no other better person than John Hanchinmani, a man of mettle and money, though secretly vindictive to my prophetic voice. He accepted readily to meet me on the mutually agreed time and place. He looked triumphed, cheerful, and full of confidence after having secured eight years of extension to his service at one go and on his own terms, an unusual happening. He said he was happy, posing confidence in him and I felt humbled by his and others' recognizing steel in my spine and maintaining good health – despite tormenting experiences. Another three to four meetings were held, followed by the first one. He asked me, how long it would go on, I said that is why I am here. In the course of the conversation, he said they would win the lawsuit; however, after the appeal was admitted, he conceded that the matter was going on, for there is no clarity on the termination of a bishop. By his opening up to the truth, I felt vindicated. After in-depth discussion, I recognized that the crush of the matter was flexible to financial claim, a little here and a little there, as he said, but barely sanguine to restoring my status, not even as a retired bishop under the pretext of the church. I perceived he was actually worried of my prophetic inclination, and the ongoing criminal case against Taranath Sagar appeared to be a hindrance. Anyway, he said he would share our conversation with bishops and others. I felt I would accede withdrawing the criminal case.

Meetings with John Hanchinmani were followed by meetings with the Friends of Convenience. By seeing me, they almost in unison said, 'You look just the same'; I felt a little flattered. I saw them after almost five to six years, the glow of glory from their faces faded and they looked sober. However, in their company, I was not comfortable as before and struggled to forget the past. I felt Sampath Kumar was sincere, but Nimrod Christian did not inspire me, and although Sampath Kumar desired to get into the restitution mode, however, then lacked courage and was parasite on Nimrod Christian's depleted bravado to lift up the matter. They could do nothing more than to speak to Pradeep Samuel, the then president of the Council of Bishops, who seemed serious and concerned; he even met me to talk to me, but at that time, he was not having strong political footing. However, he asked me to make an application to the Council of Bishops, so I did it, requesting to reconcile.

In the meantime, by chance I happened to speak to the Aggressive Opponent. I said to him, 'I was misunderstood and I had nothing personal against you.' Although not fully, but he was adequately satisfied, and to my great amazement, he became one of my supporters. Others and I felt it was anything but great change! Not long after, in our personal meeting, he said, 'Actually, there are no charges against you and there is no rule to terminate bishop.' Once again, I felt joy of vindication. He assured he would work for me with bishops and others and made his best efforts to reconcile; however, unsuccessful.

By the development, Taranath Sagar was seeing himself singled out, as only an obstacle. Then it so happened that I met him in the Methodist Centre, Mumbai. By seeing me, he was surprised and smiled. He welcomed me to sit, ordered tea and snack, and Victor Raja joined us. It was a long talk, among several things, he said, 'There was nothing between us, and now everybody is trying to be good with you, projecting me, as if I am the only person against you.' He said he did not prepare affidavits against me; 'Sampath Kumar got them to Hyderabad and placed them on my table, urging me to join him in ousting you.' In vain, he tried to justify himself; however, it was hard to rely on his story; whatever the fact was, he was party to the conspiracy. Then he divulged what Sampath Kumar said to him: 'Dinesh instigated Francis Sunderraj against me to come to Bangalore Episcopal Area.' He vociferously said, when time comes, he would put the bombshell. Regardless, what made me feel triumphant once again was that he did not deny the conspiracy of preparing false affidavits, he was not its author, was his only cry. Then he asked me, how the Friends of Convenience were to help me, on this Victor Raja said, 'What face do they have, they are the ones who moved and seconded the resolution, recommending termination and it is on the record.'

Then he said to Taranath Sagar, I was like his elder brother, sort out the matter. While, I was about to leave, I said, 'I filed the criminal case, not to harm you, but to bring out truth.' Then he asked me to withdraw it and said, 'Do not worry, I do what I say.' Then I remembered what he said long before to me, 'How can I trust you?' However, I felt, it was not wise to remind him at that moment. I was in ambivalence whether to trust him or not, and assuming, people do change with time, believed him. I proved my point and felt, it shall serve no further useful purpose, and John Hanchinmani and Pradeep Samuel were persistently saying that Taranath Sagar was resentful because of the criminal case, for they knew what role he played. Not long after, I informed Taranath Sagar that the Metropolitan magistrate was dragging the case, he urged me to make a withdrawal application, which I did, against my advocate's apprehension of his motive. After George Edward's evidence in the box, and before the summons order, at my insistence, my advocate moved the application to withdraw criminal complaint and the court reluctantly accepted it. Then he sent a sms text message, "Thank you Bishop, I'll call later." Unbelievably, he never called, despised his words, and swayed by his political ambition. I was dismayed; he chose to confine my prophetic voice in wilderness exile to secure his continuation in the episcopal office. Anyway, not deprived by reason, I did not feel wise to persist, for I felt it was like throwing pearls before deceptive and vengeful leaders, nor I was heavy with grief for doing what I said I would do, for I realized, what he did to one, he would do to Ninety-Nine as well. However, I was longing to witness the miracle of reconciliation; it did not happen despite others and my best efforts. Taranath Sagar and those under his influence did not budge, misused the power of office and John Hanchinmani's invisible hand held the political strings by imagining turbulence in their political comfort zone. Then by the turn of events, some of the Collusive Clique were lured by the prospect of Bishop House's sale/development like juicy bones and by the divine providence, the pending house maintenance bills were reimbursed as my episcopal office and travel expenses from 2006 to 2014, reconciliation was not adored because of the shift of paradigm of holiness of life. The cheque of ₹ 11,41,740/– ceremonially handed over to me in the conclave of active bishops, officers, and others; it indeed annulled the action of termination. In the meantime, they surprised me, by duplicity attempted to take the possession of the house by legal process; however, it was flop show and I, being faithful to my calling, moved out with a blameless heart on December 27, 2014 and rented an apartment.

In persistent political malevolency, I thought if wishes were horses, truth and justice would triumph in its fullness and I would ride over the conspiracy, breathe a fresh air of freedom, unshackle the prophetic voice, be relieved from the pain and agony, and witness the fervour of holiness of life. Actually, it did not happen, neither the church nor the court gave me the justice I deserved, despite my great struggle. However, I was consoled that some of the stars of the Collusive Clique were remorseful in one way or another, for their role in the conspiracy to oust me that gave me sanguine feeling. I do not claim I am a perfect man before God. No, I am not; however I am striving to be one. Regardless, as for the concocted charges, after I go the way of all the earth, I will not be ashamed to stand before the Lord. Until that happens, I am going to serve the Lord in the way he planned, for the preacher in me shall not die as long as I live.

Paradigm Shift

Ido not wish to be imprisoned in the past or write an epitaph on it, as an exclusive memory preserved, inasmuch as I feel it is wise to learn lessons from the past for the present and future, for I dared not live a presumptuous existence. I recognize that an ideal situation does not exist anywhere in the world, much less in the church. I perceived the church leaders were indifferent to the holiness of life, saving the lost, serving the poor and needy, as their focus was on narrow inclusive power ambition, which was shifting the paradigm of holiness of life, and the church's religious leaders lacked passion to preserve and perpetuate the cherished values of the Christian faith. In other words, surging ambition to occupy elected posts tended to shift the spiritual priorities of the church. The power-crazy religious hierarchy and laity were preoccupied with self-propelling goals and cared little or nothing for the mission of the church. There was barely desire and concern for the holiness of life and stereotype ministerial formation did not conform to the holiness of life, which gave rise to vengeful power politics. I remember, when I was a young minister, my senior colleagues used to say, people did not like to contest elections. They strived hard to get people on various administrative committees of the church and after much prompting, some came forward to help meet constitutional requirement. Then the political mindset in the church was different than the present scenario; no sooner the General Conference adjourned sine die than the church leaders of all cadre engrossed in the future election strategies to occupy some creamy posts or membership on church's committees, and the nearer they come to the General Conference's session, fierier and bitter, they become. I recognized it was breeding distasteful political culture, and the tendency of appeasement tactics was increasing, bending decisions and programme to influence prospective voters to achieve ultimate cherished political goals; it seemed like economic determinism. I seldom witnessed the concerted efforts to facilitate the return of the paradigm of holiness of life and the real was far from an ideal.

I perceived after 1981, when the church accepted affiliated autonomy under compulsion and perhaps with some good reasons, the paradigm of holiness of life began to shift, adversely affecting the church's growth, spirituality, leadership credibility, stewardship, and values of truth, justice, and equity. The juxtaposed paradigm of power ambition and emergence of opportunity to hold elected positions on various bodies of the church conditioned the quality of church leadership inasmuch as influenced potential leaders. More people aspired for a few posts; the accelerated election race to ascend in the church hierarchy paved the way for unacceptable means. The conflict of interest compromised the primacy of spiritual content of the Christian faith.

The church's meager resources prodigiously expensed to grease the church's administrative machinery and evangelism and church growth received mere symbolic attention and in-fights among bishops popped up; some acted like political snake, others like political ladder, and such political milieu was conducive to the paradigm shift of holiness of life. The politics of power and position was dominating the scene and right to expression was shackled, true to the words of Jean-Jacques, who said that man is born free, but everywhere in bondage, and in real sense, the values of truth, justice, and equity were depleting. Often, the Council of Bishops meetings were like kangaroo court, held at astronomical cost. A great deal of time was spent to fix brother bishops who stood for truth and justice; however, there was nothing against delinquent bishops. I observed there was tendency among the episcopal leaders to conspire against their colleagues; however, they had no time to bring out a quarterly pastoral letter for the church, as the part of their spiritual duty, at least once, not even in 2006, on the occasion of 150 years of celebration of the church. Amazingly, symbolism was thriving, spirituality was declining, and the church was awfully becoming insensitive to the prophetic voice. The excessive indulgence in the inferior church politics and the thorny property development issues dominated the church scenario and seldom spiritual uplifting and human insensitivity witnessed. The spiritual leaders were cozy with outward form of godliness, became power centric and neglected to internalize the Christian character, essential to the life and witness of the church.

Although there was manifest spiritual pathos, the passion for souls was not rekindled. As a young pastor, I heard one of the church officials expressing concern over spiritual famine in the church. Then I felt, it was sounding like a great idea, packed nicely into the catchwords, and I confess, I barely could imagine its spread effects. As the years passed by, the spiritual famine or spiritual emptiness began to spread like a leaven and spirituality was dwindling at an alarming level. I recognize that when people become worldly, they alienate from spirituality and get attracted to material things like iron to magnet. There was perception that the religious leaders were ceasing to be the role model of the holiness of life; perhaps their preoccupation and overoccupation with the power politics were driving them away from expected roles. The effect of John Wesley's spiritual experience of a 'strangely warm heart' was seldom felt in the church and it seemed by the turn of time and events, it lost its relevance. Unprecedented craze; how to hold and continue in power dominated the thinking and feeling of the church leaders; secondary issues occupied the pages of the agenda, the first never become first and the shift in the paradigm of the holiness of life remained unchecked. The great spiritual heritage of the Methodism applauded, not practiced, for the end goal of the church leaders was anything but the power ambition. Their desire to settle personal differences preceded spiritual concerns and no quality time was devoted to the planning and programmes of spiritual concerns and ministry to the poor and needy. The church leaders were unduly worried about ascending and continuing in the positions of power. I was perplexed to see that the episcopal leaders were even occupied with personal welfare schemes than dissipating worldly tendencies, as if Episcopalians were like Epicureans. The faithful churchgoers were dismayed at the state of spirituality and returned from the church worship with spiritual starvation, Sunday after Sunday.

It was pathetic, even after a half century, the church membership was more or less static, it dwindled in the northern conferences, while somewhat increased in other conferences; however, on an average, the church membership was static over a period of a half-century, it strongly suggest the spiritual decay or pathos. Not long before, a small group of Methodists visited me. I knew them for several decades. They said they felt deeply hurt by their pastor's attitude; he ridiculed their spiritual hunger, and in an inappropriate manner reacted to their assembling in the church for the Bible study without his knowledge and perhaps in his absence. They said they did not intend to undermine the pastor's authority, while the authority-conscious pastor failed to feed the flock of Christ, the spirit-filled preaching was missing, and sheep in pews returned without receiving spiritual Manna and neglected pastoral care. At the end of our conversation, they said, 'Bishop we left the Methodist Church, as others did'. I was speechless, I did not accept that they would leave the church, I could, at the most, persuade them to think it over. I felt in love and concern, pastor could have avoided making fuss over his authority, as they were merely keen to study the Bible for spiritual edification. There were such stories of spiritual hunger of people and spiritual emptiness of religious leaders everywhere in the church. I recognized most people in the church were seeking spiritual fulfilment, whereas spiritual leaders were lost in power politics and malicious deeds, so the church members tended to be indifferent to the Methodism. It was pitiable, spiritual leaders in their pursuit of power paid little attention to the spiritual ministry and care for the poor and needy. There was greater awareness that the bishops' greatest concern was to settling political score with their colleagues and others, camouflaged worldly tendency under the pretext of the church good, but the spiritual concern of the church was their least concern. I was amazed how soon they forgot who they were, anything but consecrated ones. I recognize that human memory is short; however, I never thought it would be shorter in the case of the religious leaders. Instead of leading an exemplary life, they were prompting inferior power politics and the spiritual life style of the religious leaders was causing imbalance between faith and practice and the lack of devotion to calling, shifting the paradigm of holiness of life, and dissipated the little flock of Christ to seek spiritual solace elsewhere.

The hunger for power led to divisive political formations and accelerated unhealthy competitions among the church leaders to attain the creamy positions of power and it seemed it conditioned them; they did not live by truth, conscience and ethical standard. Under the influence of negative energy, the church democracy was abused to survive in authority and bishops victimized pastors; either recklessly transferred or terminated and police cases and litigations sprouted. The spiritual mismatch of the bishops appalled all; malicious acts and deeds made negative imprint on the mind of the church community; it suggested the paradigm shift. It was painful happening, the roots of Wesleyan spirituality shook and belittled the need to internalize the holiness of life, craving for elected positions was intense and the care for spirit and body was the ritual of convenience. I recognize, historically unsatisfied spiritual needs gave impetus to 'reformists' or 'revivalist' movements. If religious leaders fail to neglect, what is first is first, then the paradigm of the holiness of life will endlessly shift and the spiritual passion or hunger may either push Christians out of the church to start a new congregation to satisfy spiritual needs or pull them together for spiritual renewal. The church, beginning from Jerusalem to Rome, the world over and from Aldersgate to India, witnessed such tendency and spiritual fervour culminating church growth.

In the past, men and women of God inflamed by the holiness of life led the great Methodist movement around the world with unbroken devotion and zeal for evangelism, and the church began to grow; such fervour is conspicuously missing and paralysis of holy calling, truth, justice, and equity observable. In olden times, priests, prophets, and kings received direct divine call, consecrated and sent out; however, now the church chooses spiritual leaders either by election or by selection in the church's great tradition. The right choice of spiritual leaders like bishops, pastors, and deaconesses is crucial for the church's mission to the world, and the lack of calling and inferior ministerial formation led to spiritual casualty. There is tendency among pastors (and church workers) to act like a professional in religious garb; it affects the spiritual ministry, resulting in pastors doing routine rituals and bishops posed like an organizational boss. Harold L. Wilansky, an American sociologist in the same vein said, 'there was such tendency among pastors to act as professional'[1]. In spiritual insensitiveness, church leaders acted like secular leaders by looking through the religious looking glass, it was pathetic, their 'sacred calling' was becoming like a profession. I recognize, although there is an element of professionalism, so far it related to specialized training; however the bottom line is that it is sacred calling.

The church was in a great hurry and anxiety to elect bishops to fulfil the constitutional requirement without caring for the sanctity of bishopric. The election of a bishop, a spiritual and temporal leader of the church conducted merely to filling the constitutional post by the utter neglect of calling and in a great haste, to continue the tradition of the infinite constitutional episcopal continuum. As a result, episcopal aspirants who lacked ministerial standards, held inferior report cards and craved for comfort and honour were elected. Not long before, I was pleasantly surprised to receive unexpected guests from south India. They came to comfort me when they heard how my colleagues conspired and victimized me. In the course of conversation, they expressed their anguish over aspiring episcopal candidates and the ways in which bishops' election won. One of them said, and then one of the newly elected bishops offered him 4000 pieces of one-rupee nickel coins to buy his vote. He said, he refused to accept it and politely said, 'Sir, how can I take money from you when we give offertory and donation for pastoral support.' Surely, such episcopal candidates with temporal paradigm are elected to lead the church at the utter neglect of holiness life. The spiritual work of the church given in the hands of the episcopal leaders who expected the church to serve them, serving the church sacrificially was their least concern. It was observed servanthood among the episcopal leaders was missing; authoritarianism and intimidation overshadowed the calling. It suggested a significant shift; the spiritual leadership of the church was not the role model of a servant leader; it seemed they were self-seeking leaders who expected others to serve them. Over the years, there was lack of seriousness and discerning sensitivity in electing episcopal leaders was rising. I observed episcopal candidates with tainted record were considered as best bet, as inferior power politics flourished, for they were the kind of persons who ideally fitted the prescription of the politically motivated active bishops who craved to form a political clique in the Council of Bishops, such pitiable political attitude, soiled the image of bishopric.

Of course, there were delegates who voted episcopal candidates on spiritual standing, while others tactically swayed and frustrated episcopal elections for the sake of monetary gain. The episcopal leaders and the church bureaucrats did horse-trading and supported those who hailed their ways. The urgency of fulfilling the constitution requirement of the church influenced delegates to cast vote in the favour of undeserving stock, the crises of spirituality had an accelerating spread-effect. It was antithesis, the bishops with temporal mindset tried to shoulder the spiritual responsibility of the church, and material and political tendency in India, too, was fertile to such potential endeavour. When questioned on their faith and practice, they raised eyebrow in intolerance. The inconsistent life style and duplicity of bishops discredited bishopric; in the public, they masqueraded as spiritual leaders; however, in private, they were crazy materialistic lots. Nevertheless, there were some episcopal candidates with a fine bend of spiritual and temporal acumen, but they lacked elective charisma to gather votes in their barn and found no favour and support among bishops who cherished power ambition more than the holiness of life.

There was rivalry among the bishops to gain supremacy over each other like struggle to be first among equals; it was an ongoing scene. The Council of Bishops meetings were the breeding ground for conspiracy, injustice, and malicious plots against their episcopal colleagues who refused to assimilate inferior political traits of the majority. It was disgusting, some bishops managed to get complaints from venal persons to destroy their colleague. The situation in the church was far from being adorable and spiritual leaders were not penitent to ruining their own great calling. Prior to becoming the affiliated autonomous church, there was a separate body presided over by an active bishop to adjudicate serious complaints against bishops. I believe, to substitute it by the unfair system was a big blunder, where Bishops act as judges to their own cause[2]. In the old system, at least there was some hope to meet the end of justice unlike in the present one, where a few Bishops driven by negative energy can script the destiny of their episcopal colleague. I failed to comprehend why such better justice system with its checks and balances substituted with unjust, unfair, and manipulative collegiums justice system that often used like Lynch law. Bishops with malicious intention could marginalize their episcopal colleagues by show of hands and uproot them from the bishopric. It was ironical; the General Conference of the church elected bishops by secret ballot without any discussion, and with two-thirds votes of the delegates present and voting, whereas only three unjust and spiteful bishops could annihilate him from the episcopal leadership itself. Three active bishops made a majority among the bishops who had right to vote; it was all that necessary and sufficient, no logic or rationale held any good and retired bishops maliciously stirred to agitate in their support, gave meaning to words in exaggeration for their own advantage. No one asked or cared to know, whether the disciplinary action contemplated had any ground, reason, or justified or commensurate, it was awful crises of love, forgiveness, and reconciliation, for self-preserving and self-perpetuating persons were elevated to bishopric in utter insensitiveness to the holiness of life.

The stewardship scenario was gloomy. Not long before, I happened to meet a church leader of another denomination who said, people bow down to the one who holds church' purse. His words fired my imagination, stretched my mental muscles, and I concurred his view. He was down to earth, in understanding the general tendency of people in the church hierarchy, who acted like Mammon. The treasurer influenced leaders who mattered and dominated the church's affairs. Long before, a senior pastor narrated a story on how an episcopal leader in the church, by seeing the then treasurer stood in adulation, exclaimed here cometh the one who puts a loaf of bread in our plate! I was at loss to hear such utterances, of no other than an episcopal leader who failed to rely on divine providence. Some bishops even asked the treasurer, how much money, I hoped it was a satire! He was magical, even the church Judiciary could not escape from him. There was a petition against him on financial misconduct, I was bewildered to read, the injudicious part of the Judicial Council's Decision No. 515, which said, 'No further petition on this matter will be entertained.' I could not believe that it could lose the sense of fairness and give sweeping judicial cover that deprived the petitioner, even right to review. It was unprecedented, not found in any other reported Judiciary's decisions. People were indifferent to what the treasurer did and obliged him despite his lack of commitment to the mission of the church and imprudent financial handlings. It seemed the need for funds to carry forward the church work operation and keeping it on hold worried the church workers, so they did not feel wise to antagonize him. He easily won support of the church leaders and enjoyed immunity due to the magic of holding the church's purse. Money is the medium of exchange for goods and services in nonbarter economy and Mammon per se is not evil; however, it can breed evil if prodigiously used for exploitative and inappropriate purpose of defeating the end of justice or such other purposes.

I believe the church treasurer can play a positive role in advancing the mission of the church. The quadrennial election of the treasurer was discontinued under the new dispensation of affiliated autonomy, while treasurers of all other bodies within the church were elected, which was inconsistent with democratic norm or tradition, and not in the interest of the church and not in line with other denominational churches. It gave impression, as if the church ran out of democratic norms to give rise to the perpetual treasurer, who ruled magically and over-ruled everything and everyone. Bishops and elected members of various bodies of the church come and go; however, the treasurer remains until he retires, and he even could manoeuvre the extension in the absence of clear vision for the church and reluctance of parasitical leadership to change the treasurer. He triumphed; the absence of credible episcopal leadership and vision for the church did not worry him of losing the crown of Mammon and big benefits. As years passed by, the treasurer mastered the skill on how to use his office to influence people and thrust his roots like banyan tree in all spheres of life and ministry of the church, secretly wrestled to elevate his favourite candidates to bishopric with oblique motive and to command their allegiance. Such bishops lacked prophetic voice, were soft on him, and left him loose to enjoy undiluted, undisturbed, unrestricted and unlimited power. It was pathetic, the church treasurer even did auditing of others' accounts; however, no one did his, and as if he was either impeccable or church' leaders worried about the disclosure of his favours. Interestingly, he managed to become treasurer of all programme councils of the church and held several other posts, as if there was dearth of competent persons in the church. I perceived the church leadership became treasurer centric and relied on him and none others, confirming his indispensability to act like a cushion treasurer. What's more, they even elected him as recording secretary to write minutes and draft resolutions; he used the occasion to cover and safeguard himself and his political clique, and to torment the voice of dissent. The general secretary of the church, often an episcopal aspirant, relinquished gladly his right to be on his side and to get his blessing for his episcopal election.

In 1993, the GBGM of the United Methodist Church raised serious concern over handling of permanent endowment income and the gain in exchange[3]. They sounded urgency to change of treasurer though not with so many words. Despite, he manoeuvred to overcome the challenges with the help of the spokesman and the leaders with vested interest. Greatly disappointed by it, the GBGM then appointed the Area Financial Executive in India to canalize income from fund accounts, directly to the church's institutions through Consortium of Missions and Institutions. The church became a helpless spectator, incapable of doing anything than to fall in line with it. The GBGM auditors found that the treasurer held funds in investment without releasing it to end beneficiaries, and gain-in-exchange misappropriated and interest from it was not credited to original beneficiaries' accounts. He misled the church, gave lame excuses, and made the age-old practice scapegoat without seeking a fresh mandate. There was chaos and confusion, however, he triumphed. The GBGM's stewardship concerns were overlooked and gave to it a political face and leaders stirred people emotionally and made them to act like a demagogue under the pretext of the church's prestige. He won the battle; however, the church lost the war. The church was asked to pay back the gain-in-exchange and interest earned on it. I remember, in the Bangalore meeting, the cheque of about ₹ 1,00,00,000/– written and signed to pay the first installment and thenceforth the GBGM funding sharply reduced.

There was lack of stewardship in other areas as well. At the time of the winding up of the IMBO operation, I was surprised to know that the church treasury staff was on the payroll of the IMBO, rendering services to the church's treasury office like outsourcing. They gave the staff full benefits in settlement of their services, and then again, the same staff re-employed at the last drawn salary without rationalizing either the salary scale or the size of work force. A few others and I balked; he managed to keep me out of the settlement committee and had his final say on the matter.

The Executive council's meetings were flooded with financial statements of various accounts; it confused than clarified; however, people were hilarious to get bulky financial statements, only to get engrossed in it, while agenda matters swiftly dealt. There was lack of flow in the balance sheet of the church, hope not, with the aim to mislead. A financial analyst, who glanced through it, said if such a thing happens in a corporate sector, he could have been even fired. There was perception that the details of the episcopal expenses highlighted to divert attention from his expenses as it was lay buried in the treasury's office budget, honorariums, perquisites, and unnecessary international travels, and although there was no budgetary provision for his out-station travels, he amazingly travelled like a busy corporate executive, keeping one foot on arrival and other on the departure lounge, barely contributing to the life and ministry of the church, giving impression to act like a glorified accountant: 'You raise funds, I pay' was his alibi mindset. There were no initiatives on the stewardship vision for the church and ability to articulate it. In my conversation with him, during our travels, on the financial short fall in the church's treasury, I was amazed, he simply said, 'Bishop, let us manage as long we are in position and leave the rest to future leaders'; he did not offer any innovative idea or new initiative to deal with it. Shifting the responsibility on others was the general tendency in all spare of the church's life that needed change. The short fall in church finance was of a great concern, but the fact that the episcopal leaders and others falling short on their calling and dedication was of still a greater worry. Curiously, on several occasions, he passionately cited stories from the great Hindu epics to hammer home his viewpoints. His focus was on easy source of money, especially income from property sale cum development and craved for more benefits. I remember, bishops' pension was reduced from two-thirds the last drawn salary, on the logic that the pension was fixed at the time when bishops' salary was low; however, he pretended, as if he was short on memory, for he knew the revised pension policy. The Executive Council appointed the pension committee under my chairmanship, which met from October 17 to

18, 2001 in Chandigarh to review then existing pension policy and bring fresh recommendations. He was on the committee and its recommendations were adopted and implemented. Ironically, he bit his own logic, less the salary more the pension, but for himself, the bigger the salary, the bigger the pension. He masterly changed his lay pension into full pension when his salary was much higher than of bishops. The spiteful bishops throttled my voice; I was disabled. In 2005, I watched silently the melodrama in the meeting held in Shillong. He acted, as if he cared for the church's economy, however, nothing was tangible. On the contrary, he did his best efforts to get for himself golden eggs out of the fluid political situation without caring for the goose. He exploited sympathy of members out of his wife's demise, and the bishops with selfish motive to get his reciprocal support to continue in episcopal office beyond their superannuation, in appeasement, approved his request[4]. It was a pity that the bishops and other leaders were yielding to his materialistic gluttony in the midst of galloping financial deficit, and then close to ₹ 16,00,00,000/– and it may increase or decrease, depending on how much property assets will be liquidated and stewardship sensitivity internalized. He was smiling; the church did not even have privilege to shed tears while paying for his prodigious paraphernalia. The expenses on greasing the church's gigantic administrative machinery galloped, the funds on hand shrunk, and the church leaders did not do more in less. Unrelenting property sale and development proceeds could not reduce the huge deficit due to imprudent administrative spending, so advances from other fund accounts were drawn to meet the ends. The greater dependence on easy source of income gave rise to tensions in the church community, paved the way for litigations, bishops were booked in criminal cases, leaders lured people to inferior means and dissuaded new initiatives. I recognized, the affiliated autonomy without adequate funds was a premature act, and perhaps, some might prefer to call it as historical necessity. Interestingly, the treasurer escaped all controversies, confrontation, and disputes, and bishops were the ones, who faced them although he was the key player and omnipresent member in all property sale and development committees. A great deal of energy and time was invested in liquidating property assets at undervaluation; however, no significant efforts were made in instilling the value of giving to the mission of the church. What he did went unnoticed, so long, church leaders kept satisfied; fed on milk and honey and lack of stewardship concern was the cumulative result of the power ambition that shifted the paradigm of holiness of life.

Obviously, the church leaders were indifferent to truth, justice, and equity, which are the indispensable expression of true piety, and defied and bent the rule of law of the church, gone by different rules to muzzle the prophetic voice, which they perceived as an obstacle to their survival in power. The religious leaders played malicious roles that tarnished the life and witness of the church; it was a potent source of disorder in the church; it was then a dominant trend unlike in the past. They seldom worried about the paradigm return and held captive the universal values of truth, justice, and equity for the sake of their craving to ascend or retain the positions of power in the church hierarchy.

They tilted justice to achieve power ambition and to victimize those who were committed to holiness of life and evaded truth and justice. The right to expression was symbolically recognized, however not adored; ochlocracy was the political way in the name of democracy and the church governance was oligarchic. In self-defense and to hold on to power, they conspired to destroy church leaders who were not hibernated to the law of Christ and the rule of law. By political collusion, bishops made others a scapegoat and defied the Discipline to remain in helm of the church's affairs. In such political milieu, there was very little or no hope of survival in the ministry of the church or get justice. In the absence of collective conscience among the custodians of the church law, they had gone by different rules and what they said was the rule when it pinched their power ambition. Regardless, truth cannot be kept in a veil too long; it shines even in darkness although by then, a great injustice is done to those who are committed to church's ideals. The vengeful politics victimized right-thinking leaders; it could not be compensated in terms of money or otherwise. The bishops paralyzed truth, justice, and equity for the sake of achieving their narrow personal power ambition that shifted the paradigm of the holiness of life. I perceived that the church leadership was living and growing with seared conscience and their priority was to hold elected positions, authority, and make money.

The church cherished the values of truth and justice; in contrast, those who struggled to uphold it were perceived as potential threat to the hegemony of power-ambitious church leaders, so they used their authority to thwart all that was lawful and just leaving nothing within their reign to ruin it.

It seemed like the way of the world, which I felt should not be so in the church. No, it was my wishful thinking, as from the time immemorial, the force of ambition devoured humanity. Yet, it was not naive to think, at least spiritual leaders of the church should live by holiness of life, not by temporal power and their inner nature should edify the great calling to which they were called. Seemingly, the ideal was far from real and intolerance to the prophetic voice barely inspired hope. The spirituality was merely ceremonial and symbolical. In the midst of the tides of power ambition, to feel spiritual warmth, I believe the paradigm of holiness life, a second wind of the 'strangely warm heart' has to return.

Appendix

Mr. Edward George Manik & Others

Vs.

Area & Presiding Bishop, South India Regional Conference, MCI

MUMBAI, 28th November, 2002

A petition dated 1-5-2002 was received from Mr. Edward George & 48 other member delegates from Bidar district of South India Regional Conference against the misconduct of the 20th Session of the South India Regional Conference held from 19th to 21st April 2002 at R MC Banglore by the Presiding Bishop in violation of the Book of Discipline, MCI and praying for declaring the 20th Session of the SIRC conference null and void on the following grounds:

1. The procedure for fixing appointments under Art 379 of the Book of Discipline was not followed ;

2. As per the conference program Election cannot be conducted on Sunday but in the Conference elections were held after the Ordination service which is contrary to the Book of Discipline;

3. The Conference has come to the final conclusion and decided several matters on Sunday at 3:15 PM instead of concluding the matters Saturday itself which also violates the provision of the Book of Discipline;

4. Under Art 378 of Book of Discipline the Bishop shall have a cabinet composed of all the D.S. , Chairman ,Board of Ministry, One layman, One Deaconess elected by their Regional conference members. At the time when Regional Conference is meeting lay members of the Regional Conference shall elect their one member for Bishop's Cabinet among their members present But in the 20th Session of the Conference held at Banglore , the lay member to the Bishop's Cabinet was not called and in the absence of the lay member the said Cabinet was conducted . So the said Conference has become ultra violation to the Book of Discipline.

5. Under Art 617 Art. IV Conference Lay Leader was removed from RBI during last year but as per Para 617 this vacancy should have been filled up during the Conference but the Bishop intentionally violated the Book of Discipline and because of this negligence there was no Conference Lay Leader and because of this reason there was no lay representative for Bishop' Cabinet;

6. Mrs. Nirmala Sunath, Mr. B.U.Patil were nominated as tellers by the Bishop for counting the election ballots They were contestants and they got elected as delegates to the General Conference

7. Rev. Moses Mamdapur was elected by RBI temporarily as Conference Treasurer in place of Mr. Anand Mundanimam till the Conference but this vacancy was not filled up by the ill motive of Bishop.

Judicial Council Decision No. 575

8. The appointment of D.S was not carried out as per Article 379(1) of the Book of Discipline in respect of Goa District;

9. No District Superintendent was appointed for Bidar District which has sent 101 representatives to the Regional Conference and in place of it only District Supervisor was appointed ;

The presiding Bishop in his response to the above submitted vide his letter No. 435/200 dated 28th May 2002 that:

1. They have not quoted any provisions of the Book of Discipline for their representation;

2. Mr. Mr. Anand Reuben says that he is a member of St. Paul's Methodist Church, Chidri-whereas there is no St. Pauls' Methodist Church in Chidri;

3. They claim to be delegates of Methodist Church –where as not one of them is a delegate to SIRC (the list from Bidar District is attached)

4. Since they did not attend the Regional Conference they are totally unaware of the proceedings;

5. All their statements are totally false;

The Judicial Council discussed the petition at great length and observed that the Presiding Bishop's response to the allegations and contentions of the petitioners were found to be inadequate, unsubstantiated by documentary evidences and denial of some of the allegation that the 20th Session of the SIRC was not conducted strictly in accordance with the provision of the Book of Discipline. The Presiding Bishop also failed to furnish documentary evidences through his Conference Secretary to counter the allegations. The irregularity committed by the Area Bishop in the matter of appointing Supervisor D.S for Bidar District and its subsequent bearing on election of delegates to the Regional Conference as alleged by the petitioners were not specifically denied with documentary evidences. Further no documentary evidences was produced to show that the business of the 20th Session of the SIRC (except appointments)was not conducted after the Ordination Service on Sunday or whether there was any specific resolution to extend the session to resume after the Ordination service.The Law of the Land also prescribes that the contestants cannot be appointed/nominated/elected as tellers to count the votes to ensure free and fair election which should prevail .

In view of the above there exist a prima-facie mis-conduct of the 20th Session of the SIRC held at Banglore in violation of 623 Art. II, 378 Art. XV,617 Art. IV and other provisions of the Book of Discipline. Therefore, the 20th Session of SIRC held at Banglore on 18thto 21 April 2002is declared null and void.

Dr. Komal Masih
Pro-tem Chairman

Dr. Frank C. Singh
Secretary, JC

JC/P/764/2002

Mr. Clerence Peter & Others, NIRC

Vs.

The Presiding Bishops & Others, NIRC

MUMBAI, 30th November, 2002

A petition dated 8th October, 2002 was filed by Mr. Clerence Peter & Others of NIRC against the 20th session of NIRC at Almora from 6th to 8th of September 2002 in Methodist Church / Adam Girls Inter College conducted in violation of the Book of Discipline, MCI and praying for saving the Church by the persons who dishonor the Law of the Land and disrespect the Book of Discipline.

The petition was filed under Para 59.1 and Para 1217.1 of the Discipline of MCI on the grounds that the elections of NIRC for delegates to the forthcoming General Conference was conducted in violation of Para 504, Art. III Sub-para 3 (2) of the Book of Discipline.

The petitioners alleged that :

(1) The Grand total of all the Ministers in full connection with the Conference comes to 6+37+4=47. This means only 6 ministerial delegates should have been elected and not 7. Out of 47 ministerial members 5 did not attend the conference hence the total number of voting ministerial members were 42 in all ballot cast. The Chair did not receive 7 ministerial candidates in full connection with the conference and were not allowed to sit in the bar of the conference and to cast their votes. Hence one Ministerial delegate and one lay delegate must be deleted from the penal of elected to General Conference.

(2) The Council of Bishops decided the dates and places for the North India Regional Conference to be held on 6th September to 8th September 2002 at Almora.

(3) Rev. Sunder S. Lal, Conference Secretary circulated the Notice of the Regional Conference dated 29th August 2002 at his own accord as the language of the notice, self evident and self explanatory and against the Para 610 Art. X of the Book of Discipline.

(4) Bishop Sampath Kumar and Bishop Nimrod Christian has presided over the Session of NIRC in the capacity of Supervising Bishops and Bishop Dr. D. K. Agarwal as observing Bishop also presided over the Session of NIRC. The acts of presiding over the session of NIRC by all three Bishops are illegal and willful violation of the Para 607 Art. VII of the Book of Discipline.

Judicial Council Decision No. 576

The Judicial Council in its letter dated 15th October, 2002 asked for Para-wise respon... the above referred petition from the Presiding Bishop Sampath Kumar of NIRC. Presiding Bishop in his response No. 435/2002 dated 23rd October 2002 filed his respon... saying that:

    (1) "Are they Methodist members in good standing?
    (2) Many matters are clubbed in the petition some of which are in the court
    (3) Some persons mentioned ,are being inquired into by the Committee appoin...
        by the Executive Council for Haldwani matters.
    (4) Most matters are sub-judice, therefore, I cannot comment."

The other defendants namely, Rev. Phillip Masih, Dr. Ashish Massey, Mrs. Mohin... Wellington , Shri William Dilawar and Rev. Sunil K. Masih complained that they hav... not received the copy of the petition .

The Judicial Council, after discussing the petition at great length, observed as under:

(1) The Judicial Council found that the response of the Presiding Bishop, NIRC wa... incomplete, ambiguous and not para-wise. The allegations pertaining to Notice :o... convening the 20th session of the NIRC were not refuted and substantiated ... documentary evidences.

(2) The allegations regarding calling the meeting under Para 610 Art. X were not r... with documentary evidences

(3) The Notice Published in the Indian Witness dated September 2002 under caption "ANOUNCEMENT" to hold the 20th Session of NIRC at Almora did not bear th... name of the Presiding Bishop of NIRC and the allegations by the petitioners in th... matter were not refuted with documentary evidences or clarification

(4) The allegation of the petitioners regarding holding the election of the minis... ministerial delegates to the forthcoming General Conference under Para 605 Art... were not refuted by the Presiding Bishop in his response with documents... evidences, nor directed the Conference Secretary to file response para-wise with documentary evidences which amounts to ignoring the seriousness of the matter and not complying with the direction of the Judicial Council in the interest of the justice

(5) The information supplied to the Judicial Council , revealed that the Notice dated 2 ... 8-2002 for the said Conference issued by the Conference Secretary was posted ar... stamped by the Post Office on 22-8-2002. This has rendered the notice illegal unde... Para 609 Art. IX (3) which did not fulfill the constitutional requirement under Para 609 Art. IX (1) which stipulates 14 days' Notice read with Para 609 Art. IX (3) " i... shall deemed to have been issued 72 hours after the time of posting". Therefore, th... service of notice should have been counted three days (72 hours) after the date (22-8 ... 2002) of the impugned Notice i.e. to be counted from 24-8-2002 for the Conferen... to be started from 6th August 2002 giving less mandatory length of service of no... requirement of 14 days.

(6) The North India Regional Conference held on 6th to 8th August 2002 did not elec... Alternate under Para 504 Art. III (6) as per the information supplied by the petitioner

(7) As per the documentary evidence says , the petitioner had dispatched copies of the petition to all the respondent / defendants .

The Judicial Council is very clear in its mind that it cannot admit any petition of a petitioner under Para 59 Art. IV (2), to determine the constitutionality of any action of the Regional Conference if not supported by one tenth of the members present and vote which means the Judicial Council cannot determine the constitutionality of the election and other matters, therefore the Judicial Council did not adjudicate the legality of the election /action of the 20th Session of North India Regional Conference because it not supported by the one tenth of the members of the Conference present and voting.

However, the Judicial Council adjudicated the conduct of the Regional conference within the boundary of the Para 609 Art. IX (3), Para 609 Art. IX (1), Para 504 Art. (6) as If any Regional Conference elect more than the required number of the representative to the General Conference than it would throw open the liberty for other Regional Conferences to elect more delegates to the General Conference affecting the composition of the General Conference. Can more members be elected than what is allowed under Para 504 Art. III (2) ?. It is not the prerogative of the Regional Conference to elect more delegates than the numbers prescribed in violation of the Discipline under the pretext of the Para 59 Art. IV (2). The silence on the part of one tenth of the members attending and voting cannot validate the violation of Para 504 Art. III (2) and (6). One extra vote has its own important bearing on the minimum number required for election of the various offices including Episcopal election in the General Conference. The conduct of the Business outside the boundary of constitutional provision is and always be ultra-vires of the Constitution and Book of Discipline, MCI and as such liable to be set aside. The majority decision cannot validate the un-constitutional conduct of the Conference.

The Judicial Council; therefore, unanimously (except Dr. Naresh Singh, Member who withdrew himself from discussion of the petition and this decision) decide and declare the Conduct of the 20th Session of the North India Regional Conference held at Almorah from 6th to 8th September 2002, illegal and null & void.

Dr. Rev. Komal Masih
Protem Chairman, JC

Dr. F. C. Singh
Secretary, JC

Resolution passed in the meeting of the Special Executive Council, MCI held on 4th January 2003, at Mumbai:

"WHEREAS it was reported by the General Secretary, MCI, that Decisions No. 569-576 has been received on January 2, 2003 from the Secretary of the Judicial Council; and

WHEREAS the Executive Council expresses its great concern that such Decisions are neither signed by the President nor by the Secretary of the Judicial Council; and

WHEREAS the above Decisions were taken under the Protem Chairman for which there is no provisions for the Judicial Council in the Book of Discipline; and

WHEREAS the procedure for entertaining petitions are not followed as per the Discipline of the MCI;

BE IT RESOLVED THAT the above Decisions cannot be given any effect and cognizance

FURTHER RESOLVED THAT any Decisions pertaining to the same matter should be examined by the Executive Council before it is acted upon.

Seconded by   Proposed by
Sd/- Dr. R. Gyani   Sd/- M. Paul

                                                              4-1-2003"

Executive Council Resolution making the Decisions
Ineffective and non-cognizable

THE METHODIST CHURCH IN INDIA

JUDICIAL COUNCIL

Dr. Frank C. Singh
M.Co., M.Com (Bus. Admn.) & II. Ph.D.
Secretary,
Judicial Council MCI

? STAFF BUNGALOW,
LUCKNOW CHRISTIAN COLLEGE,
LUCKNOW - 226 018, U.P. INDIA.
PHONE : 0522-222578

The Judicial Council, MCI is deeply concerned with the Resolution passed in the meeting of the Special Executive Council, MCI held on 4th January 2003 at Mumbai nullifying the JC Decisions Nos. 569-576 taken by the Judicial Council in its meeting held from 26th to 30th November 2002 at Mumbai.

The following concerns were expressed in the meeting of the Judicial Council held on 11th Feb.2003 at the Seat of the General Conference, Hawabagh Women's College, Jabalpur in response to the afore said resolutions passed by the Executive Council.

1. Whereas the signatures of the President and Secretary of the Judicial Council on the JC Decisions are concerned, it is a set practice that the covering letter is signed by the Secretary and the copies of the JC Decisions are sent out to all concerned for necessary and information under covering letter with the official seal of the JC affixed on each page of JC Decisions.

2. Whereas the signature of the President/ Pro-tem Chairman are taken on the Minutes of the proceedings covering and confirming each action of the Judicial Council.

3. Whereas all previous Decision of Judicial Council were sent to the concerned parties and bodies to the petitions with the JC Official seal affixed on them and the covering letter signed by the Secretary were accepted and implemented in the past.

4. Whereas if for certain reasons the signatures of the President and Secretary were necessary, it would have been better if they were sent back for the signature on each page of decision instead of declaring them non-effective.

5. Whereas provision of Pro-tem Chairman for the JC are concerned the book of Discipline of the M.C.I. Para # 1217 (10) says "to provide its own methods of organization and procedure". Beside where The Book of Discipline is Silent Roberts Rules of order is applicable and in regard of electing Pro-tem Chair person it provides for the appointment of Pro-tem Chairman in the absence of President and Vice President to conduct the business of the body and the Robert Rule of Order is well recognized in MCI. The JC was well "in order" in electing Pro-tem Chairman to transact its business. (refer Robert Rules of order chapter XV page 444)

Cont .. 2

Judicial Council's letter decrying the resolution

THE METHODIST CHURCH IN INDIA

JUDICIAL COUNCIL

Dr. Frank C. Singh
M. Com., M.Com. (Bus. Admn.) L.L.B. Ph.D.
Secretary,
Judicial Council, MCI

2, STAFF BUNGALOW,
LUCKNOW CHRISTIAN COLLEGE,
LUCKNOW - 226 018, U.P., INDIA
PHONE : 0522 222578

-- 2 --

6. Whereas in the past several decisions were made under the pro-tem Chairmanship. They were honoured and implemented.

7. Whereas the procedure for entertaining the petition is concerned the Judicial Council was within its purview and petition were entertained with the consent of the members. The Book of Discipline provides under Para 1217 (10) and 59(10) that J.C. can adopt its own procedure for the adjudication of petitions.

8. Whereas the Judicial Council is an Independent body under Para 57 read with Para 1214 Art.XIII. which says "Decisions of Judicial Council on Appeals referred to it or on the interpretation of the constitutional provisions shall be final and binding on all members and bodies of the Church".

9. Whereas the Judicial Council of the MCI is considered as the highest court of the Church vide Para 1202 of the Book of Discipline.

10. Whereas there is no provision in the Book of Discipline of the MCI that the decisions of the Judicial Council should sent for examination to the Executive Council before they are acted upon. It has never been done before.

Therefore the Judicial Council is of the view that the resolution dated 4th January 2003 taken by the Executive Council of MCI by nullifying the JC Decision No.569 to 576 has hampered and lowered the prestige and status of the highest Judiciary of the MCI which has adversely affected the administration of Justice in the Church.

Rev. James C. Lal   Dr. F. C. Singh.
Pro-Tem Chairman, JC M (Resigned from —   Secretary, JC, M.C.I.
                          Pro-Tem Chairman)

Members :
    A. E. Bose -
1. Mrs. A.E.Bose   3. Dr. Rev. G.R. Singh Abstained

2. Miss Martha Hucenappa   4. Dr. Rev. Komal Masih

                                       My vote of dissent
5. Dr. Naresh Singh   be recorded
                                       Komal Masih
                                       15-2-03

406

References & Notes

Chapter 1: Aldegate to India

1. Rowley, H. H. (ed.), <u>Student's Bible Atlas</u>, London: Lutter Press, 1965, pp.11–12, 14
2. <u>The Bible</u>, New Revised Standard Version, Grand Rapids: Zondervan Bible Publishers, 1990, p. 1111 & Tasker, R.V.G., <u>St Matthew</u>, London: The Tyndale Press, 1961, pp. 156–157
3. Walker, Williston, <u>A History of the Church</u>, Edinburgh: T & T Clark, 1959, pp. 301–368
4. <u>Ibid</u>, p. 310
5. 'John Wesley', <u>Encyclopedia of Britannica</u>, Vol. 23, Chicago: Encyclopedia Britannica Inc, 1972 pp. 414–416 & Personal Relations Influence the Choice. <u>The Works of John Wesley</u>, 3rd Ed., Vol. I, London: Baker House Co. p. 103

6. 'Historical Statement', The Book of Discipline of the United Methodist Church, Nashville: UMC publishing House: 1988, pp. 7–18

7. Doctrine and Discipline of the Methodist Church in Southern Asia, (MCSA), Lucknow: Lucknow Publishing House, 1965 op. cit., p. 14 & Minutes of the Executive Board of the MCSA, Nineteenth Session, 26–28 March 1957 p. 7

8. 'Historical Statement', The Book of Discipline of the Methodist church in India, (MCI), (5th Ed.) Lucknow: Lucknow Publishing House, 2004 pp. 6–22

9. Minutes of the Executive Board, MCSA, August 5, 1973, p. 19

10. Central Conference Twenty Eight Session, Hyderabad 14th–15th 1976 pp. 14–16 & Minutes of the Executive Board of the MCSA, Sixteenth Session, 29th September– 1st October 1954, pp. 7–10. Once again, November 29, 1973 date was fixed for the Methodist church to join the Church of North India, but it did not consummate. (Minutes of the Executive Board of the MCSA, 5th August 1973, p. 21

11. In the Biblical times, prophets did foretelling and forth telling. They warned of impending danger and judgment and courageously denounced evil practices, oppression and injustice. Here it is used, as voice against wrongdoing, achieving power ambition by lawlessness and inferior means, falsehood and injustice.

12. Babylonia is southern Mesopotamia or modern day south Iraq. It was a powerful

kingdom, flourished under Nebuchadnezzar. The Babylonian army overrun both Judah and Israel. Jews were taken into exile to Babylonia and often got barbaric treatment. In the New Testament, captivity is considered as figurative. Ref.: Bromily, Geoffrey (Ed.) <u>The International Standard Bible Encyclopedia,</u> Vol. I, Grand Rapids: William Eerdmans Publishing Co., 1979, pp. 391, 612–615

Chapter 2: Early Years

1. George Bowen (1816–1888) died and buried in the Sewri Christian Cemetery in Bombay. I was curious to read the epitaph, so I visited for the purpose. After several visits and extensive search, I was able to locate his grave with help of the pastor of the church. I was sad to see, it lay in partly broken and neglected state. I suggested the pastor to restore it; he agreed to do so. However, the words on the gravestone read as, 'A man of eminent piety, rare selfdenial and untiring zeal for Christ during a continuous residence in this city of 40 years. Truthful in every good work', Col. 1:10

2. <u>Doctrine and Discipline,</u> <u>op</u>. <u>cit</u>., 1965, p. 7

3. <u>Official Journal of Bombay Regional Conference,</u> IV Session Nasrapur, Pune: Spicer College Press, 1984, p. 17

4. <u>The Book of Discipline</u>, (5th Ed.) Lucknow: Lucknow Publishing House, 2004, p. 110

5. Weber, Max, <u>The Protestant Ethics and the Spirit of Capitalism</u>, New York: Charles Sons, 1958, p. 183

Chapter 3: Serving the Poor and Needy

1. 'Quadrennium Report of the Council of Relief and Rehabilitation', <u>The Official Journal of The General Conference,</u> Adjourned 4th Regular Session, 23–30 November, Bangalore, Lucknow: Lucknow Publishing House, 1994 pp. 215–219

2. Dalai Lama, <u>My Land and My People</u>, New York: Potala Corporation, 1983

3. Huberman, Leo, <u>Man's Worldly Goods</u>, Hesperides Press, 2006

4   Cornelius, Cyril & others, <u>The Report of the Enquiry Committee</u>: The Council of Bishops, Methodist Church in India, 29 August 1994

Chapter 4: Vision Came True

1. <u>The Official Journal of the General Conference</u>, Special Session, MCI September 11–15, New Delhi, 1991 p. 45

2. <u>The Bible</u>, op.cit p. 1348

3. There were suggestions to eliminate candidates who do not secure a certain number of votes in continuous three ballots or introduce an electronic voting system to save time and to facilitate quick election. But, no efforts were made to see that men of God were elected and candidates with tainted records discouraged to run for episcopal office.

4. <u>The Official Journal of Bombay Regional Conference</u>, XII Session, Lonavala 10–13 March 1994, p. 23

5. <u>The Official Journal of the General Conference</u>, 4th Regular Session, at New Delhi, 22–31 May 1994, p. 41

6. The property records are not properly maintained or updated and in some cases, records are missing. Most property titles deeds are not legally muted in the name of the church's trust and new properties are purchased in the name of the Methodist Church in India Trust Association. The poor property management led to unnecessary debate on legal complications. A greater reliance on the property development to raise money, further augmented problems.

7. <u>The Report of Inquiry Committee</u>, 29 August 1994, p. 117

8. <u>The Official Journal of the General Conference</u>, 4th Session, <u>op</u>. <u>cit</u>., pp. 25–47

9. <u>The Official Journal of the General Conference</u>, 4th Session, <u>op</u>. <u>cit</u>., pp. 48–78

10. <u>The Official Journal of the General Conference</u>, 4th Adjourned Session, Bangalore, 23–30 November 1994, p. 72

11. Freud, Sigmund, <u>The Interpretation of Dreams</u>, Noida: Maple Press, Script Ed, 2010, p.164

Chapter 5: Breaking New Grounds

1. <u>Doctrine and Disciple</u>, <u>op</u>. <u>cit</u>. p. 5
2. Roberts Redfield, a sociologist studied the Mexican Village of 'Tepoztl'an. (<u>Tepoztl'an A</u>

<u>Maxican Village: A Study of Folk Life</u>, Chicago: University of Chicago Press, 1930) By the concept of 'little community' or 'folk life', he meant, a small isolated, nonliterate and homogeneous group with strong sense of belonging. Redfield says that a small community is another of these prevailing and conspicuous forms, in which humanity obviously comes to our notice. In all parts of the world, throughout human history, there are and have been little communities. However, there is quality of distinctiveness: where the community begins and where it ends, is apparent to outside observer and is expressed in the group consciousness of the people of the community. (<u>The Little Community and Pleasant Society and Culture</u>, Chicago: Chicago University Press, 1960 pp. 1 & 4. I used the concept of 'little community' in a board sense to describe little communities within Christian Religious community, which are distinctive in its social traits and homogeneity, with strong sense of group consciousness.

3. Salig Harrison, an American sociologist (India: <u>The Two Most Dangerous Decades</u>, Madras: Oxford University Press, 1960) talks about centripetal and centrifugal forces that are at work in India. He says that the Indian Constitution acts, as centripetal force, bringing Indians together, whereas caste and language act, as centrifugal force or dividing force.

4. Agarwal, Dinesh & othr. (Ed.), <u>Perspectives on the Church Management</u>, New Delhi: ISPCK, 1998

5. Johnson, Harry, M., <u>Sociology</u>, Bombay: Allied Publishers Pvt. Ltd., 1960, p. 346
6. <u>The Bible</u>, <u>op. cit.</u>, p. 230
7. <u>The Book of Disciple of The Methodist Church in India</u>, op.cit. p. 105
8. <u>Doctrine And Discipline</u>, <u>op. cit.</u>, p. 14. (cf. the <u>Official Journal of Methodist Church in Southern Asia</u>, 30th Regular Session, 28 September – 1st October, 1980 p. 72, Official Journal of Methodist Church in India, 1st Session, 7–15 January 1981, p. 119 & the official Journal of the General Conference, 7th Session, November 19–25, p. 263) On, 12 March 2009. I checked with the church's office for the membership statistics. I was told that there was no actual statistical record of membership. I was dismayed, in spite of spending a good amount of money, no reliable official statistics was available. 1981 onwards, the church neglected to collect statistics through its Regional Conferences as before, now satisfied with presumptive membership figures.
9. <u>The Journal of the Special Session of the General Conference</u>, Calcutta, 17–23 February 1997, p. 84

Chapter 6: Friends of Convenience

1. Murphy, Edward F. <u>Webster's Treasury of Relevant Quotation</u>, New York: Greenwich House, 1978, p.308
2. <u>The Book of Discipline: The Methodist Church in India</u> op. cit. p. 46–47

3. <u>Enquiry Report</u>: the Council of Bishops, Action No. COB/2–6–2000

4. <u>The Week</u> (Magazine), 31 August 2003, P. 68

5. <u>Official Journal of the Adjourned Session of the General Conference</u>, 8–14 February, Ghaziabad, 1999, p.152

6. <u>Judicial Council: Decisions</u>, Lucknow: Lucknow Publishing House, 2009, Vol. III, pp. 51–55

7. Bidney, David, <u>Theoretical Anthropology</u>, New York: Columbia University Press, 1967 p.1

8. <u>Haldwani Property Inquiry Committee Report</u>, Methodist Church in India 19, December 2002 pp. 27, 39, 40 & 127

9. Walker, Williston, <u>op. cit.</u> p. 258

Chapter 7: Massive Conspiracy

1. Johnson Harry M, <u>op. cit.</u> p.367

2. Preece, Warren E (Ed.), <u>Encyclopedia Britannica</u>, Chicago: William Benton Publisher, 1972, Vol. II p. 754. In his, 17th Book of Confession, he described God, as changeless Light, the pure spiritual being and evil is non entity; darkness is, but the absence of Light.

3. Plato, a great political thinker of the Greek world, influenced him. Thomas Aquinas, a philosopher and theologian, held the belief that reason is capable of operating within faith, and Niccolo Machiavelli, an Italian theorist advocated unscrupulous, ruthless, and cunning political conduct. Vide: <u>Britannica Ready Reference Encyclopedia</u>, <u>op. cit.</u>, vol. 8, p. 27 & Walker, Williston, <u>op. cit.</u> p.167

4. Dumas, Alexandre, <u>The Count of Monte Christo</u>, New Delhi: Maple Press, Script Edition 2008. The author is a well-known French novelist, Edmond Dantes, the main character, was falsely accused of treason and he was imprisoned in the island fortress of the Chateu d'If, the place from where no one can escape, but when fortune favoured him, he escaped from the prison, and found the hidden treasure and purchased the title of count from Tuscan Government and the island of Monte Cristo. He won the victory over his enemies, though his victory does not truly lie in it and ultimately repented for his sin of revenge.

5. The revenge agenda was: Taranath Sagar was making undue haste to get the official list of delegates along with signed certificates of elected delegates from my episcopal area, presuming delay may affect his episcopal election. There was neither any delay nor it became impediment to holding the General Conference 2003. His displeasure over his daughter's confirmation was squeezed in it, although the pastor was authorized to confirm children as per rule. It seemed, he expected me to confirm his daughter, but concealed his desire, leaving it to me to guess. Sampath Kumar forced pastors, conducted confirmations to charge me for failure to perform duty. I suggested the Bombay Districts Superintendents to have MCI Day Worship for Bombay Conference for larger participation and in line with the practice in other Regional Conferences. They accepted suggestion and I

agreed to bring message on the occasion, well within my right. There was no institutional or legal deterrence to hold such celebration in other places than the Methodist Centre, the narrow preserve of supremacy. There was no word from Taranath Sagar, did not observe protocol; The resident bishop was always personally invited to bring message on the occasion, followed by a formal letter of invitation. I was puzzled at his arrogant attitude and petty politics. He held back the letter of invitation until the last minute and bypassed the protocol. However, long after I realized, the clash of timings could have been avoided. I found, genuine concerns are often misconstrued. Pradeep Ahaley was hostile to Taranath Sagar's former political mentor, who was appointed as district superintendent. They were antagonist to each other from their student days in the Leonard Theological College, Jabalpur. By taking the advantage of vicious political situation, dug up the dead matter after the lapse of many years, made the issue out of it that I appointed him without he fulfilling eligibility criteria; it was just not true, for the Board of Ministry did not say so and moreover a conference year is not synonymous to a calendar year. Curiously, in March 2010, his termination was revoked and in sycophancy Pradeep Samuel appointed him in the same post and counted his services that made him eligible to become bishop, perhaps with the blessing of Taranath Sagar and John Hanchinmani. Thus, his election is either illegal or declaring me guilty on this charge is false; both can't be true. Moreover, I was charged on its count for maladministration, ironically no such charge was made out against Pradeep Samuel. I was intrigued by the politics of convenience. Out of revenge, Pradeep Ahaley blew the trumpet of me making announcement of the appointment of another pastor as district superintendent. It was mere an announcement; in the past bishops announced appointments and afterwards made changes, if it was necessary. The poor pastor never took the charge; it was neither illegal nor irregular, however, in malice, I was charged on the count.

6. The detail antecedent given in the chapter 9

7. <u>Judicial Council: Decisions, MCI</u> Lucknow: Lucknow publishing House, 1993, Decision No. 314, Vol. I, p. 447–449

8. <u>Inquiry Report</u>, The Council of Bishops, 14 February 2006

9. <u>Judicial Council, MCI: Decisions</u>: Lucknow: Lucknow Publishing House, Vol. III, 2009, p. 142 &. 102

10. Wilding, Norman, <u>An Encyclopedia of Parliament</u>: London: Cassel, 4th Ed. P. 729

11. <u>The Book of Discipline: The Methodist Church in India</u>, <u>op.cit.</u> p. 106

Chapter 8: Wilderness Days

1. Asmal, Kader & others (Ed.), <u>Nelson Mandela in His Words</u>: New York: Little Brown & Company, 2003 p. xxxiv

2. <u>The Bible</u>, <u>op. cit.</u> p. 768

3. Hollister, John N. <u>The Centenary of the Methodist Church in Southern Asia</u>, Lucknow: Lucknow Publishing House, 1956. The Central Conference of the Methodist Church in Southern Asia appointed the Commission on Centenary Celebration and the Executive Board of MCSA appointed Hollister as historian to head the team and write one hundred years' work of Methodism in India. (Ref. <u>Minutes of the Executive Board of the MCSA</u>, Fifteenth Session, 9–11 September 1953, p.22)

Chapter 9: No Way to Justice

1. <u>Times of India</u>, Mumbai Edition, 28, August 2009, P. 18
2. Jenkins, Philip, <u>The Lost History of Christianity</u>, (1st Ed.): New York, Harper One 2008, p. 257
3. <u>Times of India</u>, Mumbai Edition, 8 August 2009, p. 12 the Law Commission under the chairmanship of Justice A.R. Lakshmanan, a retired judge of the Supreme Court of India recommended sweeping changes in appointment of judges, curtailment of holidays and uncle judges. Uncle judges are those judges who prior to their appointment as judges, were advocate practicing in the same court for many years. The uncle judges tend to indulge either settling their scores with advocates with whom they practiced or have soft corner for them.

Chapter 10: Paradigm Shift

1. Wilansky, Harold L., 'Professionalization of Everyone', <u>American Journal of Sociology</u>, Vol. 70 pp. 137–158

2. <u>Doctrine & Discipline</u>, <u>op. cit</u>, pp. 174–194 & <u>The Official Journal of the General Conference</u>, 31 December–7 January, Jabalpur, 1985, p. 90

3. <u>The Official Journal of the General Conference</u>, MCI, 4th Regular Session, 22–31 May 1994, New Delhi p.185–189

4. <u>The Recommendation of the Finance & Administrative Committee</u>, 18 May & 12–13 August 2005 pp. 2–3 & Vide EC/07/2007

INDEX

J

Jabalpur 29, 31, 38, 49-50, 73, 189, 192, 416, 419
Jaipur 140-1
Janvier, Joel 6
Jefferson, Thomas 256
Jenkins, Philip 357
Jeremiah (prophet) 1
John Paul II (pope) 232
John the Baptist 1, 282
Johnson, Harry 203
Joshi, R. D. 21, 23, 25-6, 35, 39
Joshi and Urlana 21, 23, 26, 35, 39, 144-5
Judicial Council 9, 177, 183, 187, 212, 219, 223, 254-5, 262, 357, 390, 405, 414, 417
justice 196, 225, 262-71, 275-81, 310-11, 322-4, 327-34, 338, 342-4, 346, 348-50, 352-4, 358-62, 364-6, 396-7

K

Kanakaraj, N. 33-5
Karkare, Namdeo 89, 186, 222-3, 227
Kempis, Thomas a 106
Kolkata (Calcutta) 161-3, 213, 216, 256, 342, 413
Kotdwar 57

Kumar, Sampath 91, 160-1, 168-80, 183-6, 192, 210-24, 226-32, 234-7, 242-5, 255-7, 271-3, 296-7, 315-18, 367-72, 374-5

L

Lal, James 44, 194
Lall, G. M. 50
Lance, L. R. 38-9
Lee, Stan 291
Legislative body 38, 195
Leonard Theological College 29, 31, 39, 42, 50, 416
Light of Life 285
Lincoln, Abraham 7
Locke, John 256
Lonavala 77, 208, 411
Lucknow 49, 67, 87, 172, 294, 296, 408-10, 414, 417-18
Lucknow Regional Conference 49, 172
Luke, Manoranjan 19, 21
Luke, St. 6
Luther, Martin 2-3, 5, 245

M

Mandela, Nelson 278, 417
Marx, Karl 7, 32, 68
Marxism 7
Masih, Anjana 252, 255, 258-9, 262, 267, 294
Massey, Joseph 214, 251